THE
MAKING
OF A
GOVERNMENT

Roderic A. Camp

THE
MAKING
OF A
GOVERNMENT

POLITICAL
LEADERS
IN
MODERN
MEXICO

The University of Arizona Press
Tucson, Arizona

About the Author

RODERIC A. CAMP, director of Latin American Studies at Central College, Pella, Iowa, has written numerous books and articles on Mexico. In 1982 he became the contributing editor of the Mexican politics section of the *Handbook of Latin American Studies*, a biennial publication of the Library of Congress's Hispanic Division. He served as a fellow of the Woodrow Wilson Center for International Scholars in 1983–84. Among his publications are *Mexico's Leaders: Their Education and Recruitment* (University of Arizona Press, 1980) and *Mexican Political Biographies, 1935–80* (University of Arizona Press, 1982).

THE UNIVERSITY OF ARIZONA PRESS

Copyright © 1984
The Arizona Board of Regents
All Rights Reserved
Manufactured in the U.S.A.

This book was set in 10/12 Linotron Goudy Oldstyle.

Library of Congress Cataloging in Publication Data

Camp, Roderic Ai.
    The making of a government.

    Bibliography: p.
    Includes index.
    1. Politicians—Education—Mexico.   2. Political socialization—Mexico.   I. Title.
JL1247.C34   1984   306'.2'0972   84-8811

ISBN 0-8165-0871-2

To my parents

Contents

Tables

Acknowledgments

This book has relied upon the good will and interest of many people. The research was begun in 1972 and involved many trips to Mexico. Although my debt to many Mexican public figures, both retired and active, living and deceased, is obvious, I would like to thank several who, during many years, have repeatedly given freely of their time and insights into the evolution of the Mexican political system. Among them are Sealtiel Alatriste, Antonio Armendáriz, the late Praxedis Balboa Gojón, Ernesto Enríquez Coyro, the late Luis de la Peña Porth, Manuel Hinojosa Ortiz, Hugo B. Margáin, Daniel Pedro Martínez, Antonio Martínez Báez, the late Alfonso Pulido Islas, Raúl Rángel Frias, and the late Víctor Manuel Villaseñor. Without their assistance, and that of many other Mexicans, this work would have not been possible.

Furthermore, my own ideas and interpretations about Mexican life and the themes in this book have been greatly influenced by three North American scholars: Peter H. Smith, James W. Wilkie, and John Womack, Jr., each of whom I owe an intellectual debt. In addition, Enrique Krauze, Jean Meyer, and Gabriel Zaid have contributed to the appearance of this work in Mexico. And, most importantly, I wish to thank my wife Emily and my brother Roger for the literate suggestions that have made this a more humanistic work.

Lastly, I wish to express my appreciation to Central College for a sabbatical which stimulated this work, and to the American Philosophical Society, which helped to fund some of my research.

R.A.C.

1

Politicians and Their Socialization in Mexico

The education, or what social scientists like to call *socialization*, of public figures in Mexico is revealing not only to the specialist interested in Latin American governments, but to the reader interested in learning about the complex influences affecting the builders of a nation emerging from a violent, twentieth-century revolution. To achieve insight into this process, and, more particularly, into the people who contributed to its growth, the researcher could follow one of two broadly conceived routes. First, using documentary sources or statistical data, the social scientist might describe the results of government policy and attempt to attribute values and goals to the men and women who forged them. Or second, using a methodology borrowed in part from the oral history tradition, the scholar might attempt to converse with many survivors who were actors in this political and social drama, and attempt to record and analyze their own views about their activities and values, as well as the decisions they made. Neither approach is inherently better than the other. But, while the first is far more common than the second, I have chosen to follow the second approach, with supportive evidence from the first, in an attempt to provide an unusual perspective on a group of influential leaders in our time.

There are certain weaknesses to an approach which relies on the recollections of any group, including a group which, by virtue of the positions it

1

has held and the influence it has wielded over decision-making in Mexico, could be accurately described as a political elite. These weaknesses have been pointed out by James Wilkie.[1] People tend to have a selective recall, especially in front of an inquiring social scientist. Supportive or positive experiences are recounted more often than unpleasant ones. Despite these difficulties, interviewing—without recording—mitigates the figure's belief that a written, irrefutable record of what he says may be used against him. Using this technique, I believe I have elicited the most objective evaluations possible under the circumstances.[2]

In an examination of the survey approaches which have been used to analyze the political socialization process, I found numerous studies of large groups, but very few studies of elites in any country. In general, the study of elites is one of the least developed areas of research on political socialization.[3] In fact, there is very little available in the whole area of adult political socialization, as distinct from the experiences of individuals before the age of eighteen. However, the studies of political elites, which have been done primarily in the United States and European countries, have generally focused on local and national legislators, rather than on the heads of executive agencies. In Mexico, as in the case of most Latin American and developing nations, it is the executive branch, rather than the legislative, which wields power over government decision-making. For this reason, the interviews have focused on those persons who, while they may have held legislative positions, more frequently have been sub-directors and directors of major federal agencies in Mexico. They have not been randomly selected, but rather were purposely chosen from those who responded to letters and requests for interviews which were sent to all living public figures known to have held an office at the highest level in the political system. Because those political leaders raised and educated since 1910, during the immediate post-revolutionary decades, are of primary importance to this study, most of the interviewees are people who spent their youth in the 1920s and 1930s, although I have not entirely excluded some from the 1910s and 1940s.

The individuals who formed the core group of interviewees for this study are part of a larger group which, with the exception of a few individuals, has been part of a select pool of political leaders holding public positions in Mexico from 1946 to 1970 and having considerable control over federal monies spent on national policies. During that twenty-five-year period, only two hundred and four persons have held such positions. Of those, ninety-one were known to be deceased at the time of the interviews. Of the remaining one hundred and thirteen, I corresponded with and/or interviewed thirty-eight persons (34 percent), of whom I selected twenty-four to interview for this study. The members of this core group were selected on the basis of the following criteria: they could be located, they represented a carefully chosen cross-section of the administrative political elite in Mexico during this period, they each held a position in at least one of the four administrations during this period, they represented diverse ideological viewpoints within that political leadership, and they were all graduates of the National University, with one exception, during the 1920s and 1930s. Each of these individuals has answered a number of open-ended questions about how he was socialized, about his family background, and about how he became interested in public life. It is a modal group in that it does not include non-college graduates, graduates from institutions other than the National University, graduates before 1920 or after 1940, or office-holders who have held only elective positions. However, the focus of this study is on the socialization experiences of public figures who have held offices with the potential of formulating or implementing national policies in Mexico during the post-World War II period. The individuals who have held such offices in Mexico during the years 1946 to 1970 were college-educated, graduated from the National University from 1920 to 1939, and largely followed bureaucratic careers.

These interviews have been supplemented by others with an expanded group of individuals who have held electoral positions and who graduated at different times from various institutions, and therefore fall outside of the immediate focus of this study. Information gathered from this larger group was used to expand and complement the data drawn from the core group. There is little if any bias in the type of individual who responded to these interviews, since only one person refused to grant me an interview, and many granted me the first interview regarding their personal lives or their first public interview in many years. I believe their views are representative of the political elite which has held policy-making positions in the Mexican government since 1946, and I have selected these persons on the basis of an intimate knowledge of career patterns and background data of Mexico's political leadership since the 1930s.

Unfortunately, there is no foundation on which to build an examination of elite socialization in Mexico. To my knowledge there are no existing studies of the socialization experiences of public figures in Mexico or Latin America. As one scholar suggested in a review of Mexican literature, how political socialization takes place and how it affects public affairs is a gap in our knowledge of that country.[4] Therefore, in suggesting some hypotheses and determining avenues for focusing our research, I have had to rely on comparative studies of other countries and of different types of political leaders. Because of this situation, I have attempted to examine a number of broad questions related to socialization research everywhere, rather than to specify a number of individual hypotheses concerning the learning experiences of prominent Mexican officials. My overall emphasis, then, is to answer some relevant questions. First, why did these men and women enter public life rather than private careers? Second, what was the impact of their parents on their choice of career and on their values? Third, in relation to other agents of socialization, how important were significant historical events in the turmoil of the first three decades of this century? Fourth, what impact did the educational environment of the National Preparatory School and the National University have on the men and women educated there? Fifth, how influential were preparatory and university professors on the values and beliefs of this group? Who were these persons and what were their views? Sixth, as a passive agent, how important were books, both inside and outside of the classroom, on the education of these political leaders? And seventh, what did these experiences ultimately contribute in the way of universal values among public officials from these generations?

As implied above, we must look beyond Mexico for ideas and conclusions concerning the socialization experiences of political leaders. In doing so, we are led to further speculations and to suggestive conclusions, since most socialization data is inconclusive. For example, if we examine background data for various political elites, of which parents are an important part, we find that we are unable to predict the effects of these variables from one culture to the next.[5] The reasons why political leaders entered public life are equally mysterious. After making a careful study of North American legislators, one political scientist concluded that "one's over-all impression is one of great diversity, suggesting that many roads may lead to an interest in politics for those whose careers lead them into legislative office."[6]

As will be seen in the following pages, this situation is applicable to public figures in Mexico. Not only has it been difficult to determine a clear set of experiences relevant to the political leader, but such experiences do not occur at any fixed period of time in the individual's life. As Richard Dawson and Kenneth Prewitt have suggested, "political learning is cumulative. Orientations learned early in life determine much of the form and substance of orientations acquired later. Political attachments acquired early both open up the possibility for some types of later learning and limit the likelihood that other types will occur."[7] This is precisely why no single source of influence is equally important to all subjects studied, and also why any one source, particularly at an early stage in a person's life, can be highly influential. While the subject may recall a certain individual or experience as important, the same subject may not fully realize how it opened him up to or closed off future learning experiences. For these and other reasons, then, I have confined my efforts to acquiring some knowledge about how public figures in Mexico see themselves as having been socialized, rather than making highly speculative and unfounded hypothetical predictions about their socialization.

In selecting the sources of socialization for public figures, I have, however, allowed myself to be influenced by conclusions from other studies. Although the evidence from most studies indicate, as suggested above, that individuals are influenced by experiences throughout their lifetimes, most people
acquire their beliefs when they are young, largely because this is the period in
which they are most receptive to outside influences. As Robert Dahl has
noted, "typically, a person is highly receptive during, and only during, the
first two decades of his life. At the end of this period, one's outlook becomes
fixed or crystallized."[8] I believe this to be true in the case of Mexican political
leaders. It is for that reason that I have decided to examine five basic sources
affecting these men and women from childhood until their mid-twenties: parents, teachers, friends, educational experiences, and books. Events will also
be examined, with an emphasis on those which took place during a subject's
early years. In addition, this study is limited to several generations of Mexicans, largely because I believe that these generations form what Karl Mannheim labels a "community of location." In his words, generations may be described as similar, or having a "community of location," when "they are in a
position to experience the same events and data," and especially when those
experiences play upon a similarly "stratified" consciousness.[9]

Certain sources of socialization have been selected for detailed study
not only because they were most likely to be those influential during the first
three decades of a public figure's life, but also because studies of political elites
from other countries indicate that they might be of some importance. For
example, all five sources examined in this study were seen as important by
state legislators in the United States. However, their importance varied depending on when the legislator himself thought he was socialized. Kornberg
found that "if the person thought he was politically socialized as a child, 88
percent claimed family as the agent; if as an adolescent, 100 percent claimed
self (e.g. read on own); if an adult, 100 percent claimed external events and
conditions, e.g. campaign, exposed to a charismatic leader, attendance at
college, depression, war, etc."[10]

This work gives substantial emphasis to the educational experiences of
the subjects because education encompasses their experiences from age fifteen
to twenty-two. In addition, as Searing indicated in his comparative analysis,
one of the strongest relationships between social background factors and attitudes among Venezuelan leaders was level of education.[11] Public figures in
Mexico have had an educational experience very similar to that of Venezuelan political elites.[12] Furthermore, the public men with whom we are dealing
have had a very homogeneous formal education, in terms of both level and
place. If such experiences, combined with similar social background characteristics, were important in determining Venezuelan elite attitudes, they
might also be relevant to political leaders in Mexico.

Another socialization source of interest is the teacher as an agent distinct from the larger, more complex educational experience. As Dawson and Prewitt have noted,

> The teacher's role as conveyor of consensus values is so widely assumed that few students of political socialization have investigated it. One major reason why teachers operate so effectively in this connection is that they are products of the same political socialization for which they serve as agents. Teachers generally do not need to be taught to laud the virtues of the nation. Their own political selves have been shaped in accordance with the very consensus values they now transmit.[13]

This statement would be true for a period of stable political and social growth, but not necessarily for the several decades of post-revolutionary upheaval in Mexico being examined here. Mexico provides us with the opportunity to examine the durability of traditional ideas and professors at the preparatory schools and universities and the conflict between the old and the new.

Lastly, this study examines, in some detail, the family background of political leaders. In all general studies of political socialization, family influences have emerged as significant. This is equally true in Latin America and Mexico. In a study of the attitudes of students who became the leaders of Panama and Costa Rica, Daniel Goldrich found that students from both countries most frequently talked about political ideas with their families, and that when in need of political advice, more than 70 percent from each group went to some family member.[14] In a more recently completed study of non-elite students in Mexico, Rafael Segovia found that both family and school were important places for discussing politics. But he also concluded that there was a greater possibility among the more informed children for ultimately participating in politics.[15] Since more knowledgeable children generally come from better educated parents, family background would appear to be crucial to entering a public career. If this relationship is true of present generations, it is of interest to know if it has actually been true of past generations during a period of renovation in political leadership. Family background and education, combined with major historic events, are thus the factors most likely to have had an impact on the attitudes and values of Mexican political elites.

2

Choosing a Political Career

A question asked by all students of political socialization, regardless of whom they study, is when their subjects first became interested in politics. Because this study examines a representative group of high office-holders in Mexico, it is equally of interest why they first became *involved* in participating in public life. Often, initial interest is confused with involvement in politics, largely because the two may occur simultaneously and the cause of interest as well as involvement may be one and the same.[1]

Reasons for Interest in Politics

The time at which most political leaders have been socialized is important, since it may help to determine the agents of socialization most likely to have contributed to their interest. For example, a person who claimed to have become politically interested as an adult is more likely to have been influenced by his peers or by his participation in civic activities rather than by his education or family environment. In addition, Kenneth Prewitt and his colleagues found that North American state legislators and city council members who date their interest in politics early in life systematically differ from their colleagues with respect to their socialization experiences.[2]

The Prewitt study is one of the few that has determined the time of initial interest in public affairs for a sample of political leaders. Although the sample is confined to state and local representatives, and is therefore not representative of a more elite group, at least 10 percent of Mexico's political leaders held equivalent positions before reaching high national office. The Prewitt respondents from the state legislature remembered their initial interest in public affairs beginning during childhood or grammar school (38 percent), adolescence or high school (15 percent), college or equivalent period (11 percent), after college or equivalent period (16 percent), and at the time of entry into public life (20 percent). These findings are revealing for several reasons. First, in support of assertions that socialization studies are neglecting posteducational periods in an individual's life, the Prewitt data indicate that at least 36 percent of the legislators and city council members had taken on an interest in public affairs *after* they had finished college. Furthermore, the data, while indicating a substantial impact from childhood, also reveal considerable diversity among legislators and council members as to when their interest in politics occurred.

The importance of the posteducational years has also been supported by studies of a more comparable group of political elites in Canada and the United States: members of Parliament and Congress. In that study the authors found that 46 percent of the national legislators claimed childhood as the time of first interest, 13 percent remembered it occurring during adolescence, and 41 percent had not become interested until they were adults.[3]

The data also illustrate, as suggested above, that, even for political leaders, participation and interest frequently occur at the same time. If we can assume that anyone holding public office is, by definition, interested in public affairs, then Mexico's political leaders would date their initial interest in public affairs within these same time frames, most frequently before the age of 30. Unlike many North American office-holders, more than 95 percent of Mexico's high-office-holders are career public officials, in either the bureaucratic or the electoral sphere. For example, there is very little exchange among business people and political leadership in Mexico. Fewer than one percent of Mexico's political leaders were in business prior to their public careers, whereas North Americans frequently exchange business and political roles. Because successful political careers in Mexico require a long apprenticeship in the public sector, nearly all office-holders have embarked on their careers upon graduating from college, and rarely later than age 30.[4]

Mexican political leaders attribute their initial interest in politics to equally diverse periods of time. However, their interest occurred far more heavily during adolescence and in college. Mexicans differ from North American legislators and council members for several reasons. As indicated in chapter 1, the core Mexican sample of this study is representative of the majority of administrative office-holders, who are college-educated. Therefore, one would expect a bias in favor of the college or equivalent period because all of the respondents actually had a college education.[5] In spite of this inherent bias, I believe an analysis of how the public figures first became interested in politics, combined with a study of the background of each individual, will reveal reasons other than the educational level of the Mexicans for the distribution of these responses.

Another study of the political socialization of public figures focused on Canadian party officials (Table 2.1). It contains more comparable data on the question of why political leaders became interested in politics because it looks at college-educated leaders. The responses reflect a number of agents active during each of the time periods suggested in the North American studies cited earlier. In the case of the Mexicans, because the group under study grew up during the Revolution of 1910 or shortly thereafter, one might expect a high response for public events. However, the respondents revealed that friends, either in school or in young adulthood, were most responsible for developing their interest in political affairs. It is difficult to say why the Revolution did not stimulate greater interest in political activities among those persons born after 1900, as it undoubtedly did for political leaders, whether from civilian or military backgrounds, who were born in the last two decades of the nineteenth century. The reason might be that the Revolution was already becoming a historical event, especially to the post-1910 group, and, that without their active participation in the Revolution, it contributed little to involving the post-1900 generations in politics. However, its impact on political, economic, and social attitudes among these same leaders was more significant.[6]

It is easier to suggest why school friends have had a substantial influence on developing political interests. First, Mexican political leaders became interested in politics during the time they were in school, a time when one would expect peer group influence to be increasing and family influence to be decreasing, particularly since most Mexicans were educated in preparatory schools and universities away from their families.[7] Studies of North American students reveal that peer groups do play a consequential role in the development of political orientations, and that students and their friends are more alike than unlike in political terms.[8] Furthermore, Rafael Segovia, in his study of Mexican schoolchildren, has found that public schoolchildren talk about political ideas most frequently with their friends, followed closely by family and teachers.[9] Friends are also an important agent for determining political interests because of the strong need which middle-class Mexicans seem to have for friendship. Rogelio Díaz Guerrero, a prominent Mexican psychologist, suggests that

**Table 2.1 Agents Associated with Changes in
Political Interests of College-Educated Canadian Party Officials**

Agents	Percentage of Officials Who Identified Them as Responsible[a]
Public events	42
Public figures	40
Work	21
School friends	19
Kin	15
Friends	13
School materials	12
Recreation	12
Teachers	·9

Source: Adapted from Allan Kornberg, Joel Smith, and David Bromley, "Some Differences in the Political Socialization Patterns of Canadian and American Party Officials," in Jack Dennis, ed. *Socialization to Politics* (New York: Wiley, 1973), Table 5, p. 444.

[a]Percentages are greater than 100 because the authors counted multiple responses.

> the need to have friends is uncommonly intense in the Mexican; all our lives we are searching for friends; we constantly delight in coteries, parties, gossip, disputes, and all that sort of thing. This even provokes problems; as executives you probably complain, and your bosses probably do too, of this never-ending formation of coteries.[10]

Lastly, as will be suggested in a later discussion of peer group influence on the development of political ideas and participation, friends play a crucial role in political recruitment in Mexico.

If the backgrounds of individual respondents are examined, other explanations are encountered for why certain individuals recall first being interested in politics at a given period in their lives. For those Mexicans who were first interested in politics during their childhood or adolescence, there was often the presence of a politically active family. Not surprisingly, Prewitt and his colleagues found the same relationship. They noted that

> whether or not there is a politically active family in the background is strongly related to time of initial political socialization. Better than half (52 percent) of the legislators and nearly half of the councilmen (45 percent) who note early interest report family political activity. This compares with 7 and 18 percent, respec-

tively, of their colleagues who perceive adult experiences as first ushering them into the political world.[11]

Of the three Mexicans who date their interest from childhood, two were from politically active families. The third individual, indirectly affected, describes the importance of family activity, even though such involvement pertained only to his grandfather:

> I was born into a wealthy family. My father was the son of a sena-
> tor. My grandfather was a strong supporter of Benito Juárez. De-
> spite the fact that he was a landowner, he was a liberal. We were
> what Mexicans call creoles, but my family environment was that
> of a nineteenth-century liberal. My grandfather supported Lerdo
> de Tejada when Juárez died. He was governor of Mexico during
> this period, but when Porfirio Díaz revolted and succeeded in ob-
> taining the presidency, my grandfather was forced out of office. In
> spite of this, and his dislike for Díaz, he retained his popularity
> and contacts in the state of Mexico, remaining a senator for many
> years. He was a member of a small group not addicted to Díaz. All
> of this suggests that while I grew up in a privileged environment,
> I was very much surrounded by political activity. During the 1910
> Revolution my grandfather did not support Francisco Madero and
> had to leave the country. In 1920, at the invitation of his old sen-
> ate companion Venustiano Carranza [then President of Mexico],
> he returned to Mexico and died that same year.[12]

One of the two respondents whose family initiated his interest in politics dur-ing his childhood gives a similar reason:

> I was very preoccupied with revolutionary questions as a youth,
> because my father . . . participated in the Revolution. I was also
> aware of the constant battles against the postrevolutionary gov-
> ernments. My father interested me in the problems of the average
> Mexican. Also, when I was in primary school, I had many pro-
> fessors who were participants in the Revolution. Although I did
> not understand the ideology, and they spoke little of the issues,
> the fact that they had participated encouraged my interests in po-
> litical affairs.[13]

Of those Mexicans who developed an interest in politics as adults, only one had a family actively involved in political affairs. Not only does an early interest in politics often relate to family background, but, perhaps more im-portant, it is indicative of different socialization experiences. The Prewitt study found that those North American legislators and council members who believed that they were first interested in politics as youngsters were strongly influenced by the study of politics in school or by participation in school poli-tics. Not surprisingly, those who dated their interest in politics as adults rarely saw such activities as an important part of their socialization. Only one of the Mexicans who became interested in politics after college had been involved in student politics. On the other hand, those Mexicans who became interested in politics during their childhood and adolescence were very active in school politics. Miguel Alemán, for example, sponsored a student newspaper and in 1927, as a young law student, supported several opposition leaders in a bid against the official candidate for the presidency.[14]

Student intellectual activities have long been important to future political leaders in Mexico, especially those who had become interested in politics at an early age. Martin Luis Guzmán, a first-hand observer of Francisco Villa's revolutionary activities and a leading revolutionary novelist, was such a person. He became interested in politics as a child because his mother, who was an avid reader of newspapers, read aloud to him. He suggests the importance of this experience:

> To me, the most important part of the newspaper were the articles on politics. This explains why when I was thirteen I formed a small paper called *Quincenal* with another friend, Feliciano Bravo, in the sixth year of our primary school. We directed our newspaper to the youth of the port of Veracruz, where we were going to school. We had exactly fifty subscribers, at a cost of only 30 cents a month. We commented mostly on Veracruz political questions from the point of view of an adolescent.[15]

Other adolescent political activists joined political clubs. During the pre-revolutionary events, liberal clubs were common throughout Mexico. F. Javier Gaxiola, for example, who came from a prominent political family in the state of Mexico, became interested in politics at a young age. As a result, he joined a liberal club in Toluca in 1910 at the age of twelve and participated in a number of student demonstrations.[16] Other Mexicans were first interested in politics as a result of their participation in strictly student political affairs—not a surprising response, since most Mexican universities were characterized by internal and external political activities. Many of the respondents participated in historic student strikes at the National Preparatory School and the National University in Mexico City. Others, who initially attended normal school during their young teens, date their interest in politics from that period. One such individual was Alfonso Pulido Islas, one of the few Mexicans who attributes his pre-adult interest in politics to a political event, the reelection of General Alvaro Obregón for president in 1927.[17] Surprisingly, only one respondent, a senator during the 1940s, believed that the Revolution and the environment it created was responsible for his political interest.[18]

For most Mexican political leaders, unlike the North Americans, initial interest began during the college years. This finding is not altogether unexpected, since future Mexican political leaders were most frequently recruited during their college years, especially at the National University.[19] Furthermore, of all the traditional background variables, only an education at the National University has been strongly related to success in politics.[20] I believe there are several additional reasons why a large proportion of Mexican political leaders first became interested in politics during their university years. As implied above, timing is important to the Mexican public figure. Unlike the North Americans, very few enter political careers after the age of 25. This means that for almost all Mexican political leaders, interest and involvement both must take place by the early twenties, a situation which focuses attention on the years from age 12 to 22, most of which have been spent at the university. Furthermore, Mexican political leaders are more homogeneous in background than the legislative sample used in the North American data because, like the majority of successful Mexican politicians, they have graduated from two institutions: the National Preparatory School and the National University. Moreover, since both institutions are located in the political, social, and economic capital of Mexico, the psychological impact of attending school there puts students into an obvious political environment, similar to that found in Washington, D.C. Lastly, because the majority of students are from the provinces and are away from their parents, or have already declared an interest in politics as a result of politically active parents, only four probable sources remain: peer influence from fellow students, influence from professors and books, the impact of the university and preparatory school environment itself, and the impact of national political events magnified by proximity to the capital.

All of the Mexican political leaders who were first interested in politics at the university were from middle-class families, none of which was involved in politics. Moreover, all of them were law students. Law school curricula, and, after 1929, the economics school curricula, were by far the most politically and socially oriented at the National University, as well as at state universities. One graduate of the National Engineering School describes his political formation during these years as minimal. Although he remembers the election of 1939 and the popularity of the opposition candidate, General Juan Andreu Almazán, among engineering students, he believes their preference was based on a superficial knowledge rather than on an intellectual choice.[21] But for law students the commitment often rose from their studies. One such student, a graduate of the late 1930s, remembers his first participation as a voter: "I first voted in 1934 without being a member of any party. I voted for Cárdenas, but the majority of students in our guest house voted against him. I think I voted on impulse. But when I studied agrarian law, I then became really interested in politics."[22]

The study of agrarian law, which was introduced as a result of the revolutionary emphasis on land tenure questions in the late 1920s, opened up many vistas to the law students of the 1930s. In general, though, it was the study of public law which most stimulated students to take an interest in politics:

> During my professional school days I began to see the light when some of my professors began talking of new laws produced by the Revolution, in particular the labor and agrarian laws. It was a beautiful period because the Law School professors discussed many of these issues. We formed a student association of which I was president. I would call it a democratic-socialist group. In 1925, we supported a movement to develop a new civil code which would introduce new norms to society. Later, I participated in many presidential campaigns.[23]

Law students became interested in politics not only because of their studies and their participation in intellectual discussions with professors and fellow students, but also because professors admonished them to do so. Mariano Azuela, son of a well-known novelist of the Mexican Revolution and later a senator and justice of the Supreme Court, first "became interested as a student because of the impact of the Seven Wise Men, especially Antonio Caso and José Vasconcelos. . . . Our professors argued that we should enter public life to contribute more culture and rationality."[24] The reasons which persuaded National Law School students to become interested in politics were not equally apparent in some of the regional law schools. For example, Raúl Cardiel Reyes, one of the most prominent student leaders from the provinces during the 1930s and a native of San Luis Potosí, became interested in Mexican political affairs during that period, but his interest developed through his literary activities. He was not preoccupied with such issues before because, unlike professors in Mexico City, his professors did not analyze political questions at school.[25]

Although the North American politicians who first became interested in politics during their school years were fewer in numbers than the Mexicans, they were influenced in much the same way. The Prewitt study notes that "the interview schedules are rich with quotations attesting to the 'inspirational' nature of the educational experience."[26] This important relationship between student and teacher has been especially true in the Mexican context.[27]

Law school students at the National University may have also become interested in politics in an educational environment largely because it was new to them. Heinz Eulau, in making some general conclusions about his studies of North American legislators, commented that an immigrant population might seize upon political and social activities to make itself feel at home in a new environment. He further noted that "in newly created communities, fewer legislators are 'born into' politics, more become politically interested and active in the process of community life." [28] The Mexican preparatory school and university environment is a new situation confronting the student from the provinces, comparable to a new community environment for the immigrant. [29] Respondents observed repeatedly that proportionately more Mexican student leaders are from the provinces than from the Federal District. Provincial students perhaps felt a greater need than local students to integrate themselves into their new and more sophisticated urban environment by becoming active in social, literary, and political student groups, since participation in student activity is one means of receiving recognition and acceptance.

We have analyzed some of the reasons for the differences in initial interest in politics among North American and Mexican political leaders during childhood and through their college years. But what about the minority of Mexican leaders who became interested in politics after graduating from college? Mexicans who became interested in politics as adults did so in several ways. The smallest group did so as a result of circumstances. For example, another graduate from the National Engineering School, Luis de la Peña Porth, believed he developed certain ideas and goals from his professional education, but that his interest in politics occurred after working for several mining firms. It was then that he became interested in achieving some of these goals, most prominently the one of putting Mexican natural resources back into the hands of Mexicans. [30] Others, similar to the largest group of respondents in the Prewitt study who indicated an adult interest in politics, became interested through socially related political activities. Víctor Manuel Villaseñor, who later managed three major decentralized agencies for the Mexican government, describes how his political interests emerged:

> The Claims Commission stopped its work temporarily during 1931. I had a lot of time on my hands so I began to read and write for *El Universal*. This was about the time that Vicente Lombardo Toledano began to change his written views from those of a Christian Democrat to those of a Marxist. In 1932, Manuel R. Palacios, who was then a Marxist, asked me to give a conference. It was through this conference that I met Lombardo Toledano. He invited me to dine with him the next day, and, as I was very impressed with him, we soon became good friends. Narciso Bas-

sols, who was Secretary of Public Education, published 40,000 copies of my speech. This is how I came to know him and Lombardo, and how I was introduced to political activism.[31]

For others, political interests came as the result of specific events, even late in life. For one Mexican, it was a move to Mexico City combined with the international events of World War II.[32] Political interests for some public figures developed simultaneously with their work, either early or late in life. The experience of Eduardo Bustamante, who later became a cabinet secretary in the 1950s, illustrates how a first position stimulated his political interests:

> When I was in the Secretariat of the Treasury study group, I became very interested in political activities. I was commissioned by the Secretary of the Treasury to help reorganize the government financial sector of the state of Nuevo León. I was only twenty-three when this happened. I was supposed to help Governor Aaron Saénz. His closest collaborator was José Benítez, an intelligent man who had studied in Germany. The three of us developed a great friendship, and we discussed many problems of local government. Saénz later became campaign director for Obregón's presidential candidacy in 1927. Benítez then became Governor of Nuevo León. I was close to him, and we constantly talked about political questions. Really, in such a position, I had no choice but to be interested in what was happening in politics. I met and knew all of the prominent politicians of the period. When President Pascual Ortiz Rubio made Saénz Secretary of Public Education, Saénz in turn asked me to be his private secretary.[33]

The most uncommon type of Mexican political leader is an individual who has not developed an interest in politics until after he is in his thirties. Such persons became interested at that late date because they are asked to fill positions having political implications. Their interests coincide with their participation. Ernesto Enríquez exemplifies this unusual type, both because his grandfather had been politically prominent and because his own political interest began at age thirty-five. In describing important personal changes in his life, he suggests how such a change took place:

> I then went through one other major change when my Free Law School companion, José A. Ceniceros, then Subsecretary of Foreign Relations, asked me to become a member of the Claims Commission on Water Rights for Mexico and the United States. I had to learn English. This forced me into reading dozens of

books in English as well as on the history of international water problems. This was the first time I had an interest in politics and the first time I participated in public life.[34]

Prewitt found that the political leader who converts to public affairs late in life generally has a different view of politics, one that is usually lacking in glamor. Of those few Mexicans who later found many characteristics of politics distasteful or actually believed themselves to be non-politicians, all had become interested in politics and participated in public affairs as adults. This finding agrees with others which suggest

> that at each level the "home-grown" politicians have a more realistic, "political" conception of their role than do late starters, are more professional in their approach to politics, have stronger programmatic interests, and harbor stronger ambitions for political advancement. These distinctive traits no doubt help explain why early starters make it to the top of the political hierarchy in disproportionate numbers.[35]

Mexican political leaders bear out this general rule, and, since 1946, those individuals most successful in politics, who are often called members of the "Revolutionary Family," are those political leaders with decades of public service, not adult converts to politics.

Reasons for Involvement in Politics

Becoming interested in politics is only the first step for a future political leader. A question of equal interest is why people ultimately choose public careers. Those agents responsible for stimulating a first interest in politics are often equally responsible for encouraging individuals to become involved in politics. I have attempted to determine the practical reasons why Mexicans went into public careers during the 1920s and 1930s. The respondents indicated at least five broad categories which contain their reasons for entering politics: a personal decision (arising from a desire to achieve certain goals, the need for employment, a sense of obligation, ambition, or an interest in politics), the influence of a personality, an experience, the world's environmental situation, or an external event (Table 2.2).

Other scholars have used such diverse categories to indicate the reasons why politicians entered upon public careers that comparable data is hard to come by. Table 2.2 makes it clear that the majority of Mexicans were influenced by a variety of personal reasons for choosing political careers. For North American legislators, the most common reason appeared to be a "sense

Table 2.2 Why Mexican Politicians Entered Public Careers

Reason Given	Response	
	%	No.
Personal decision	53	20
Goals		
Employment		
Obligation		
Ambition		
Interest		
Personality	34	13
Political leader		
Family member		
Professor		
Friends		
Experience	5	2
University days		
Environment	5	2
Resource shortage		
External event	3	1
Vasconcelos campaign		

Note: Expanded group responses are recorded here. There were thirty-eight responses. No multiple responses were recorded. See chapter 1 for a description of this group.

of obligation" (Table 2.3). Of all the responses a person might give, this one seems to be most suspect, since it is a self-effacing, modest reason, allowing for no self-interest, and does not appear to conform with the personalities of most political leaders. Mexicans, however, did not give this reason in large numbers, although within the category of personal decisions listed in Table 2.2 it was the most frequent response. This finding may be the result of the sample, since almost all of the respondents had retired from politics or were considered senior statesmen, whereas the Prewitt sample was an active group of legislators. However, if the responses are confined to the five categories which Prewitt used—admiration for politicians, ambition for political power, sense of indignation, other, and sense of obligation—of which the first and last were most common for North Americans, we find that proportionately, Mexicans did admire politicians and felt a sense of obligation strikingly similar to that of the North Americans as shown in Table 2.3. They fail to corre-

Table 2.3 Predispositions of North American Legislators and Mexican Political Leaders for Entering Politics

Predisposition	North Americans[a] (%)	Mexicans (%)
Admiration for politicians	30	35
Ambition for political power	12	12
Sense of indignation	20	6
Sense of obligation	34	35
Other (desire for sociability, etc.)	7	12

[a]Information adapted from Prewitt et al., Table 6, p. 577, in which I have collapsed the responses for pre-adult and adult categories.

spond with North Americans in only one category, a "sense of indignation." This finding is not surprising, however, since, when broken down according to time when political interest occurred, only 9 percent of the North Americans claiming pre-adult political interests gave indignation as a reason for becoming involved in politics. Since many of the Mexicans first became interested in politics before the adult years, one would expect the Mexican response to be closer to the pre-adult North American response than to the combined figures.[36]

The majority of Mexicans went into public careers on the basis of personal reasons, and, as suggested above, among them was a sense of obligation to their country. Some Mexicans describe their obligation as similar to the North American concept of a "sense of duty." One political leader sees it as a part of the public figure's mentality: "I decided to become involved in public life because I have an idea that one should serve his society and that he has a responsibility to serve. There are really two types of people in this regard— those with a private mentality and those with a public mentality."[37] Others compare public service with life in a private law practice: "Public service was more interesting than my private law practice. I felt that I could have some influence on the direction Mexico would take through a public career, and it would be better to serve at least a little than not at all."[38]

Many other Mexicans from various generations of students believed that they had a collective responsibility to serve their country, not just to fulfill a sense of civic duty, but rather to implement goals or policies which had universal acceptance among their fellow students. Graduates of the engineering school, who were small in number and were concerned with the domination of natural resources by foreign private interests, seemed to be particularly influenced by such thinking. "I wanted to participate in public life in order to carry out [certain] goals. I think this was true of the other eight members of my generation. We were always close and we hoped to achieve these goals together." Still other Mexicans had decided long before their graduation that a public career was the only one of interest to them. In all of these cases in the sample, such individuals came from families having a history of political movement. Ambitious for political power, they still defined their reasons in terms of goals. For example, Miguel Alemán recalled his reasons in the following way:

> I wanted to be active in the affairs of my country. It was not really an accident, but resulted from the experiences of my family. I finished my law career in three years. I may have been a good or bad student, but I wanted to complete my degree quickly so I could participate in activities that would accomplish some of the goals I had established during my youth.[39]

A small number of Mexicans were attracted to politics because of the excitement or interest it seemed to offer. Those Mexicans who made their decisions to embark on a public career as adults did so largely by accident. This type of experience has been well described by one of these men:

> My participation in public life was totally accidental. I had no intention of going into it. Once involved, I became quite interested in the question of administration. Also, as a result of my experience on the Claims Commission, I was so interested in the water rights issue that I became a special consultant to the government.[40]

The most common reasons given by Mexicans who made their decisions in an internal fashion, after that of "a sense of obligation," were entirely practical. Some chose public careers because their value systems would not let them adjust to private careers: "I did not like private practice. I have always believed that private law helps to maintain the interests of the wealthy and the conservatives. I am basically an idealist, and I thought I could live an independent life in the judicial system." Or, "I had studied law for three years, but I decided that to be a successful private lawyer you have to pay or make bribes to get things moving rapidly. In a sense, I felt you were helping to corrupt the system or to continue the corruption which already existed, and I decided I could not do that." Others, while not expressing it in obvious terms, were interested in the material benefits which they might obtain, both honestly and dishonestly. Many Mexicans did not justify their practical decision on moral grounds but implied that there were few alternatives for employment. This finding was particularly true of economists.

> No private organizations had trained economists. In 1933, I was first employed as an economist under Professor Ramón Beteta in the Statistics Department of the Secretariat of the Treasury. All of my experiences up to and during this period gave me a greater sense of humanity toward dealing with people and problems. Because of the lack of opportunities in private enterprise, a career in the public sector was a necessity.[41]

After a personal decision of the kind described above, the second most important reason for Mexicans entering public careers was the influence of some personality, whether a politician, family member, professor or friend. Among those personalities influencing Mexicans to go into politics, professors were most common. Professors have not been of substantial importance to the political careers of North Americans. The explanation for this difference is quite clear: student politics in Mexico are a microcosm of political activity at the national level, and, more important, many professors and deans are very much a part of the political world. A former student explains how he became involved in politics through a professor:

> When I was a student at the School of Economics I had a very famous law professor named Mario Sousa, who later became quite active in the 1945–46 presidential campaign. Sousa organized a group of professors and former students to support the civilian candidate for president, Miguel Alemán, and this organization circulated a manifesto signed by a number of students or former students of Professor Sousa. I signed the manifesto and campaigned for Alemán. This resulted in my being offered a position in the Federal District.[42]

Many political leaders believed that their professors were indirectly responsible for encouraging them to participate in public life because they emphasized the need for competent persons in government.[43]

Of almost equal importance with professors were political leaders themselves. Most political leaders attracted individuals to political careers because of their charismatic behavior and values. The two most frequently mentioned leaders of this period were Lázaro Cárdenas and José Vasconcelos. Vasconcelos was a professor and educational leader turned politician. He appealed to several prominent generations of students because of his criticism of General Obregón's reelection and his opposition to the official candidacy of Pascual Ortiz Rubio in 1929, after Obregón, as president-elect, was assassinated.[44]

Cárdenas, on the other hand, who had no education beyond secondary school, impressed many Mexicans as an acquaintance or from afar. Respondents made statements such as, "Cárdenas got me interested in politics because of what he did as President of Mexico," or "Cárdenas had a natural ability to get things done, and this made a great impact on me personally." Even some world leaders impressed Mexicans sufficiently to get them interested in politics. During this period, it was Franklin D. Roosevelt and his attempts to deal with the depression which encouraged some Mexicans, as adults, to participate in politics.

Others entered political careers because of friendship with a person who became prominent in politics. Such persons were actually recruited by a political leader. One of them, who became a cabinet secretary in the 1940s, describes how he initially became a reluctant politician:

> I was a consulting lawyer to various agencies of the Mexican government. I gave advice and made recommendations on various problems for the Secretariats of Foreign Relations, Economy and Treasury. For some time I served as Director of the Office of Public Debt for Treasury. I also worked in the National Bank of Mexico and served as the President of the National Banking Commission. Although I served in these public positions, I did not have a political career. It was due entirely to the efforts of Alemán, and his respect for his professors, many of whom were from my generation, that I became a member of the elite group serving in high posts in his administration. Although I never taught him, he chose many of us to be members of his campaign group and of his cabinet. This was how many individuals, without previous political experience, entered his cabinet.[45]

Personal contact with a politician has been a reason for many political leaders to enter public careers and has provided ambitious aspirants with a key link to success in such careers, but it would be incorrect to assume that even those with political careers always took advantage of such a relationship to become involved in politics. A small number of our respondents turned down opportunities at some point in their lives because they were not yet ready for a public career. In general, because most authors describe a political career in Mexico as long and intensive, the impression exists that ambition would never allow an individual to turn down an important appointment.[46] There are many cases of delayed careers, however, among Mexican political leaders, especially among those who became involved in public careers as adults. One interviewee's experience is representative:

In 1938 during the Cedillo rebellion in San Luis Potosí, I served
as sort of a private secretary to the then Secretary of Defense
Manuel Avila Camacho. Later, when he became president in
1940, Gilberto Flores Muñóz (a prominent politician from San
Luis Potosí) told me that Avila Camacho had been very impressed
with me and wanted me to run for a political office in San Luis
Potosí. But, because I was not interested in participating in politics, I turned him down.[47]

One of the more common ways in which North Americans became involved
in politics was through social relationships. For North Americans, a group of
friends often acts as a catalyst to get a person involved in politics. In his
analysis of why city council members go into politics, Kenneth Prewitt concluded that

political choices are no less influenced by primary groups than
other types of choices. We expect to find, and we do, that a man's
decision to become politically active and eventually to seek a
council position will have been influenced by the advice, the
suggestions, and the social pressures from other individuals. In
tracing the experiences which led from their general interest in
politics to their political activities to their candidacy for office,
two-thirds of the councilmen cite the importance of small, informal groups of friends or acquaintances.[48]

Because of the domination of the official party in Mexican politics, *non-
political* social relationships as an agent of political involvement are rare, although within the official party itself, local political activists may encourage
someone they respect to become a candidate or pre-candidate for an official
party nomination. One respondent became involved as a young student in
state politics after numerous friends from his home state of Veracruz suggested
that he become a candidate for federal deputy. He remembers that "at first I
was not interested, but finally I became an egoist and accepted the opportunity. I had a lot of faith that I would win, but I lost the nomination, and the
candidacy went to another person. I was only twenty-six when that occurred."[49] Others, however, were initially more successful, and received their
original opportunities as well as encouragement to participate through
friends. Such was the case of the late Julián Garza Tijerina, who ultimately
became a senator:

I was serving as a medical doctor in Monterrey, where I later became director of the military medical facilities. A friend of mine

was named as Director of Medical Services for the state of Nuevo León. This friend asked me to serve as his secretary, but he resigned after six months, and I became head of those services. This position required that I check the quality of medical services throughout the state of Nuevo León. I did this with great frequency. When a political campaign came up, someone asked me to run for public office primarily because I knew Nuevo León extremely well—both geographically, by visiting most of the towns, and economically and politically, by knowing many of its problems from first-hand experience as well as many of the towns' inhabitants. I became a federal deputy as a result of this campaign.[50]

The other personality most commonly responsible for an individual's choosing a public career is someone in the immediate family, generally the father. This is a frequent characteristic among other political leaders. Robert Putnam found that political involvement for British, German, and Italian members of parliament was often a family legacy. Nearly half reported that some older relative of theirs had been active in politics.[51] Other scholars have implied that some political leaders have sought political power because of a loss of parental affection brought about through the death of one or both parents in childhood. Two-thirds of the British prime ministers over the last two centuries had lost one or both parents in childhood.[52] This condition appears to be rather common among the Mexican political leaders about whom parental information was available, but it is difficult to determine whether such deaths were uncommon among the general population. In fact, since life expectancy was rather low in Mexico during the 1900s to the 1920s, one might expect the early loss of one or more parents to be typical.[53]

Mexicans who mentioned parents as responsible for their political careers were referring to a politically active father. Typical of such persons is Hugo Pedro González, who became governor of his home state of Tamaulipas in 1945. He attributes his political involvement to the political activities of his father, who was active in local and national politics until the early 1940s.[54] In a study of why political leaders in Russia became revolutionaries, Jerome Davis found that the influence of family was the second most frequent reason, accounting for 17 percent of the responses of Communist leaders.[55] But he found that family members were responsible for two reasons: first, a legacy of political involvement or the values of influential family members; and second, a negative reaction to family members' beliefs or political activities in support of the czarist regime. Some Mexican leaders reacted against the Porfirian beliefs of their fathers, but the reaction was not important in explaining their political activism, although it was important in the development of their political beliefs.[56] It is quite probable that the Russian Communist leaders stated that they became revolutionaries in reaction to their families' beliefs because Davis phrased his question in terms of becoming a revolutionary instead of becoming just a political activist. Furthermore, the group under study here is from Mexico's post-revolutionary generation and thus not directly comparable to the Russian revolutionary group which made up part of Davis's sample.

The remainder of Mexican political leaders, although in small numbers, were involved in politics through a personal experience at the university, as a result of the general environment prevailing in Mexico during their young adulthood, or through participation in or observance of an external event. As an experience, the university, particularly for law students, was most important. Such an experience was also cited by North Americans as a frequent cause for entering politics.[57] One Mexican leader, a prominent party official and later director of a cabinet-level department, remembers such an experience at law school:

> The Law School was a place of many unsettling ideas. Many students thought they should participate in politics. There was a Grupo Universitario de Orientación Revolucionario, among whom was First Captain Alfonso Corona del Rosal (later President of the official party). It was made up of about twenty to thirty students, and I was a member. We supported Manuel Ávila Camacho in 1940, but we were surely a minority among the students.[58]

Not only was the experience of passing through a university environment conducive to stimulating political careers; the post-revolutionary environment itself, for those individuals pursuing careers in the early 1920s, also encouraged public careers. Ignacio Chávez, on the fringe of political activities as a prominent professor and dean of the National Medical School and who later became rector of the National University, has clearly expressed this feeling: "The environment of the times, that is, the Revolution and the changes it brought about, gave many of my companions the idea of serving the public, as well as becoming teachers or professors."[59] Least influential in encouraging Mexicans to become involved in politics were external events, whether political campaigns, economic or political crises, or changes in the international environment. The only such event mentioned by Mexicans was the Vasconcelos presidential campaign. One respondent, who was a student supporter of Vasconcelos, explains its impact:

> I believe this event was the most important political event for those Mexicans who are now between the ages of fifty-five and

seventy-five, because it occurred when they were young and impressionable. I believe there was considerable disillusionment resulting from the circumstances in which the campaign took place, and not because of the ideas of Vasconcelos. We had the opportunity to control the political apparatus of Mexico, but we lost—so then we had to learn how to win. I believe this loss became a prod which prompted many of the young students and intellectuals who became extremely capable politicians who did know how to win to go into political life.[60]

Comparisons of this study with findings from other studies of political leaders indicate certain similarities as well as differences among Mexicans and their counterparts in North American and European cultures. Mexican political leaders become interested sooner than North Americans in political subjects; friends are more important for developing this interest among Mexicans; the university environment and professors have a greater impact in involving Mexicans in politics; and Mexican leaders start their political careers earlier than North Americans.

The most significant contrasts among Mexican and North American political leaders appear to be caused by a major structural difference in the educational systems of Mexico, the lack of political party competition, and perhaps may be complemented by a need for friendship greater than that found in the societies from which the comparisons were drawn. Mexicans started political careers sooner because politics in Mexico is a full-time career, requiring the development of political and administrative skills, and, equally important, the early development of a network of personal relationships essential to success in Mexican public life. Furthermore, the nature of private enterprise in Mexico, especially during the period in which these figures entered public life, was one in which family dynasties controlled most managerial positions in successful firms, limiting opportunities of educated Mexicans for public or independent (and risky) professional careers. Mexicans also became interested in politics sooner than North Americans because of the relationship between interest and involvement, which suggests that, since most successful political leaders in Mexico started their careers during or immediately after college, their interest had to either coincide with that initial involvement or precede it by some time.

Mexicans also chose several agents more frequently than did North Americans or Canadians as being important in developing their interest because of certain structural and cultural differences. The university environment was prominent because of the location of the institutions responsible for political elite education in Mexico, and because of the domination of the National University and the Preparatory School in the education of Mexico's political leaders. This situation, combined with the fact that many political leaders teach at these two schools, explains their special influence on Mexicans' involvement and interest in politics. Friends have also had a more important role in influencing Mexicans because children are removed earlier from another source: influential parents. Friends are also an essential ingredient in the formation of personal cliques, which sustain the patron-client relationship in Mexican political culture.

Certain similarities are also apparent among North Americans and Mexicans. The politically active family has an impact in both cultures in developing an early interest in politics among future political leaders. Furthermore, Mexicans and North Americans usually became involved in politics for the same reasons, and the differences which occurred are related to structural differences in the political and educational systems. Overall, the findings support those few studies already in existence which suggest some typical patterns for political elites in general. They also suggest the importance of immediate forces on the choice of public careers by political leaders, an area generally neglected in past research.[61]

3

Parents, Friends, and Events
as Socializers

Most studies of socialization have found that family and friends are among the more important influences in this process. Political leaders provide no exception to this pattern. It is logical to look at the family as a source of socialization because most studies have shown that individuals "tend to have political attitudes and values like those of their parents."[1] As has been pointed out by Wayne Cornelius, previous works have been preoccupied with what is learned and in what sequence, but my focus, similar to his, will be on who or what was responsible for political socialization.[2]

Parents

Studies of North American legislators indicated that of those who attributed their earliest political interest to persons with whom they were in a direct and sustained relationship, many more mentioned family members than friends and associates as having been instrumental in this respect.[3] Twelve, or 25 percent, of the respondents from this study's expanded sample who answered this question indicated that one or both parents were most important or of equal importance to any other socializing influence.[4] None of the Mexicans mentioned other family members as primary agents of socialization, although several listed brothers as secondary agents.

A substantial portion of the respondents (24 percent) indicated that parents had had the strongest influence. Given the importance of family and kinship in Mexican culture and political life, one might expect the response to be larger. Heinz Eulau has speculated on what he believed to be a smaller than·normal role for the family in socializing California's legislators, suggesting that it might be due to the fact that California was still an immigrant state when his study was conducted, and it "may be that the formation of stable primary groups which can act as effective agents of political socialization have not been able to form."[5] Eulau's suggestion is applicable to Mexico, because the Revolution caused substantial uprooting, and, as the process of urbanization took place, parents frequently shifted their places of residence. Such moves can be seen in the majority of the biographies of Mexico's political leadership from this period.[6] Furthermore, the Revolution, like the process of industrialization, produced a new set of values that created pressures on traditional socializing agents.[7] As in all transitional societies, traditional family values came under attack. Moreover, in a previous analysis of the impact of the family on political interests, I found that most Mexican political leaders left their parents at a young age to go to school. This might be a further explanation for a low rate of family influence.

Several reasons have been suggested for why the majority of Mexican political leaders were not socialized by their parents. But what about the sizable minority which was so influenced? There are a number of characteristics common to many of them. Twenty-five percent of those who identified parents as the primary socializing agent also had been first interested in politics in their youth. One of these was Antonio Armendáriz, who recalls, "As a young child I began to understand many of the problems facing Mexico. I remember thinking that I should go to school in order to change my situation by taking the better alternative to improve my life."[8] But early interest in politics, while more common for this group than for those who were influenced by other sources, was not prevalent among the majority. Other characteristics were more significant than early interest, especially the occupation and economic background of the parents. The most prominent feature among family-socialized political leaders was the presence of a politically active family member. Of the twelve, six had fathers who were active politically or in the Revolution, and two had grandfathers who were prominent in state politics. This finding is unusual for Mexican political leaders, since data from the general population show that only about 30 percent of all prominent political leaders in Mexico during this period had relatives holding political offices.[9] Although more complete information would, I believe, increase that figure, the figure for this group of twelve is still quite high.

Politically active families are characteristic of the backgrounds of political leaders in other cultures. For example, one study of British party activists noted the degree of political activism present among their parents.[10] Heinz Eulau's study of North American legislators concluded that "it is likely that legislators too tend to come from families which are much more involved in politics than the average American family."[11] Individuals with relatives in political office have certain advantages over other aspirants to public office. One reason is that such a person has grown up in an environment conducive to political knowledge, interest, values, and participation.[12] Eulau has recorded a statement from a North American legislator illustrative of this environment:

> My first recollection of politics was when I was four years old and my father was a member of the House. . . . I played in this room [my father's office] when I was a little boy. Then, too, I experienced a brief congressional campaign when my father was a candidate for Congress. He was defeated, but the whole thing left a deep impression on me. I met lots of people in politics through my father.[13]

The late F. Javier Gaxiola, a Mexican whose father was a prominent politician in the state of Mexico, recalled similar images of his home, where his father entertained many prominent intellectuals and public men.[14]

　　The political activity of a parent was not alone responsible for parents being important socializers of future leaders. Perhaps of equal importance was the personality of the parent. For example, Mariano Azuela was more impressed with his father's personality than the fact that he had participated in the Revolution:

> My father was the most influential force on my ideas. He was a vigorous person—a person with great moral austerity, with few friends because of this and because his books became successful long after he had written them. He was deceived by the Revolution when he participated in it. He joined Villa believing he was invincible. When Villa was defeated by Obregón he was greatly surprised. I believe this defeat affected my father greatly.[15]

Furthermore, on the basis of the responses, it appears that closeness to the parent is of equal importance in determining the socializing influence of that parent. A lack of such closeness is quite probably responsible for Kent Jennings' and Richard Niemi's finding among North American students that the reason students and parents are not even more like each other is that some students adopt incorrect perceptions of parental attitudes.[16] Mexicans who believe that their parents were most influential have indicated they spent a lot of time with them, as did Miguel Alemán and his father, who was the most important influence on Alemán's intellectual formation during the years of post-revolutionary activity.[17]

The fathers of Mexican political leaders were the most influential family socializers. This response is not surprising, since they were the ones who participated in politics. Furthermore, the father plays a strongly authoritarian role in the Mexican family, and did so particularly during the period in which these Mexicans were raised. Even in cases in which the father was active in politics, however, some Mexican leaders recalled that their mothers were more important to the development of their ideas. Mothers who exceeded the impact of a politically active father did so either because the father was not close to the sons or because the mother was much more receptive to the changes in attitudes brought about by the Mexican Revolution. Víctor Manuel Villaseñor explains why his mother was so important:

> My mother had a much greater role in the development of my ideas in spite of the fact that my father was a federal deputy under Díaz and was the first Federal Inspector of Petroleum. But he did not have the political complexion of my mother. She was part of the oligarchy, but she understood the problems of the Mexican people and was a Maderista. When I became a Marxist in the 1930s, she began to read many of the classic Marxist works.[18]

Every fourth leader who chose his family as most important selected his mother as being more influential than his father. For some Mexicans, mothers took on a significant role because the fathers had died.[19] An example is Antonio Armendáriz, whose childhood was influenced in many ways by an intelligent mother:

> My father was a peasant who died in 1910. My mother was the person who influenced me most. She read most of the literature accessible to us during this period, works by Victor Hugo, Alexandre Dumas, and those of a famous astronomer. There were also many serialized books which came out in 10-to-15-page sections, and if you collected all of them you would have a complete book. These were sold everywhere. For example, I remember the novels of Riva Palacios. In addition to her secular readings, my mother read many religious works. The Bible and the various stories of the Jews and their fight for freedom and liberty all contributed to my intellectual development and environment. She had an above-average intelligence, read a lot, and played the violin. She felt the only way out for me was to go to school. She believed the best place for this was the Federal District. She was a supporter

of Madero, and she emphasized two solutions to the problem of Mexico: that "the only form of saving the people of Mexico was through education," and "that it was indispensable that all farmers should receive the fruits of their labor." I often heard these words from my mother during her lifetime. I believe that the cultural importance and influence of my mother was far more important than whether or not we had money.[20]

Politically active families are characteristic of Mexican political leaders who were influenced most by their parents. In addition, parents who had a significant impact on future political leaders were mostly from professional backgrounds and income levels which would put them in the middle or upper classes. This finding is not surprising, since anyone who was a politician during the pre-revolutionary years generally came from these classes.[21] But the parent's occupation is important to the socialization of political leaders in other ways. In the first place, other scholars have found that the higher the parent's status the more important the family as a socializing agent.[22] Only 63 percent of Mexico's general political leadership was from the middle and upper classes, whereas 75 percent of the political leaders who were primarily socialized by their parents came from such backgrounds. As Jennings and Neimi have suggested for North American adolescents, parents with higher levels of education, more often those from professional backgrounds, create an atmosphere conducive to a child's acquisition of political knowledge.[23] This condition is equally true of Mexicans. In his study of Mexican children, Rafael Segovia concluded that "the occupation of the parent has a fundamental weight on the orientation of the children towards politics, and the interest which develops in politics."[24]

Parental occupation may not be the only reason why some children are more readily socialized by their parents than others, but the location in which they are raised may be of some relevance in giving children an early awareness and interest which might make them more susceptible to their parents' views. Segovia found that children from the Federal District exceeded all others in qualitative and quantitative knowledge about politics.[25] It is difficult to substantiate the importance of parents' socio-economic background, political activity, and place of residence on the socialization of future political leaders because the three variables are interrelated. Politicians come from the middle and upper classes, which in turn are made up of professional people living in the major cities and state capitals of Mexico. But of the three variables, only one is not common to all political leaders: family political activity. Therefore, while the professional background of their parents and familial residence may have been of some importance, since precocious political maturation would have made it more likely for future leaders to have been influenced politically by parents before leaving for preparatory school and college, a parent's political activism still remains the important factor in socializing Mexican politicians.

Because parents' political activism was of considerable importance to political leaders socialized by a family member, and because the parents of most of the respondents were eligible to have participated in the Mexican Revolution, it would be revealing to know the activities of their parents during the Revolution and their attitudes toward the Revolution. The parents of the enlarged sample fall into four general categories: active revolutionaries; pro-revolutionary but inactive; anti-revolutionary; neutral. Unexpectedly, the largest group of parents was anti-revolutionary (35 percent). This figure is surprising because of its size, and because I had expected the interviewees to exaggerate the pro-revolutionary behavior and attitudes of their parents. Although the combined responses for active revolutionaries and inactive pro-revolutionaries (52 percent) exceeded that of the anti-revolutionaries, the latter group is substantial.

The anti-revolutionary parents were generally professional people who could not identify with the aims of the Revolution; self-made businessmen who, while sympathetic to the needs of the poor, did not want structural changes or saw violence as a threat to their newly achieved transition to the lower middle-class; or office-holders in the Díaz era. Alfonso Pulido Islas, whose father initially had welcomed the ideas of Madero, is representative of the transitional middle-class, which could not accept the resulting changes:

> With the death of President Madero and the reinitiation of the Revolutionary movement in 1913 with multiple manifestations and initiatives of the class struggle and the destruction of typically capitalist structures such as large landholdings and the community of interests of the State, the Church, and entrepreneurs, my father rejected the new audacious and aggressive objectives of the various revolutionary factions (Carrancismo, Villismo, Zapatismo, Floresmagonismo, etc.) and preferred the restoration of a system which would assimilate (because of his homesickness for the Porfiriato) the hateful dictatorship. From then on, until his death in 1950, my father was a most severe and rude critic of all the acts and achievements of public power, as well as of all tendencies toward socialistic structures and doctrines. His wife, less intolerant and more flexible, listened sadly to the frequent discussion which I had with him defending my revolutionary, anticlerical, and nationalistic points of view.[26]

Such families were important because, while they contributed to the positive development of certain moral qualities in their children, they also encouraged their politically inclined children, who in some way had to be sympathetic to the Revolution in order to succeed, to go outside of the family for their political ideas.

Of the pro-revolutionary parents it is surprising how many, whether active or inactive, had parents who were liberal supporters of Benito Juárez in the middle of the nineteenth century, a finding which suggests that for many of the Mexican political leaders, political sympathies have had a long tradition. In four cases, political sympathies extended to activism in the independence era during the second and third decades of the nineteenth century. In categorizing individuals as active revolutionaries, I have used a liberal definition which includes political office-holders from 1911 to 1917 as well as military activists from 1911 to 1917.[27] Of the revolutionary parents, all but two had been federal office-holders, generally under Madero. Only two parents had actually been involved in the fighting. César Sepulveda, who has held several positions in the middle levels of the federal bureaucracy, including the directorship of the Institute of Foreign Relations, describes his father's experience:

> He was a pure liberal, of those called *chinacos* or *jacobinos*. Deeply anti-imperialistic, he believed in Juárez and his ideas. He was one of the first to launch the Revolution from the 2nd of April of 1907—the first blow falling in Monterrey. As a schoolfriend of Emilio Madero, Lorenzo Hernández, Rafael Hernández, Lorenzo Aguilar, and others, in 1910, he formed the San Luis Rifle Company. Much later, when Emilio Madero joined Villa, my father was on the staff of the Zaragoza Brigade, in the financial section, because he possessed banking experience, having been one of the founders of the Merchants Bank of Monterrey. Ricardo A. Sepulveda saw the Porfiriato as a sickness, a decadence in the country, and opposed the lack of political liberty and the tremendous social inequality. He was of the opinion that Díaz, from 1884, had been a traitor to the Reform and the 1857 Constitution.[28]

For some families in Mexico, the Revolution, like the Civil War in the United States, served as a wedge to split family loyalties. In Mexico, at least among political leaders, such a split was rare, especially within the immediate family. Only one of the political leaders interviewed by the author had such a divided family, a father and two uncles who were against the Revolution and a brother who actually fought under a prominent revolutionary leader.[29] A small group also identified their parents as neutral toward the Revolution, evaluating its pros or cons or not discussing it at all in front of the children.

Regardless of their background, professional status, or participation in or attitude toward the Revolution, parents generally had the following influences on their children: political, philosophical, or professional. The first category has already been discussed earlier in the analysis of parents who politically socialized their children. But what of the other three quarters of the expanded sample who identified socializing agents other than parents: did parents have any influence on them? It is quite apparent, with few exceptions, that parents were remembered by these political leaders as forming their personal or moral values. Such values are important because, as Dean Jaros has suggested, culturally defined values of a general nature may have political consequences.[30] For example, one of the most significant might be honesty. Angel Carvajal saw his own father in such a light. "My father was a small rancher. He did not have any advanced studies, but was a very honest man. My principal purpose as Secretary of Government was to set a moral tone by my own behavior."[31] Others were influenced by more spiritual qualities: "As was common in my period as a student, my family suffered from great poverty: their culture was very limited (my father never went to school and he learned to read and write on his own); his religiosity was sparse (which perhaps influenced my atheism and my humanism and humanitarianism)."[32]

Many Mexican political leaders were influenced professionally by their parents; that is, they followed the same profession or established professional goals advocated by their parents. Twenty-seven percent of our enlarged group followed the same professional careers as their parents, usually as lawyers or engineers. One public man put it this way: "In general, the life of a person has much to do with his home environment. My father was a professional engineer and raised me in a middle-class environment. This had a great influence on my life and my own profession, but it did not really influence my ideas."[33] Other Mexicans from less fortunate circumstances hoped to give their children an improved life through better preparation. This situation was typical of many Mexican families from these circumstances and has been vividly described by Luis González:

> They "looked for the best way to do things" so as to derive the maximum ˋadvantage. Their conformity with the way of life handed down by their ancestors was nearly total; but the worm of ambition still gnawed at them—the wish to be more respected, richer, and wiser than their parents. Above all, they wanted their children to be better than themselves.[34]

Compare this literary description with Mario Colin Sánchez's recollection of his parents: ". . . they belong to what in Mexico we call the popular class, descendants of agricultural workers on both sides, and the great merit which they always had was their preoccupation with giving their children all of the economic elements at their means in order to prepare us and give us a profession."[35]

Friends

Although family members, especially parents, have had a substantial role in the formation of political leaders in Mexico, friends have also been important. Their influence, however, has been felt differently. General socialization studies reveal that friends are important in the formation of political values. As Jaros has concluded, "Peer groups seem to have most prominence as competitors to traditional socialization agents."[36] Because most Mexican political leaders left their families at an early age, one might expect friends to have a stronger socialization role in Mexico than in similar situations in the United States. But among the respondents in the enlarged group, not one mentioned friends as a primary socializing agent, although they were frequently mentioned as having some influence.

There may be several explanations as to why Mexican political leaders were not strongly influenced by peer groups. It appears that students search for reinforcement of their values and ideas in their choice of friendships. A University of Washington study indicated that student friendships became stronger and more like-minded from the freshmen to the senior year.[37] Furthermore, several studies of Latin American universities suggest that many students are predisposed to select departments or schools which philosophically are oriented to their own existing beliefs.[38] Future political leaders, like the average student, often select an environment in which they will encounter a homogeneous group of fellow students.[39] Therefore one would expect that young people with similar ideas would have little influence on each other. A study of Jamaican students supports this conclusion: ". . . we find that homogeneous peer groups function to reinforce working class political norms and the existent political cleavage between the working class and other social classes."[40] Not only do peer groups reinforce the future leaders' ideas, but many of the future leaders, because of personality characteristics, were themselves at the head of these student groups. Not surprisingly, almost all the political leaders about whom complete information was known, were prominent student activists, in the top of their class intellectually, or leaders of an intellectual group or literary activity. As one interviewee put it, "I would not say that my friends were too important, because, to speak immodestly, I was the head of my student group." In short, if anyone was influential on peer groups, it was the political leader himself.

Friends did not have a negligible role, however, because for many of Mexico's political leaders they served as transmitters rather than catalysts of new ideas. As Antonio Armendáriz commented, "as students we talked a lot about the ideas in newspapers and we exchanged books. Without television and radio we had to talk to one another and that was important in our learning about new ideas."[41] Friends served as a means of interchanging ideas, but, if future leaders were influenced by another source, most often professors, students reinforced the retention of these ideas. In his classic study of Bennington College, Theodore Newcomb concluded that "a recently changed attitude is most likely to persist if one of its behavioral expressions is the selection of a social environment which one finds supportive of the changed attitude."[42] I believe that fellow students often provide this social environment, and, in fact, continue to do so throughout their lifetimes. As I suggest elsewhere, Mexican political leaders retain student friendships throughout their lives, and use those friendships as a basis for entering political life or recruiting others to political life.[43] Newcomb also concluded that the husbands of the students in his college sample were most responsible for providing a supportive environment contributing to the continuation of certain attitudes among Bennington women for three decades. Since no wives were mentioned by Mexican political leaders as important to their socialization process, and, because until recently, wives have been uninvolved in political affairs, I would argue that friends, often from student days, play the same role for Mexican political leaders that husbands did for the Bennington women in Newcomb's study.[44]

Friends also played an important role as young adults because they provided a homogeneous socializing environment for the one dissident peer group—students from lower-class and provincial backgrounds. But, as several leaders mentioned, such students were easily influenced: first, by the city itself, and second, by the absence of their parents. Furthermore, Michael Langton, in his Jamaican study, found that students from lower classes, when mixed with peers from middle and upper classes, tended to be resocialized in the direction of higher-class political norms.[45] This finding seems to be true in the Mexican case, and it explains in part the conservative tone of political administrations in Mexico since the mid-1940s, administrations dominated and led by middle-class graduates of the National University who moderated the reformist views of their less fortunate but more socially conscious schoolmates.[46] As will be seen, middle-class students provide a reinforcing social environment, whereas professors, political leaders, or events were more important agents of political socialization.

In general, this analysis of the role of parents and friends on the socialization of Mexico's political leaders suggests two important findings. First, although parents had a substantial influence on political leaders, especially if they were themselves political leaders and/or professional people, the continuity of political ideas from parents to children was not as common in Mexico as it has been in other societies. In North American studies, where the political party preferences of children and their parents have been compared, only seven percent of the children had completely opposite party identification from that of their parents.[47] Yet in Mexico, even though it would be more likely for a political leader, because of the mythology surrounding the Revolution of 1910, to say that his parents were revolutionaries or pro-revolutionary, more than a third identified their parents as having views politically opposite to their own. This substantial change between parents and political leaders may be attributed to three factors: 1) the extraordinary nature of the transition taking place after the Revolution, 2) the more independent personality of the future political leader versus the average child, 3) the realities of Mexican politics, making some degree of confirmation to pro-revolutionary views a necessity, especially after 1929. At the same time, because of the middle- and upper-middle-class backgrounds of the majority of parents, peers, and professors of Mexican political leaders, these public figures have retained a certain conservatism in their views.[48]

The second finding is that friends are of secondary importance in the socialization of Mexican political leaders even though they are of primary importance to the success of their political careers. This finding appears to be due to the personality of the highly successful political leaders and to the homogeneous background of peer groups. However, it may also be due to two paradoxical attitudinal attributes of Mexico, one of which suggests that Mexicans give power to those who are most familiar, and the other of which describes the Mexican as very oriented to hierarchy. In short, Mexico is what Rogelio Díaz Guerrero calls an "affiliative and hierarchical culture."[49] The paradox is that while the Mexican political leader gives power to close friends or even family members, he looks to an authoritative figure for developing his own political ideas, not to an equal. In the family, it is the father who serves in this capacity; in the case of a missing father, sometimes a strong, intellectually oriented mother can play this role. At the preparatory school and the university it is the prestigious professor and administrator rather than the student who is the authority figure.

Events, Activities, and Environment

Most studies of political leaders show that political activities and historic events raised their political interest in addition to influencing their political outlook. One might expect such influences to be particularly important for the Mexican political leaders examined here because four events of world importance took place during their youth and young adulthood: the 1910 Mexican Revolution, the 1917 Russian Revolution, World War I, and the Depression of 1929. Furthermore, studies have shown that all elites, including political leaders, are affected more strongly by political and social changes than are the masses.[50] Of the respondents in the expanded group, 23 percent claimed that some important historic event, participation in a political activity, or the social environment of the times had a primary impact on their socialization. Although this group is sizable, and equal to that of Mexican leaders socialized by their family, it is a smaller group than I had expected. Even though many of the Mexican leaders mentioned specific events as having a secondary importance on their political, social, and economic ideas, it appears from their responses that unless they actually participated in an event or were directly influenced by the consequences of that event—however extraordinary—it had little significance.

In what way did the Revolution influence Mexican political leaders and how did they perceive the environment in which they grew up? For those who were adolescents during the first decade of the 1900s, the Revolution was a significant event, because this group saw firsthand the results of the Revolution (or had actually participated in it). Many of the leaders in the sample who grew up during the second and third decades of the twentieth century, on the other hand, missed the interruptions which the Revolution brought to the lives of earlier generations. Students in the 1900s often joined in revolutionary activiies.[51] The Revolution dominated the socializing experiences of these students. As the late General Juan Barragán, leader of the Authentic Party of the Mexican Revolution, wrote, "I retain fond memories of my student life, but my formation as a man really was the result of my participation in the Mexican Revolution, in which I dealt with all of the great leaders made possible by that movement."[52] Political and intellectual leaders who grew up during this period saw themselves as forming a new generation of Mexicans, the generation of 1915.[53] The Revolution was equally important in stimulating social changes and in creating, for the first time, an excited interest in political affairs among the rural population.[54]

For most of the Mexicans who were prominent in public life after 1946, the Revolution was a childhood memory or a recollection of secondhand accounts of relatives and friends. Only five percent of Mexico's political leadership after 1946 was born before 1900. The majority of these figures grew up between 1900 and 1920 and received their university educations in the 1920s and 1930s. They were Mexico's post-revolutionary generation. Of the leaders from this post-revolutionary group who selected events, activities, or environments as most important, 36 percent considered the national environment to have been most influential.[55] For some individuals, the knowledge of Mexico's past and its historical traditions was largely responsible for their political development. Martin Luis Guzmán has best described this influence:

> The history of the development of Mexico since 1810 had the most important influence on my ideas. This influenced me greatly in a spiritual way and in my political ideas. The most important figures, historically speaking, were Morelos, Juárez, and the reformists of the nineteenth century, such as Miguel Lerdo de Tejada, Melchor O'Campo, and the later Mexican educators Gabino Barreda and Justo Sierra.[56]

But for the majority, the national historical environment was overshadowed and influenced by the Revolution.

For the post-revolutionary generation, the most important characteristic of the environment was the prevalence of violence and instability. This atmosphere has been described rather carefully by Manuel Maples Arce, an intellectual who grew up during these years:

> Life in Mexico during those years was full of difficulties and potential military outbursts. After each presidential election there was only one pause, relatively brief, for public tranquility, before the political groups and military elements again returned to their agitation for the control of power. This was responsible for hours of unrest, parliamentary agitation and armed violence. Given this fate, a state of anguish reigned which made an impression on all of the spirits and did not leave without having a psychological impact on the life of the youth.[57]

The other environmental flavor which dominated the Mexican political scene during the 1920s and 1930s was the conflict between socially liberal and conservative elements, complemented by their attitude toward the issue of the separation of church and state in Mexico. Many young people, educated by clerics during their primary-school years, struggled with the fanatical positions held by representatives of both sides of the church-state issue.[58] Political partisanship and intellectual factions were present in the provinces, as recalled by Raúl Cardiel Reyes:

> During this period as a student in San Luis Potosí, I had many intellectual battles with students from the Catholic student organizations. At the same time, like me, many students who considered themselves "liberals" opposed what were then known as

communist student groups. The majority of students in San Luis Potosí adopted a philosophy which they called "liberal socialism." [59]

For the post-revolutionary generation, political instability, violence, and political-religious partisan conflict contributed to the national social environment which surrounded their adolescent years.

Another condition, less obvious or visible than the others but having an important environmental flavor, was the presence of foreign influence in Mexico and the growing sense of nationalism. As Henry Schmidt has noted, Mexico in the "1920's witnessed an enthusiastic nationalism as scholars, critics, novelists, poets, painters, and composers sought to capture the spirit of the Revolution and the meaning of Mexican history."[60] Growing nationalism seemed to be most important to the Mexican leaders of this period who became engineers. Luis de la Peña Porth has expressed this feeling as representative of the generations of the late 1930s and early 1940s:

> I think the most important influence on my generation and myself was a condition which existed in Mexico—that of foreign control over the mining industry. This environment played a significant role in the development of my ideas and my professional orientation. I surely believe this was a general condition of my generation at the university, where we discussed this situation.[61]

Among the conditions least mentioned by Mexican political leaders, perhaps because of its obvious presence, was poverty. The individual in the sample most influenced by it was Daniel Pedro Martínez, a doctor who came into direct contact with frightening social conditions:

> Two years after my graduation as a doctor, I worked for the public leper prevention service and had the opportunity to examine that disease in more than 2,000 homes throughout Mexico. This four-year experience opened a new panorama of medicine and human life to me. In reality, it was my major lesson in epidemiology, psychology, sociology, and politics. I have had the fortune of living many other experiences like this, but I am convinced that the most important in my life was the environment of my work and the social environment of Mexico.[62]

It is probable that other Mexicans were also influenced to some degree by social conditions, even though they were unaware of them or did not themselves conform to the norms of their own social environment or that of

Mexico.[63] One of the interviewees, Ernesto Enríquez, attempted to provide an example of the continuous importance of social environment on the interests and attitudes of Mexico's leaders. He noted that he, his father, and his son had all been raised in a similar social environment, one of considerable wealth. Each had received a law degree, his father in the 1890s, he in the 1920s, and his son in the 1960s. Unaware of his predecessor's topic, each wrote his law thesis on an organizational problem, though the subject of each thesis was directly related to Mexican social and economic conditions at the time of its writing. In short, Enríquez suggested that the homogeneous nature of his family environment produced a similar emphasis on organizational themes over three generations, but that changes in the social environment produced completely different topics mirroring those changes.[64]

For other Mexican political leaders, actual experiences or contact with important events were more influential than general social conditions in Mexico. Not surprisingly, of those who mentioned events as most important to their process of socialization, the Revolution ranked first. What is surprising is that only four individuals from the enlarged sample were most influenced by the Revolution, although most of them grew up during the Revolution. Several individuals, without actually having participated directly or indirectly in the Revolution, ranked it as most important to their philosophical formation.[65] Others, because they came into personal contact with the Revolution, usually through their parents, received lasting, vivid impressions. For example, Salvador Azuela recalls that

> life was more important than school since I had to suffer painful days in the period of the Revolution as a child and adolescent because of the participation of my father . . . in this historic episode. Because of his participation, during the first years of my preparatory training my class attendance was not normal on account of family necessities and the problems of subsistence during the revolutionary fighting.[66]

Still other men, while not perceiving the Revolution as the most important socializing influence in their lives, saw it as having a profound effect on their attitudes. One of them witnessed the consequences of the Revolution as a youth:

> I helped my father take pictures of men who were to be executed by the various sides during the revolutionary period. As a young boy, I saw and talked to men who were brave, melancholy, or crying just before they were killed. I also helped my father . . . pick up the dead men in the streets after an engagement by opposing

forces. All of this made a lasting and profound impression on me, and is something I would never want my children to witness.[67]

Other Mexicans, while not witnessing the Revolution, were forced to undergo experiences because their parents were in some way involved with the military or political groups competing for power in the post-revolutionary atmosphere. Among them was Miguel Alemán, who had to stop his studies because of the military activities of his father, General Miguel Alemán. During this break in his studies, he went to work as an employee of a petroleum company in Veracruz. A change in the political situation of the state, combined with the activities of his father, forced Alemán to flee for his life. He finally was able to join some regular government troops in Tampico, where he received a safe-conduct back to Mexico City.[68]

The remainder of Mexican political leaders who were primarily socialized by events were influenced by historic events from afar or by campaigns in which they were actual observers or participants. The most important events which they listed were

> Revolution, 1911
> Death of Francisco Madero, 1913
> Seizure of Veracruz by the United States, 1914
> World War I, 1914
> Pershing Expedition in Northern Mexico, 1916
> Constitutional Convention of 1917
> Russian Revolution, 1917
> Death of Venustiano Carranza, 1920
> Cristero Rebellion, 1926
> Reelection Campaign of Alvaro Obregón, 1927–28
> Death of Alvaro Obregón, 1928
> Presidential Campaign of José Vasconcelos, 1929
> World Depression, 1929
> Establishment of the National Revolutionary Party, 1929
> First Five-Year Plan of the USSR, 1928–32
> Debates of Antonio Caso and Vicente Lombardo Toledano, 1933
> Expropriation of Oil Companies, 1938
> Presidential Campaign of General Juan Andreu Almazán, 1939

Of these events, the most important were World War I, the Russian Revolution, the Great Depression, and the Oil Expropriation of 1938. For some, the first two of these events had a greater direct impact than did the Mexican Revolution, because they were old enough to understand their implications yet young enough to romanticize them. Manuel Palacios, who was a teenager during World War I and the Russian Revolution, believes that his generation saw both events in a very romantic light and that many members of his generation, who had read numerous Russian novels, were rabid supporters of the Russian Revolution.[69] The attraction of World War I to most Mexicans came from their interest and admiration for the French culture, a characteristic particularly true of political leaders from upper-class backgrounds and those with literary interests.[70] Of lesser importance to Mexican political leaders was the Depression. Initially, this finding seemed surprising, since the Depression had strongly affected the United States during these years and appeared to have influenced young people there.[71] After querying a number of political leaders as to the reason for the Depression's slight influence, however, I found that its actual effect could not be seen as dramatically in Mexico as in the United States and Europe.[72] In fact, the Depression was mentioned only by those political leaders who had traveled outside of Mexico during these years, an experience best described by Víctor Manuel Villaseñor:

> The 1929 Depression very definitely affected my ideas. The reason for this is that Eduardo Suárez had resigned from the United States-Mexican Claims Commission and I was appointed in his place. This circumstance brought me to the United States during the period you call the "Roaring Twenties," and, when the crash came, it had a tremendous influence on me because I was able to see the changes in the American economy, especially when I came back to the United States after an absence in 1931. . . . We had a period of rest, and I traveled to Pittsburgh, which made a deep impression on me. Then, when the first plan of the USSR was published, I began to see capitalism on the decline and a new ascendance of the Russian system.[73]

The last event of considerable importance was the expropriation of the oil companies by President Cárdenas in 1938. This event made a strong impression on student-age political leaders who were studying economics and engineering.

Other Mexican political leaders, like their North American counterparts, were most influenced by presidential campaigns or administrations, which together were of equal importance with the Revolution and the social environment as socializing influences. For North Americans, state or local political campaigns followed in importance, but they went unmentioned by Mexicans. The reason for this omission is probably the centralized nature of Mexican politics, in which, psychologically and pragmatically, political careers and participation occur at the national level. This situation explains why so few Mexicans actually begin careers at the local and state level, develop a regional reputation, and then move on to the national political scene. Instead, they leave their states at an early age to complete schooling in Mexico City, enter political life there, usually through the bureaucracy, and, several decades later, perhaps become the party's gubernatorial candidates without having spent much time in their home states. Generally, if a campaign was important enough to have attracted a person's attention and socialized him, often through actual participation, it did so in part because the individual attended school in the capital city or was involved in national student politics.

Two campaigns seemed to be of particular importance to the generations of Mexican political leaders under examination. The first, which was quite controversial, was the presidential reelection campaign of Alvaro Obregón in 1927. One of the principles of the revolutionary movement had been a ban on reelection. Obregón had been able to revise the 1917 Constitution to permit nonconsecutive reelection. In any case, the campaign attracted young people opposed to his reelection, and others who thought he still had much to contribute to Mexico's development. Alfonso Pulido Islas, one of the latter individuals, was in normal school when the election took place. He was active in student politics and attended several national congresses. In 1927, he recalls,

> We celebrated our Fourth Normal Congress, in which we decided to support Obregón for reelection. We formed a student group to carry out this goal, and I became president. I traveled all over Mexico with Obregón during that campaign. I was only 20, but I became friends with older politicians who were extremely important in that era, such as Aaron Saénz. Obregón called me *Chilipequín* [a small variety of Mexican chili] because I was the youngest. From this Obregonista group of students came such political leaders as Luis I. Rodríguez (President of the Official Party), Gustavo Corona (President of the Committee to deal with the petroleum companies) and Antonio Mayez Navarro (Head of Political Control under Cárdenas).[74]

The second campaign of considerable significance was a special presidential campaign in 1929, which was held after Obregón, who had won the earlier election, was assassinated. A disenchanted member of Obregón's earlier administration, known to numerous generations of students, decided to wage a campaign against the official candidate. The leader of this opposition campaign was José Vasconcelos. Vasconcelos drew most of his supporters from the urban middle class and from those students who would dominate political administrations after 1946. After the Revolution, this was the single most important event for Mexican political leaders, probably because, unlike the Revolution, most were old enough to participate in it.[75] For the most committed, it was a dividing line in their lives. As Mauricio Magdaleno, who was Subsecretary of Education in the 1964–70 administration, has written, "years later I felt my life was divided into two portions: before Vasconcelos and after Vasconcelos."[76] Others were captivated by his personality and his ideas, making it difficult to separate Vasconcelos's personal impact from the impact of his campaign. This was true of Angel Carvajal, one of the most successful Vasconcelistas, who lost out as a presidential pre-candidate in 1958 to another Vasconcelos activist, Adolfo López Mateos:

> I was a friend of Vasconcelos, a good friend, and my generation was captivated by his ideas, mainly because of his honest conduct in public office and his achievements for Mexico. I fought with him during his campaign in 1929. . . . I really wanted to moralize political life after that campaign. That was my main goal.[77]

For the generation of Mexican political leaders who have dominated politics in the 1970s it was the violent presidential campaign of 1933 between the official candidate, Manuel Avila Camacho, and the disgruntled loser of the official candidacy, Juan Andreu Almazán, which was most influential. This election affected a group of individuals who are outside the focus of this study, those holding offices in the 1970s.

Although presidential administrations were important as socializing experiences for North American legislators, only one presidential administration stood out in the minds of this group of Mexican political leaders, that of Lázaro Cárdenas. This finding is not surprising, because, as one respondent suggested, the transition from the period dominated by Plutarco Elias Calles to that of Cárdenas was marked by a change in the emphasis of social ideas.[78] Cárdenas impressed many of his younger contemporaries with his effort to cope with the social problems of the Mexican people. His image was further enhanced by his move against the oil companies in 1938 at a time when he was generally unpopular among students and middle-class groups.[79]

Among Mexican leaders who chose an event, activity, or the overall social environment as being important in their development, the Revolution stands out as being most significant, but not overwhelming as a socializing influence. The social environment of the post-revolutionary period, experienced by most of the members of the enlarged sample during their youth, was equally significant. Both of these influences overshadowed the importance of presidential campaigns for Mexicans, although campaigns have been most important to North American political leaders. Even to an elite group from middle-class, urban backgrounds, the Revolution and the environment it created made a much more significant impression on the fabric of society than did the Depression for a similar type of individual in the United States. The dynamic changes in Mexican society, more than individual events, will continue to affect the attitudes of Mexicans for many generations.

4

The Social Influence of the School Environment

Family, friends, events, and social conditions have all been influential in the formation of the philosophies and values of Mexican political leaders. But a sizable group of Mexican leaders was more influenced by three other sources: school, professors, and books, all of which were part of the academic experience. Sometimes it is difficult to separate these three influences, because each is interrelated and contributes to the overall university environment. As Dean Jaros has suggested, students can be socialized at school in five different ways: 1) by curricular content alone, 2) by curricular content mediated by educational quality, 3) by teachers' overt expression of their own values in classroom situations, 4) by teachers' more casual expression of their own values in less structured, out-of-class situations, and 5) by pupil identification with particular teachers and adoption of values these teachers are perceived to hold.[1] In some cases, individuals believe they have been influenced by an amorphous combination of all of these experiences, something they label the university's social environment. Although several Mexicans were influenced by grammar-school teachers and school literature, nearly all who mentioned some aspect of the school environment as being important referred to their preparatory and university experiences.

There are few studies of the importance of the university on the socialization experiences of students in Latin America, but a study by Kenneth Walker of three Latin American universities concluded that "the kind of socialization experience undergone by university students undoubtedly had a persisting effect on their future orientations, as a number of studies suggest. . . ."[2] Schools and the universities are likely to have such an influence on Mexicans as well, since Segovia's study of grammar and secondary school students revealed that publicly educated children (from among whom come the majority of Mexican political leaders) chose school as the second most important place in which they spoke about politics, after their own homes.[3] The importance of the school environment is not foreign to North American legislators either, since many have suggested that their study of politics at the university was responsible for their becoming interested in political affairs.[4]

The educational system deserves a close examination because most political leaders, regardless of the culture, are well educated and thus have passed through such an environment.[5] Moreover, as suggested earlier, most Mexican youngsters leave their families and attend preparatory school and the university at the age of 15 to 16, thereby reducing the influence of family over their youth and increasing the likelihood that the educational environment will be important.[6] Not only is the physical distance important in this process, but, as Harold Lasswell has suggested, under

> various circumstances the culture of one's early years is rejected in whole or part, especially if it is perceived as a handicap to a successful career in politics. Individuals reared in minority cultures not infrequently break away and acquire the majority way of life; and local or regional figures reach out to achieve enough sophistication to pave the way to the playing of an active part in the larger national or transnational arena.[7]

Again, as suggested earlier, many Mexicans mentioned the ease with which they were drawn to the middle-class, urban environment which pervaded the university.[8] Lastly, in the Mexican and Latin American context, there is considerable intervention by political and economic groups in secondary and professional education, a phenomenon which we know little about.[9] The more politicized nature of the Mexican university environment is an important aspect of this environment's socialization of Mexico's political leaders.

The Mexican university environment deserves our attention for other reasons, too. One reason is indicated by the suggestion of several respondents that their graduating class seemed to be a generation with a shared set of experiences.[10] What it means to be a member of a generation has been best defined by Karl Mannheim:

> The fact of belonging to the same class, and that of belonging to the same generation or age group, have this in common, that

> both endow the individuals sharing in them with a common loca-
> tion in the social and historical process, and thereby limit them
> to a specific range of potential experience, predisposing them for
> a certain characteristic mode of thought and experience, and a
> characteristic type of historically relevant action.[11]

Being a member of a generation does not necessarily imply that each individual accepts the values and goals of his fellow members, but that each has similar perceptions and values as a result of shared experiences. As one respondent suggested, "I think that members of my generation did have the same
ideas even though later they followed different paths."[12] And, as will be argued in a later chapter, certain values appear to have been shared by members
of the same generation.

Educational environment deserves special attention in the Mexican
case because of the overwhelming prominence of two institutions in the educational backgrounds of Mexican political leaders: the National University
and the National Preparatory School. Studies indicate that the type of school
as well as the discipline chosen by the student both have an effect on pre-
disposing a person toward politics in general and specific political attitudes in
particular.[13] Among Mexican children in general, Segovia found that students from public schools expressed a greater interest in going into politics
than students from private schools.[14] Among Latin American university students in general, including in Mexico, Arthur Liebman found that certain
faculties had higher percentages of conservative students. At the National
University, the schools of Philosophy and Engineering ranked highest in this
regard.[15] Such orientations are important because they may well affect the
values of future professionals, including political leaders. Joel Verner, in his
study of Guatemalan legislators, seventy-five percent of whom had received
their college educations from the University of San Carlos in Guatemala City,
found that both the location of their university education and the fields they
studied were important and significantly related to their political orientations.[16] The social environment of the university and the professional school
has also undoubtedly had an influence on Mexican political leaders. The reason for such an influence, as suggested by Kenneth Prewitt and his colleagues,
is that "social groups nourish ambitions and provide definitions and directions
for the career aspirant. The logic of this position is persuasively supported with
reference to group theory, which points out that the cues picked up from others
determine how we view the world and our place in it."[17] One study has suggested that attending a university which dominated the education of a political
elite heightened the sense its students had of belonging to an educated class.[18]

The preparatory and university experiences also deserve an examination because of the age at which most Mexican political leaders are exposed

to that environment. Adult studies of partisanship have suggested that partisan beliefs increase steadily during the adult years. At the same time, it appears that people are most susceptible to independent political, economic, and social views at some time during their adolescent years.[19] Most Mexican political leaders were at school during these susceptible years. Furthermore, Kenneth Prewitt and his colleagues, in their study of North American council members and state legislators, found that among those who believed their socialization had taken place as pre-adults, the study of politics in school and participation in school politics were two of the three experiences most frequently mentioned.[20]

Last, but not least important, the National Preparatory School and the National University play a major role in the recruitment of future political leaders.[21] This factor is important to the socialization process of future political leaders because the structure of a political system may be significant in shaping the ambitions of the individuals who occupy offices within it. As Gordon Black has argued, "the structure of a political system acts as a filter that allows some types of individuals to move up through the system, while others are either stopped in their progress or diverted in less risky and costly directions."[22] Furthermore, in a system in which the political elite largely recruits the incoming elite, or what Ralph Turner has described as a closed system of sponsorship, "the elite recruits—who are selected early, freed from the strain of competitive struggle, and kept under close supervision—may be thoroughly indoctrinated in elite culture."[23] The Mexican academic environment may well be characterized by peculiar conditions which have shaped the ambitions and beliefs of students who have passed through it.[24]

During the 1920s and 1930s, what was the general intellectual environment of the university? Students from the period and historians of Mexican education during these years agree that ideological diversity characterized the intellectual environment at the National University. Unlike the students who were educated in the conservative ideological environment at the end of the Porfiriato, the students who formed the generations of later Mexican political leaders were exposed to all varieties of intellectual viewpoints, including nineteenth-century positivism.[25] Antonio Armendáriz, who studied at the National Preparatory School in the 1920s, likened this period to a rebirth of education in Mexico. He remembers that professors expressed varying social and political views.[26] By the 1930s, however, the university had begun to return to its earlier, conservative tone, although professors continued to hold various views. The right tended to predominate in the 1930s for several reasons. First, greater numbers of individuals with more conservative ideas had had the fortune to receive an education which would qualify them to teach at the preparatory school and the universiy. Furthermore, they had income from

other sources and were economically able to teach.[27] Second, the National
University had achieved autonomy in 1929, and for a short while it tended to
remain outside the control of the state.[28]

As this conservative emphasis was recognized by intellectuals and politicians, they supported the introduction of socialist education, the goal of
which was to make education more relevant to society and to eliminate the
elitist nature of access to education in Mexico.[29] At the university level,
Lázaro Cárdenas in 1938 tried to counteract the influence of the National
Polytechnic Institute in Mexico City. But, as one respondent pointed out,
the National Polytechnic Institute never attained the prestige of the National
University and never produced a substantial proportion of Mexico's political
leadership. Students formed political groups to support conflicting ideological
views, the leftists being known as *rojos*, and the reformists or moderates as
amarillos. Professors and political leaders who were not supporters of the conservative educational ideology established a Workers University to help less
fortunate students and workers get an education. Vicente Lombardo Toledano soon converted this institution into a politicized curriculum characterized by socialist and Marxist teachings. In the provinces during these same
years, conditions were slightly different. Raúl Cardiel Reyes, who studied at
the University of San Luis Potosí in the 1930s, recalls the environment in
great detail:

> Most of the students and the professors did not differ a great
> deal from those in Mexico City. We had different views and phi-
> losophies from those of our professors, and on the whole, we were
> much more liberal. I received many of my ideas from publications
> which were circulating at that time outside of the university. Our
> student publications also reflected these liberal ideas, ideas which
> were from some of the European thinkers like Bergson and Mohr.
> I believe that we were in a period of renovation, or a period
> in which we had a revolutionary generation (in an intellectual
> sense).
>   Many of my professors were from the Porfirian period, that is,
> they were professors who by and large had lived most of their lives
> before 1910. For example, my professor of philosophy stressed
> Spencerian ideas, which, of course, were part of the nineteenth-
> century positivist thought. Positivism was still very strong during
> my student days at the University of San Luis Potosí. . . . We
> were in an intellectual environment which was slightly back-
> ward, inherited from the Porfirian period.[30]

Not only were the students faced with an intellectual environment in
constant flux and agitation, but student activists and intellectuals debated

the issue of whether or not students had the moral obligation to participate in political affairs.[31] The philosophical debate over whether or not to participate in politics was part of the broader university environment which exposed students to the subtleties of political activities on the student level and the skills one might need to participate in public affairs in later life. This environment was part of the socialization experience of students who attended the National University, and many respondents contrasted it with the straightforward academic experience one would encounter in the prestigious private schools.[32]

The most universal educational experience shared by political leaders in Mexico was at the National Preparatory School in Mexico City. In the years immediately following the Revolution of 1910, the preparatory school was still characterized by a predominance of positivistic professors and by a lack of students sympathetic to revolutionary ideals.[33] This situation began to change as young students-turned-professors, stimulated by the social and cultural changes wrought by the Revolution, began to interject new currents of thought into the preparatory school, both inside and outside of the curriculum. Furthermore, an increasing number of students who previously had not had ready access to preparatory education because of their class background, began, by the late 1910s and early 1920s, to attend the preparatory school. The preparatory school soon began to serve as a melting pot and sometimes boiling cauldron of ideological views and social backgrounds. Adolfo Zamora, who entered the National Preparatory School in 1920, remembers it this way:

> The National Preparatory School during my generation became a very important social institution in bringing students from different family backgrounds together. It served as a sort of unifying institution in Mexico. During the years 1909 to 1925 there were some professors who were actually holdovers from the pre-1910 period. There were also revolutionary professors who were trying to conserve a cultural attitude in Mexico in spite of the revolutionary violence, the moral breakdown, and the physical upheavals characteristic of the time. Most of the professors during this period from 1909 to 1925 were either very young or extremely old.[34]

Professors were not the only ones who accounted for the intellectual stimulus. As Zamora implies, the school drew together students from diverse socio-economic backgrounds. The associations and activities of the students themselves were often more important than the classroom environment. In recalling the opening of a new world of political and social ideas, Andrés Iduarte, another student of the period, has written that it was not his classes, but his companions—who chatted in the corridors and published student newspapers—and the atmosphere of the street which contributed most to his mental images.[35] As another student pictured it, neither professors nor students alone but the interaction between the two were responsible for the environment:

> I believe it is a bit erroneous to judge the importance of the National Preparatory School by the work of certain distinguished teachers. It is more precise to understand this importance as born in the confluence of teachers and students who tried to translate to an academic language the unrest and the external problems of Mexico and those who surrounded her.[36]

But did the social environment of the National Preparatory School have an influence on the values of public figures? Such a role has been suggested for the secondary schools in Turkey and even more strongly among the public schools in England.[37] Rupert Wilkinson argues that the public schools in England "bred mental flexibility rather than imaginative foresight. Faced with an urgent need to change, the Old Public School-boy was usually resourceful in his adjustment; confronted by crisis, he would 'muddle through.' What he frequently lacked was the interest in new ideas. . . ."[38] Robert Putnam further describes the public school experience as producing an 'elite culture demonstrating "a reliance on internalized norms rather than on codified rules to govern the exercise of power, a preference for amateur generalists rather than technically trained specialists, a finely tuned sensitivity to emergent consensus, a gradualist approach to problems of social change."[39] Mexico's political leadership since the 1940s could be described in similar terms. In fact, one of the distinguished members of the Revolutionary Family, Antonio Carrillo Flores, has suggested that the leaders of his generation and thereafter put great emphasis on practical solutions, but had little interest in ideological issues, issues which might have provoked an interest in new ideas and solutions to Mexico's problems.[40]

The National Preparatory School paralleled the British public school in another regard—the sense of public service instilled in its students. Byron Massialas has suggested that in England, "once in school, students were socialized to norms of political leadership and to high expectations for political participation. On admission to one of these prestigious schools, one was almost assured of membership in the politically important circles."[41] A number of Mexicans received this impression during their preparatory years. Sealtiel Alatriste, for example, believes that his experience had a great influence on and preparation for his career in public life. He described his generation as part of the first generation ready to do things for Mexico.[42] Another Mexican felt, like many other political leaders, that his preparatory education gave him a strong sense of humanism. His studies were responsible for his belief that he must serve in government in order to change Mexico.[43]

As was suggested earlier, the desire to serve was a reason given by many of the respondents for entering public life in the first place, and, in many cases, that desire was the result of a preparatory school or university experience. For many Mexican political leaders, the preparatory environment was more important to their philosophical formation than were professional schools at the National University. This finding seemed to be almost universal among political leaders graduating from the more technical professional schools, particularly those of engineering and medicine. Pedro Daniel Martínez, who in an earlier chapter expressed a strong feeling of social consciousness, saw his preparatory and university education as two different experiences:

> Preparatory education was much more important for this kind of later role [career in public affairs]. It was a much better education, and, as a result, I was very frustrated and disappointed with my medical training. One of the reasons why I was so disappointed is that there was no emphasis on public service; in fact, we received a very negative appraisal of public service being "bureaucratic medicine." In preparatory school, an emphasis was placed on serving all Mexicans and Mexico.[44]

Even for some political leaders who went to law school, where the courses had a more humanistic emphasis, preparatory school still was seen as more important to their philosophical formation because of its breadth and its emphasis on values.[45] But whether political leaders thought their preparatory school was more important than their professional experience or first became interested in politics at the time they entered preparatory school, the preparatory education undoubtedly influenced Mexicans in a variety of ways. Mario Colín Sánchez, himself a political leader and historian, has captured (with a vivid eye) the significance of this experience for ex-president Luis Echeverría:

> The National Preparatory School, probably the school most loved by all university graduates, notably influenced a good part of the students who passed through it in their cultural formation as well as in their political ideas. This occurred concretely with my generation. I met Luis Echeverría, the present President of the Republic, in the preparatory school, and together we com-

mented on diverse occasions on the social message of the frescoes
of Orozco, Siqueiros, and Diego Rivera, all of whom captured our
sensitivity to and unrest about the problems of our country.

I am sure that the National Preparatory School very much influenced the initial formation of Luis Echeverría, and that it
was here where his vocation toward public service was first
accentuated.[46]

Students who attended preparatory schools in the provinces also seem to have
been equally influenced by the social and intellectual environment.[47]

Preparatory students who entered politics also appear to have been influenced by this common experience in developing a sense of team play, similar
to, but not as well-developed as, that characteristic among the British political elite. Robert Putnam notes that in England, "school customs and extracurricular activities have been even more important in inculcating the peculiar blend of initiative, strong leadership, self-restraint, loyalty, conformity,
and team play that characterizes products of the public schools."[48] Many of
the Mexican respondents expressed dismay at the violence and behavior
characterizing student political activities in the 1960s and 1970s, not because
of a "generation gap," but because they seemed to believe that there were
certain rules of the political game, one of which excluded the use of violence,
even though many had themselves participated in opposition campaigns and
movements against official government candidates. In this sense, the preparatory school, by centralizing the education of the majority of future political
leaders in one institution, contributed to a common socialization experience
for most leaders and made them familiar with certain unwritten rules.

The major difference between the English public schools and the National Preparatory School of Mexico is that while each contributed to a certain outlook among its graduates, provided a central pool of future political
leaders, increased the homogeneity and integration of the leadership, and increased their ability to cooperate effectively, the British public schools recruited from a more established and selective social and economic group than
did the more accessible Mexican National Preparatory School.[49] But, while
the British schools were dominated by an upper-class social and economic
elite, the National Preparatory School became an institution producing a
new, middle-class elite, which, like generations of British aristocracy, sent its
children back to its alma mater. Although the Mexican institution had much
greater social diversity in the backgrounds of its students, it—like the British
public schools—quickly absorbed the lower classes into its social environment, one characterized by middle-class, moderate values; urbanity; and professional training. The significance of this experience for the Mexicans may

well be that they have had a socializing experience shared by few other Mexicans, something which may accentuate a difference between the views and values of the masses and those of the political elites. The values of Mexican leaders and their significance for the stability of the Mexican political system will be analyzed in some detail in a later chapter.

The professional schools at the National University had less influence on the intellectual views of some political leaders than did the National Preparatory School, but for others they were more stimulating. Among the professional schools, the National Law School was most important, first because it graduated more political leaders than any other school or university in Mexico, and second because it had inherited a humanistic tradition, much like that of the National Preparatory School. Although the law curriculum was more limited than that of the preparatory school, students did not study in an environment isolated from the contemporary issues of the 1920s and 1930s. Lawyers dominate Mexican politics for many of the same reasons that lawyers dominate North American politics. Kornberg and Thomas have suggested that the law-school environment is partially responsible in the United States:

> The dominance by lawyers of public offices involved in administering law in this country suggests that the embryo American legislative leader probably found himself in an environment in which politics and the political process were salient topics of conversation. He soon realized, or was made to realize, the possibilities inherent in combining a legal with a political career.[50]

Mexican law students studied in an environment influenced by national politics, particularly since their professors, like those in the National Preparatory School, were divided, at least until 1930, into two groups, those sympathetic to positivism and those sympathetic to the Revolution. For example, Antonio Carrillo Flores, a student during the 1920s, remembers a feverish speech by Narciso Bassols, a distinguished educator and public man who exhorted professors to remember that the Law School in 1925 was not the same as it had been in 1912, and that they had the obligation to form a generation of students who would promote the new law, that of the Mexican Revolution. He was rebutted by an equally renowned jurist, Miguel S. Macedo, who, as a distinguished representative of the pre-revolutionary educators, replied that they were here to teach the science of law, not conservative or revolutionary concepts.[51] Furthermore, as suggested previously, students were involved in numerous political activities, newspapers, and intellectual and social societies, all of which contributed to the overall climate of the Law School.[52] Many of these same students enticed their classmates to dabble in national politics, participating in presidential campaigns for both opposition and official party candidates.[53] Moreover, several major political-intellectual issues also flavored the campus environment in the 1930s. One of the respondents, a prominent student leader during this period, describes one of the more important conflicts:

> At that time there was a strong Catholic element which manifested itself in an attitude expressing greater appreciation for Spanish values than Mexican, in seeing reforms as bad for Mexico, and, of course, in taking an anti-Marxist stance. This group saw humanism as a guide to education in Mexico, a movement which places more emphasis on cultural factors than on economic interests. The other group was the liberals, made up largely of the middle classes, who accepted the indigenous values as more important than the Spanish, who defended the efforts of Juárez, and who attacked Porfirio Díaz and accepted the Mexican Revolution. They did not support a classical economic system, but rather advocated a mixed economic system. I was a member of this latter group.[54]

Many future political leaders did not go to law school. Of those who did attend a university, particularly the National University, a large number were drawn to the National School of Economics, orginally created within the Law School but emerging as an independent school by 1934. It is worth discussing briefly the intellectual environment of this school, for although it too was characterized by a left-right or liberal-conservative conflict in the early years, by the early 1930s it had established itself as having a leftist orientation.[55] In general, this leftist philosophy has predominated at the school through the 1970s.[56] Unlike law-school students, economics students were trained for positions in the federal government.[57] The private sector had not yet accepted economists as desirable or necessary, and, as one author has pointed out, the stated objective of the school was "to train leaders in economic science for governmental policy positions."[58] Therefore, the intellectual and professional environment was more delineated at the School of Economics than at the Law School, especially during the 1930s, when, as described earlier, the intellectual environment at the National University was conservative, while the economics school was leftist.

The majority of future political leaders were socialized to some degree by the educational environment at the National Preparatory School and the National University, but a smaller group attended preparatory school or received their professional training in the provinces. The social environment of

Mexican provincial institutions has varied widely at different periods in the twentieth century. Some provincial institutions, similar to the National School of Economics, were characterized by a certain intellectual flavor. Private schools at the state level have had a negligible effect on political leadership since so few public figures emerged from their classrooms. For example, the most well-known private institution located in the provinces is the Monterrey Institute of Technology and Advanced Studies. It, however, was not founded until 1943 and was established and supported by the industrial community of Monterrey, Nuevo León, which employs many of its graduates. Its intellectual and social environment is in no way comparable to that found in public institutions.[59]

Some of the public universities have been comparable to the National University in their social and intellectual environment. For example, the University of Oaxaca, originally the Institute of Arts and Sciences of Oaxaca, was an institution influenced by pre-revolutionary and post-revolutionary ideologies during the period of this study.[60] Other universities have changed their intellectual environment from one era to another. The University of Guanajuato, whose students have been compared in the Myers study with students at the National University, shows little indication of an environment which would be compatible with the views expressed by most Mexican political leaders. Yet in the 1910s, groups of students at the University of Guanajuato were prominently involved in intellectual activities promoting the achievements of the Revolution, and many of these same leaders became important politicians in the 1930s.[61]

Still other schools came under the influence of local or regional political leaders and movements. Students at the University of Guadalajara, for example, were abruptly drawn into the church-state conflict through the Cristero rebellion, which centered in Jalisco during the latter half of the 1920s.[62] On the other hand, the University of Michoacán (formerly the Colegio de San Nicolás de Hidalgo) came under the influence of a key political leader of twentieth-century Mexico, Lázaro Cárdenas, who, as governor, met weekly to discuss social and intellectual questions with students and professors of that Morelian school.[63] Regardless of the provincial public university attended, most studies and memoirs indicate the presence of two common themes equally important to the environment at the National University: ideological diversity and the surrounding political instability and violence.

Only a few students avoided this university environment, and those were young people fortunate enough to travel and study outside of Mexico. As suggested in a previous chapter, they not only missed the larger social environment in which the university students found themselves, but, equally important, they missed the Mexican university environment. While it is difficult to generalize about the foreign university experiences of Mexican political leaders, it is definite that each individual experience was of considerable importance to the formation of the person involved. Ernesto Enríquez, who studied in Spain in 1914–15; Miguel Bustamante, who studied in the United States in the 1920s; and Gilberto Loyo, who studied in Italy in the 1930s, all have recognized the influence of these experiences on their development.[64] Some political leaders indicated that their foreign educational experiences were more influential than their domestic education. For example, Jesús Puente Leyva mentioned that his studies in Santiago, Chile, were more important than his other educational experiences. Also, his studies in the United States had clarified his ideas about this country and made his views of it much more realistic.[65] In the 1970s Mexico had two presidents, Echeverría and López Portillo, who received some of their education in South America. Commentators in the Mexican press have suggested that Echeverría's sympathy to Salvador Allende, and to his government, stemmed from the Mexican leader's days at the University of Santiago.

Without specifically analyzing the content of the preparatory school and the university curriculum or the intellectual orientations of the professors, what, if any, has been the socializing influence of the school environment on future political leaders? Studies of student experiences in other cultures are contradictory. One study of male students at Miami University in Ohio concluded that graduates were characterized by a significant increase in political liberalism as compared to when they entered as freshmen.[66] A study of Argentina, Colombia, and Puerto Rico, all countries having an educational system more similar to that of Mexico, found that education may actually enhance skepticism about the political process.[67] This phenomenon has surely occurred among future political leaders in Mexico, many of whom as students actually opposed the government in election campaigns or in strikes provoked by government policies. But this opposition was an initial, youthful reaction and obviously had to be overcome in order for them to become successful active participants in the political process. As suggested earlier in the study of the 1929 presidential campaign, activities against the government actually reinforced the desire of many future political leaders to participate in the system and to change it. However, other studies of college students, such as that by McClintock and Turner on North Americans, conclude that "four years of college experience had little, if any, impact upon the political knowledge, involvement and values of college students."[68]

Even though general studies of college students are contradictory, Mexican political leaders, as well as political leaders from other countries, have indicated that the university environment was important to their socialization. Kenneth Prewitt and his colleagues, in their study of North American political leaders, noted:

> The interview schedules are rich with quotations attesting to the "inspirational" nature of the educational experience. One respondent followed up his classroom interest "by making a habit of attending city council meetings every Monday night." Others were so absorbed by their new interest that they have maintained life-long contact with the teacher first responsible for their political introduction.[69]

This statement could just as easily have been written about Mexican political leaders, many of whom have followed similar patterns and had similar experiences. It is probable that political leaders, unlike the general student population, are much more susceptible to political influences. The university environment is an indirect catalyst in forming their ideas. One Mexican respondent suggested that as a teenager he did not have any definite ideas, but when he attended the university, he began to think more clearly in ideological terms.[70] The social environment of the university not only stimulated many young students to put their views in an ideological framework; for some students, the general environment actually determined definite ideological views.[71]

Furthermore, although a review of general studies on the impact of education on socialization shows that there are no clear results about the effects of student involvement in school-wide decision-making as opposed to classroom decisions, Mexican political leaders were actively involved in such decision-making roles in student-faculty governing bodies.[72] Mexican students generally have participated in school discussions and debates to a greater extent than is found in some other western cultures. Such participation and the learning which results from it, especially when external political conflicts became part of the university or classroom environment in the 1920s and 1930s, have been shown to contribute to increased interest in and knowledge of politics.[73]

An eclectic, pragmatic approach to politics evolved from the Mexican political leaders' educational environment, in which certain universal influences were present. Students were exposed, both at the preparatory schools and the universities, to considerable ideological diversity, an experience which would suggest that the source of their philosophies is an eclectic education. In addition, because of the students' exposure to and participation in intellectual and political activities, and because of the encouragement of many professors, there seemed to be an emphasis on public careers, an emphasis which went beyond the typical personal desires of some individuals to make politics their profession. For many, public life was the only professional alternative. Furthermore, because of certain common experiences shared by members of this generation at the National Preparatory School and the National University, most of these leaders developed a certain sense of unity through identifying themselves as part of a special group. Lastly, exposure to the vagaries of political instability and violence on and off campus seems to have made a universal imprint on those student generations.

These common themes running through the university experiences relate to the ideological beliefs which characterize Mexican political leaders. Important among those beliefs is the emphasis on a pragmatic and eclectic approach to development, the need for peace and order, and a sense of cooperation among members of those generations to achieve certain goals. Although other sources of socialization have been essential in engendering these values among Mexican political leaders, the social environment of their preparatory and university school days contributed substantially to those values.

One of the most important of those values was the belief in a commonly shared experience and a sense of unity among these generations. This is not to suggest that these individuals agreed on ideological means as a result of these experiences; rather they gradually developed an elite culture characterized by certain unwritten rules or beliefs. Among these beliefs was one agreed-upon means: orderly transition without large-scale violence. But several other patterns developed out of these socializing experiences, and they seem to have been duplicated, interestingly enough, in the experiences of British political leaders from the public schools and from Oxford and Cambridge. One of these informal cultural patterns is what Rupert Wilkinson calls political manners:

> The purpose of manners is to subordinate selfish impulses and to standardize outward behavior, with the accent on moderation and courtesy. Political manners create a common ground of communication between different interest groups and tend to make compromise a good in itself. A disadvantage of setting great store by political manners is that it may encourage hypocrisy, concealing conflict from the public eye by wrapping it in the mists of official harmony.[74]

Political leaders in Mexico, regardless of personal or ideological faction within the official family, have demonstrated their ability to communicate with each other and to make the transition from one administration to the next, even in cases in which there was considerable opposition to the chosen pre-candidate.

This pattern has some important implications for the Mexican political system. Not only does it imply certain ground rules to which the players must agree in order to stay in the game, but, as one scholar has suggested, it may well influence the content of the political process.[75] The contributions of the preparatory and university environment to this process are strongly enhanced by the nature of political recruitment in Mexico. Most of Mexico's leaders from these generations were recruited by professors at the University who themselves were public men and who were those most influential in contributing to the ideological positions and values among these students.[76] This pattern has occurred in generation after generation, helping Mexico's leaders to create a supportive environment in accepting the informal rules of political behavior, and playing an important role in socializing new political recruits.[77]

The implications of the environmental contributions to the socialization of Mexican political leaders are twofold, both for Mexico and for countries with similar educational systems and leadership structures. It could be argued that this environment aided Mexico to develop a political elite which allowed it to cope with serious problems from 1940 to 1970 without succumbing to the chaos of political instability so apparent in many other Latin American and Third World countries. On the other hand, while this educational experience strengthened the ability of Mexico's leaders to provide political stability, it also reduced the possibility that fresh ideas from outside their shared experience would find ready acceptance among an increasingly homogeneous elite culture, ideas essential to Mexico's leadership if it is to successfully cope with a multitude of problems without plunging Mexico back into the violence of an earlier era. Moreover, the sharp differences in educational environment between the private universities which have produced Mexico's industrial leaders and the public universities which have produced its political leaders have contributed to important differences in perceptions between these two groups, differences which have led to serious tensions and outright conflict.[78] In addition, both these groups of leaders are isolated from the masses whose future they control because they have received the socializing influences of two educational experiences which even in the 1980s are unavailable to ninety-eight percent of the Mexican people. The educational environment undoubtedly helped to determine the modern political culture and the problems it has produced.

5

The Impact of Books

The overall environment of the university has had an important influence on the socialization of Mexican political leaders. Another influence on political leaders, particularly Mexican leaders, has been literature, both inside and outside of the classroom. The reading of books, which is a self-initiated process, has complemented and has been a part of the university experience. Davis found that, of the various socializing influences on Russian revolutionary leaders, literature ranked above *all other sources* of influence. Slightly more than one-fifth of the Russian leaders ranked it as most important.[1]

Studies of school curricula suggest that they do have a socializing influence on students, whether that influence occurs through the transmission of new values or the reinforcement of old values.[2] Because the social environment of the preparatory schools and the universities in Mexico during the 1920s and 1930s was one of dynamic transition from pre-revolutionary to post-revolutionary values, both forms of influence operated equally on students. For example, the process of reinforcement has been clearly shown in a study made of United States political-science students.[3] In general, it appears that the influence of a curriculum on political values is much greater when the values being taught are in harmony with those expressed by other sources of socialization, such as the family, friends, and professors themselves.[4] Furthermore, the type of curriculum, even controlling for other factors, may determine the political outlook of students. The values inculcated in students vary from discipline to discipline and school to school, but studies of United States institutions reveal a general trend of increased liberalization of values for students as they go through college.[5]

.Even without such comparative empirical data, the interviews with Mexican political leaders reveal quite clearly that many new values were learned in preparatory and university years, values to which they would not have been exposed had they remained in the small villages and provincial cities of their youth. The lack of communication in post-revolutionary Mexico would have made exposure to these ideas unlikely without classroom experiences. In the broadest sense, education was a liberalizing experience, but Mexican political leaders, like students in the United States, received more emphasis on political and social values and issues in some curricula than in others. As shall be shown, the curricula at the National Preparatory School and the National Schools of Law and Economics were most conducive to inculcating in the students new social, political, and economic ideas. The preparatory schools during these years required courses in such diverse subjects as world history, Mexican history, economics, philosophy, logic, foreign language, literature, mathematics, geography, physics, botany, and Spanish. In fact, under Article 4 of the Study Plan for the National Preparatory School approved by the Secretary of Public Education in 1924, one of the goals of the curriculum was to provide concrete information about the production, distribution, and circulation of wealth in Mexico.[6] Each student, depending on his future professional discipline, followed a particular track of courses, but all students took a number of common courses, many of which were in the social sciences.

The National School of Law was also important in socializing students because of its curriculum. Studies of United States law schools suggest that curricula are less influential than in Mexico on the political values of law students since "attempts in the law schools to establish significant interrelationships between law and economic and social problems have failed because they have been scattered, incidental, and lacking in a sufficiently broad basis in knowledge on the part of both students and instructors.[7] Although the legal curriculum in United States law schools has some similarity with that of the National Law School in Mexico, the latter institution, born out of a humanistic, scholastic tradition, required students to take sociology, economic policy, and several courses in public law and Mexican constitutional law. It should also be remembered that the law in Mexico was undergoing tremendous changes as a result of the 1917 Constitution and the heritage of the Revolution. In the fifth year of law school, students could choose three electives, among which were Mexican Economic Policy, the History of Mexican

Civil Institutions, Labor and Social Welfare Legislation, and Mexican Banking and Credit Institutions, all of which involved considerable emphasis on new ideas and institutions created since 1915.[8] The emphasis on economic courses in the Law School is also reflected by the fact that the National School of Economics was created and first staffed within the Law School. The other professional programs responsible for the education of most political leaders have been engineering and medicine, but I have omitted them from the following discussion of literature because respondents from those schools indicated that their readings and classes had little influence on their political, economic, or social ideas. Their evaluations are confirmed by a careful analysis of the courses required in these professional schools.

Classroom Readings by Mexican Authors

During the 1920s and 1930s there were two broad categories of academic literature used in the classroom: native and foreign. It is the purpose of this section to analyze only that literature written by Mexican authors used in classes emphasizing social, economic, and political issues. In the following sections, predominant foreign authors and their works will be dealt with, followed by a description of literature read outside of class. The analysis will focus primarily on the classes at the National University, where most political leaders were educated. It will discuss only those ideas of individual authors which were attributed to them by Mexican politicians.

Those classes making the greatest use of influential literature were the sociology courses required of law students, the public-law courses, and the economics courses dealing with economic philosophy and Mexican economic institutions. All law students were required to take the same introductory sociology course. One of the prominent teachers of this course at the National University during the years of this study was Luis Chico Goerne, who used few works by Mexican or other Latin American authors. The only major Mexican works mentioned by students as having been used in this course during this period were José Vasconcelos's *The Cosmic Race* and Antonio Caso's *Concept of World History*. Both authors have been identified by political leaders as extremely influential professors in their individual socialization process, and their writings and personal philosophies will be discussed in the following chapter. The first work represented the efforts of Vasconcelos to formulate his ideas about the mestizo "race" in Mexico and Latin America, and the second book, like so many of Caso's, emphasized the spiritual importance of man in his society.[9] Although some students remember reading prominent South American writers during this period, the sociology courses appear to have been dominated by European and some North American writers.[10]

Economics courses, more plentiful in the Law School than those in sociology, were more important in the formation of Mexican political leaders. Furthermore, many political leaders enrolled in the new economics discipline established within the Law School, and, by 1934, they had begun to graduate. "Economics courses tended to be value-oriented through the 1950's because they inherited the humanistic tradition which became linked to a Marxist ideology and the rejection of mathematics and quantitative methods. . . ."[11] Furthermore, because the study of economics in Mexico was not officially established until 1929, there were no trained economists either to teach or to write texts for economics courses.[12] The school and the curricula were patterned after the London School of Economics because one of the founding members of the National School of Economics had attended this school.[13] Many of the original professors were Law School graduates and professors, so that students of both disciplines often had the same teachers.[14]

Although books by Mexican authors were scarce at the beginning, the professors who taught economic theory, general economic history, and economic policy used works from Mexican sources. Among the sources used in the economic policy course taken by all students of the National School of Law were Article 27 of the 1917 Constitution; the Agrarian Law of January 6, 1915; and the Agrarian Code of 1927. The course focused on, among other issues, agrarian problems and justifications for agrarian reform. During this period, the agrarian question seems to have been the domestic economic issue receiving the greatest attention in economics courses.[15] In addition to the agrarian issue, the general economic history course dealt with a subject of considerable interest to Mexicans, the importance of imperialistic economic systems on the development of Latin American countries. But the only Mexican work on economics which students read during this period was by Enrique Martínez Sobral, a notable professor, novelist, and self-taught expert on Mexican economic questions. He published the first Mexican textbook on economics, entitled *Principles of Economics with Special Reference to Mexican Conditions*. This was the text used at the National Law School, and his book was influenced by the thought of Charles Gide, an important French thinker.[16]

Mexican authors had little influence on students taking economic courses during these years, but political leaders have suggested that such courses were important for their socialization. Values received from this influence will be analyzed in a later chapter, but it is worth noting that a study done from 1926 to 1928 at the University of Chicago on the impact of an economics course entitled "The Economic Order" concluded that changes in students' attitudes could be ascribed to the influence of the course. Furthermore, there was a tendency toward slightly increased radicalism among the students taking the course.[17] Based on what they consider their own ideological preferences and those of other notable Mexican leaders, it appears that the respondents who were graduates of the National School of Economics have views which are further to the left than those of political leaders who were graduates of the Law School. I have no information on their ideological views before they became students, but there are no apparent differences in their social background, family, or education which would account for this difference prior to entering the two professional schools.

Law courses, although less likely than economics courses to allow for emphasis on social and political issues, were much more likely to include the work of Mexican authors because of the long tradition which legal studies have had in Mexico. The courses at the Law School reflected the ideological emphases of the professors who taught there, professors who were exponents of both old and new views. Even into the 1920s and 1930s there were many conservative professors at the School of Law.[18] Antonio Carrillo Flores has even suggested that his law-school generation of the 1920s was a "post-humous child of positivism" because it comprised students of positivist professors who were teaching a dying or dead philosophy.[19]

Even though readings by Mexican authors were in a definite minority in law classes, they did exist. The reasons for their presence can most frequently be traced to the legal changes occurring during the Revolution and to the numerous legal codes in the early 1930s. Changes in the legal system were reflected not only in the subject matter of the courses, but in the curriculum itself. Changes were made to allow for new courses in labor law, administrative law, and fiscal law.[20] The one Mexican document used in numerous law courses and described by Mexican political leaders as influential is the 1917 Constitution. The 1917 Constitution was studied in some detail in the constitutional law course taken by all law students. It is not surprising that the Constitution of 1917 is mentioned frequently by political leaders as an important source of their political views, first, because of its historic importance as a document reflecting the ideological tenets of the 1910 Revolution, and, second, because it was analyzed in some detail in other courses, namely Guarantees and *Amparo*, Labor and Social Welfare Legislation, and Administrative Law.[21] The first course, taught for many years by Narciso Bassols, analyzed all of the basic rights of the individual as they are spelled out in the Constitution. The second course, taught for several years by Vicente Lombardo Toledano, focused particularly on Article 123, dealing with labor questions. The administrative law course used the Constitution as a basis for discussing many new codes in the fields of government relations, petroleum, minerals, and railroads which emerged in the decade after 1920.

Certain specific articles also served as a basis for discussion in several law courses. In particular, Article 27, which deals with the agrarian problem, appears in many course syllabi, including that of public law under Manuel Gómez Morín, a course on the history of law, and the new course in agrarian law. This last course, taught by Luico Mendieta y Núñez, emphasized twentieth-century agrarian issues in Mexico. But because there were no texts written by Mexicans available for this subject, Mendieta y Núñez's class notes, like those of many of his colleagues, soon formed the basis of a text on agrarian law, published in the 1930s.

The lack of Mexican texts was apparent in other courses, such as the course in labor law taught by Eduardo Suárez and Vicente Lombardo Toledano, both of whom became prominent public men. Those courses dealing with new legal areas in Mexican law were particularly deficient in Mexican works. Other legal documents in the field of agrarian law also served as primary text material: for example, the 1915 law, the 1922 agrarian code, and the 1927 code. The fact that the new agrarian and labor legislation was incorporated in these courses affected the interests as well as the education of political leaders. An examination of law theses written by political leaders from the National School of Law in the 1920s and 1930s reveals a heavy emphasis on labor and agrarian questions.[22] Miguel Alemán, for example, describes the importance of the labor question on his initial formation and his early political career:

> My thesis reflects some of my ideas. I believe it might have been the first one written on the subject of work compensation and hospitalization for workers in Mexico. After my graduation I began working in this same field. Because of my interest and activities in this area a number of union leaders proposed my name to President Cárdenas as a supreme court justice, but I was too young to be eligible for such a position.[23]

The remaining books which were authored by Mexicans and used by law professors were of two types: strictly professional law texts with little social, economic, or political interpretation, and books dealing with ancient civilizations in Mexico and their laws.[24] None of them was mentioned by Mexican political leaders as having any influence on their formation.

Before arriving at the schools of Law and Economics, students were exposed to a wide range of literature at provincial preparatory schools or the National Preparatory School. For the students who attended the National Preparatory School during the late 1910s and early 1920s, the emphasis was on a positivistic education. Still, many professors during that period were advocates of liberal or even revolutionary ideas. As one student of the period has suggested, preparatory-school students were taught that they should conserve the life they had and be inspired by the past to change the future.[25] Two books by Mexicans seemed to have been of particular importance to students during this period: a work on logic by Porfirio Parra, and Justo Sierra's *The Political Evolution of the Mexican People*. Parra's work, because of the subject matter, had more relevance for students' beliefs concerning the process by which they might make future decisions. But Sierra's work, dealing with social and political questions, argued for concrete goals. Among the most significant of these, in light of what actually happened in recent Mexican political history, was his analysis of the importance of a political party: "The day that a party succeeds in maintaining an organization, political evolution will resume its progress, and the man, more essential in democracies than in aristocracies, will come later: the function will create an organ." [26] Furthermore, Sierra argued that Mexican social evolution would ultimately be futile unless it attained its final goal of liberty. It is interesting to note that the evolution of the official party and the concomitant political stability, along with the ultimate failure of the political system to reach the goal of widespread political liberties, have been two of the most widely discussed characteristics of Mexico's political history since 1929.

Mexican authors in the classroom appear to have been less influential than legal documents published during the early twentieth century, but, in the area of foreign literature which affected law, economics, and preparatory students, there are greater numbers of influential authors. These predominant foreign authors wrote in the areas of sociology, economics, and law during the 1920s and 1930s.

Classroom Readings by Foreign Authors

Foreign writers had considerable impact on individual courses at the National Preparatory School. Three authors, one German, one North American, and one British, were most important to political leaders. The German author was Arthur Schopenhauer, whose ideas were discussed in philosophy classes. But Schopenhauer's emphasis is on moral issues, and his writings have little to do with broader social and economic alternatives. The influence of the North American writer, William James, was similar, but his basic concept, that concrete experience is essential for clarifying and resolving philosophical issues, may well have contributed to the pragmatic emphasis among future Mexican leaders. [27]

The works of John Stuart Mill were those most often cited by the respondents as having had some importance in their formation at the preparatory school. Some of his ideas relevant to the Mexican experience include his view that various forms of paternalism and enlightened despotism may be the best policy for a given nation if those governments prepare it for

the next steps. Furthermore, he attached more importance to political education than to day-to-day efficiency in government.[28] His recognition that representative institutions are not suited to all peoples, depending on their education and independence, provides a justification for Mexico's official party
and semi-authoritarian system, at least during the early years.

Preparatory-school students during these years also discussed Marxism
and the role of the government in the economy, but it does not appear, at
least through the 1920s, that Marx's works were actually used in classes. The
dominant foreign influence in class was French, extending back to the 1910s,
when the texts for math, physics, chemistry, sociology, and botany were untranslated French works. Furthermore, French, as well as English, was studied intensively for two years by preparatory students.[29]

The study of sociology was required by all law students and all economic students when economics was offered within the Law School. During
these years, professors Antonio Caso, Luis Chico Goerne, and José López
Lira were the instructors in the general sociology course. As noted in the next
chapter, Caso and Chico Goerne were remembered by former students as
having had a significant influence on their formation. In fact, of all the professors mentioned by former students, Antonio Caso ranks as the most influential during the 1920s and 1930s. His class on sociology was dominated by
foreign thinkers, particularly the French.[30] This foreign influence was equally
apparent in Chico Goerne's course, which centered on individual theorists,
only two of whom were native Mexican thinkers: Caso himself and José
Vasconcelos.[31] Among the foreign writers discussed by both professors and remembered by students as having had some impact on their ideologies were
the Frenchmen Gabriel de Tarde, Henri L. Bergson, and Émile Durkheim;
and the Anglo-Americans Lester Ward, James Mark Baldwin, and Herbert
Spencer; also influential were Polish sociologist Ludwig Gumplowicz and
Oswald Spengler, the world-famous German author.

All law students during this period were exposed to the ideas of these
men. A brief examination of their work suggests some of the political and
social ideas which young Mexican students discussed. Of the three French
thinkers, Durkheim and Bergson had the most to contribute in terms of ideological orientations.[32] Bergson is considered to be an important leader of the
Romantic philosophical movement of the late nineteenth and early twentieth centuries. As Harold Randall has suggested, this is a movement against
construing human experience in terms of reason alone. It is characterized by
its open-mindedness and its receptivity to whatever truth and whatever value
any experience may reveal.[33] This orientation was important to Mexican students of the 1920s because it provided a rationale for breaking away from the
positivistic influence still present in the Law School and suggested to the

Mexican that he could find much of value in his own historical experience. Caso himself stressed both of these ideals.[34] On the other hand, Durkheim, in his book *The Rules of Sociological Method,* was an advocate of rationalism, or extending scientific rationalism to human conduct. For the contemporary Mexican political context, he had two ideas which were relevant. In terms of goals, he hoped "to transcend partisan ideological struggles and to forge a dialectical reconciliation of conservative, radical, and liberal traditions in modern thought."[35] However, he

> did not present the competition of interest groups as the desirable end state of modern society. . . . Durkheim's concrete goal was the formation of communal groups controlled by norms under aegis of the democratic state. This was the basis of his idea of a revitalized corporatism respectful of individual liberties.[36]

It can be easily argued that, although the democratic state did not develop, since the 1930s Mexico has evolved its own form of corporatism.[37] Furthermore, Durkheim's philosophical reconciliation parallels the ideological practice of the ruling party in Mexico.[38] At this point I am not suggesting that Caso and Chico Goerne were advocates of these ideals, nor that students were influenced by them to the extent that they may have applied them in a highly modified way to the practice of politics, but only that they were definitely exposed to them.

French writers dominated the teaching of sociology in Mexico during the 1920s and 1930s, but Anglo-American influence was also significant. Two writers dominated the Anglo-American contributions: Spencer and Ward.[39] Spencer made his contributions in his *First Principles* (1862). His "basic principle was that society is an organism, like all other organisms, and subject to the same evolutionary laws as all others. Any attempt, therefore, to remove human society from the laws that operate uniformly and implacably upon nature is foredoomed."[40] More relevant to our thesis however, was his view of government. Henry Steele Commager succinctly describes it as follows:

> Indeed, where government was concerned, Spencer was not merely a Manchester Liberal, he was almost an anarchist. He believed that because government is based on the necessity of dealing with evil in man, it is itself a reflection of that evil; if men could but learn to cooperate with nature, they would not need government at all. Like the Marxists, he looked forward with confidence to the eventual withering away of government.[41]

Presenting an opposing and more positive view, Lester Ward argued against laissez faire capitalism and social Darwinism, and for the role of the government in the development of society. He thought of government as far superior to private enterprise in any tasks it might undertake and believed it had a role in the organization of the energies of society for beneficent purposes.[42] In comparing the two men, it would not be fair to say that Spencer was an apologist for the capitalist entrepreneur, but only that he believed that individuals and groups were the greater creators for society.[43] While Mexico's governmental system has evolved along the lines of Ward's thinking, it would be accurate to say that among the majority of entrepreneurs in the Monterrey group, and even among a significant minority of political leaders in Mexico, Spencerian views still exist.[44]

Two other Europeans who contributed to the philosophical education of young Mexicans were Spengler and Gumplowicz. In his highly controversial *Decline of the West*, Spengler presented a number of interpretations concerning the efficacy of political systems. He did not see democracy in a favorable light; instead he perceived it as the prime agent in the destruction of cultural values.[45] But perhaps more relevant was his analysis of political ideologies, as described by H. Stuart Hughes:

> If this is the reality of politics, then political ideologies are essentially meaningless. They are merely slogans. "In the world of facts, truths are simply *means*, effective in so far as they dominate spirits and therefore determine actions. . . . But, *as* catchwords, they are for about two centuries powers of the first rank." The question of whether they are "deep, correct, or even merely logical," is quite unimportant. Their practical effectiveness alone counts.[46]

The symbolic use of ideology as a mask for pragmatic political behavior has been a hallmark of Mexican politics. Spengler, of course, is not the source of this phenomenon in Mexico, but those leaders who were to practice this belief with considerable effectiveness were exposed to this view early in their philosophical formation.

The last of these important foreign sociologists, Ludwig Gumplowicz, also perceived political institutions with a pessimistic eye. He saw political life as a conflict between classes and the emergence of a state as arising from the subjection of one group by another in the economic interest of the latter.[47] Gumplowicz and the other foreign thinkers contributed a variety of views for the Mexican student of sociology to ponder. Although there is no single theme prevailing among these views, in general the authors are critical of past and present political institutions, and in no way do they suggest imitating a contemporary regime. It can be justly argued that these foreign thinkers supported the explorations of Mexican intellectuals and the intellectual temper of the times in finding an eclectic, and, in part, native solution to the problems of Mexican society.

In a sense, part of the eclectic approach was reflected in the establishment of the study of economics at the School of Law in 1929. Furthermore, during this period, all law students were required to take a course in political economy during their first year. As was suggested above, because of the newness of the discipline of economics in Mexico, the literature was almost exclusively foreign. Among the economic writers and theorists who were discussed in the political economy course and who influenced generations of law students were Adam Smith, David Ricardo, Alfred Marshall, Sidney Webb, John Maynard Keynes, and Karl Marx. All were British, with the exception of Marx, who spent much of his life in Britain.[48]

The most traditional view of economics represented by this group, is, of course, in Adam Smith's *Wealth of Nations*. At the risk of over-generalizing, I suggest that, for this discussion, he might be considered the Herbert Spencer of the economists. Like Spencer, he has often been misrepresented and misquoted. Robert Heilbroner carefully explains Smith's view of the role of government in economic growth:

> . . . Adam Smith is not necessarily opposed—as his posthumous admirers made him out to be—to *all* government action which has as its end the promotion of the general welfare. . . .
>
> What Smith *is* against is the meddling of the government with the market mechanism. He is against restraints on imports and bounties on exports, against government laws which shelter industry from competition, and against government spending for unproductive ends. Notice that these activities of the government largely have the interest of the merchant class at heart.[49]

While Smith provided part of the foundation for modern laissez faire economic theory, David Ricardo became one of its first critics, suggesting that the landlord was the ultimate profiteer in such an economic system. His view of the economic world was not a pleasant one. His conclusions about the landlord, if applied to the large landowner in the Mexican context, might be considered an appropriate analysis of the pre-revolutionary period.[50]

In a more contemporary vein, Mexican students were strongly affected by the views of Alfred Marshall and Karl Marx. These two critics of the nineteenth-century capitalist system provided a fruitful and significant comparison for future political leaders. Clark Kerr, in an insightful analysis of their thought, suggests the extent of their impact:

Both Marshall and Marx left an historical residue of understanding and prescription. The new liberalism was overcoming the old *status quo* and Marshall helped to liberate the new liberalism. Workers were rising as a new element and Marxism helped draw attention to the importance of the workers; and the realization of their importance helped lead to their absorption into society, helped encourage the formation and acceptance of their unions and cooperatives and labour parties. The new liberalism made possible the acceptance of the workers and their organizations; the new socialism made this possibility an urgent necessity. Thus these contrasting approaches, represented by Marshall and Marx, made progressive contributions *together* to the new synthesis of modern society where the workers were integrated within the framework of liberalism. Marshall and Marx, with their understandings and their prescriptions, in open contemporaneous conflict yet unwitting historical cooperation, helped shape modern capitalism. They also gave rise to Keynes and to Tito—to guided capitalism and to market socialism; and thus to potential reconciliation between the worlds of capitalism and socialism.[51]

The reconciliation to which these two thinkers contributed is part of the mainstream of the economic thinking of the Mexican political leaders who graduated during the two decades under examination.[52] While it is often difficult to separate the private ideological views of a political leader from his public statements, most students of the Mexican political scene suggest that its leaders are neo-liberals and social democrats in their political ideologies, rather than Marxists or classical liberals. Interviews with Mexican political leaders support this view, although privately most of them seem to believe that they hold ideological views which are left of center. Coupled with the impact of Marx and Marshall, it is not difficult to understand the influence of Keynes on a generation of young Mexicans. Keynes went much further than Marshall in his revisionistic view of capitalism, suggesting that only a comprehensive socialization of investment would secure full employment conditions.[53] It is Ruben Vargas Austin's contention that Keynesian economics, as adapted to Mexican problems, has been more important in the development of economic policy than any other single influence. Keynes book, *General Theory of Employment, Interest and Money*, was widely read in Mexico after 1936.[54]

The economic views which most impressed the future political leaders were highly critical of abuses and weaknesses in the traditional capitalist system. The authors were influential, not just because they were critics, but because they suggested practical policy alternatives which their readers might follow. The Mexican students, learning in a milieu of declining positivist influence and the openness of the dynamic post-revolutionary period, listened intently to criticisms so applicable to their historical time and experience. Although many of the inadequacies criticized then still exist in the Mexican economic system, some concrete solutions were attempted by the political leaders of the post-1930s.[55]

Finally, basic law courses were strongly influenced by foreign literature. In fact, until 1930, French ideas dominated the law courses.[56] Students had to be able to read French since many of the texts used in these classes were untranslated.[57] Despite the predominance of European ideas in the teaching of public and private law in Mexico, the ideological impact on the students was much less, in view of the number of law courses, than in the few courses in sociology and political economy. Among the many French works used during these years, one by Leon Duguit, entitled A *Treatise of Constitutional Law*, stands out as having influenced many future political leaders. Students from the 1925, 1929, and 1935 graduating classes have remarked on Duguit's influence.[58] Antonio Carrillo Flores believes that many of Duguit's phrases have been used in the expression of social ideas in Mexico.[59] Perhaps his most relevant idea is that law should stress the benefits to society as a whole rather than just to the individual.[60] His work was discussed in Manuel Gómez Morín's and Manuel Borja Soriano's courses. The other most widely used law text in Mexico during these years was that of a German, Gustav Radbruch, who wrote *Introduction to the Science of Law*. His book was translated from German into Spanish in 1930. The text often focused on arguments concerning the purpose of law and its relationship to liberal and conservative political ideologies.[61] The book also contained an excellent discussion of socialism.

Even though French ideas continued to be of great significance during these years, by the late 1920s French dominance began to decline. Javier Malagón has explained why:

> There were two main causes for the loss of primacy by the French doctrines: the incorporation into the school of professors of German and Spanish origin (the latter influenced by the German and Italian doctrines which dominated the Spanish universities), and the fact that numerous works of other origin were translated beginning in the second decade of the twentieth century.[62]

In addition to the European professors who came to Mexico City during the 1930s, two young professors who were named as influential teachers visited Germany and Austria and returned to teach during these years. They were Mario de la Cueva and Eduardo García Máynez, who taught a course on the

philosophy of law during this period.[63] Other German works most often mentioned by former students included those of Georg Jellinek, Karl Jaspers, and
Hans Kelsen. Again, like most of the French authors, these legal theorists
were generally concerned with the philosophy of law rather than social uses
of the law.[64] But what is important to understand is that many of the courses,
such as Manuel Gómez Morín's public-law course, exposed students to different ideological views, including Marxism, Bolshevism, Communism, and
fascism.[65]

Anglo-American influence in law courses per se, while present, does
not appear to be significant. José Vallejo suggests, for example, that, when
law students studied North American legal ideas in the 1930s, they often did
so indirectly through European sources.[66] Anglo-American ideas were most
significant in the law course on guarantees and *amparo*, which dealt with such
diverse sources as the Marshall decision involving *Marbury vs. Madison* and
the *Federalist* papers. The most important British scholar mentioned by Mexican students was Sir Henry Sumner Maine. His work, the *History of Law*,
attempted to discover some common principles for correlating legal and social change in different societies. Perhaps more important on an ideological
basis was his general thesis that the individual's self-determination actually
increased as central political authority grew, rather than the reverse.[67] This
concept is important in the Mexican context because it provides the Mexican libertarian with an argument for the increase in government control in
social and economic spheres since 1930.

Some readers may wonder why the North American influence was not
greater. In addition to the extensive Spanish legal heritage in Mexico and the
fact that North Americans were not as prominent as the French or Germans
in the philosophy of law, the ambivalent attitudes of the Mexican toward his
northern neighbor were important. As one public figure recalled:

> In addition to these two individual acts of violence [the occupa-
> tion of Veracruz and Pershing's expedition], the attitude and be-
> havior of foreign investors, both North American and European,
> also began to have a significant impact on our philosophy. One of
> the things I did not do was to learn English, and this was true of
> many of my friends, primarily because at the time we believed
> that this was the language of foreign imperialists. Of course, now
> I regret that I never learned the language, but this feeling in our
> youth is illustrative of the general feelings we were developing to-
> wards foreigners and of our developing sense of nationalism.[68]

As is made quite clear by Frederick Turner, the North Americans and British
were the most prominent, and probably the most deserving, targets of this

nationalism.[69] In intellectual areas, then, it is difficult to separate the impact of Anglo-American ideas from the Anglo-American actions which contradict or complement them.

What, then, was the significance of Mexican, European, and North American ideas on future political leaders in Mexico? Without a doubt, interviews with and the writings of political leaders suggest that these and other intellectual influences inside and outside of the classroom had a strong impact, even though the educational experiences varied from one student to the next. In general, despite the presence of several influential positivistic or conservative thinkers, the emphasis was upon a strong role for the government in the social and economic development of society. Furthermore, criticism was leveled at capitalism as distinct from democracy, although the majority of writers advocated a limited form of individual liberty. Many of the ideas presented in the works studied were implemented by the political leaders in Mexico since the 1930s. The role of the Mexican government in the economy is great, and individual liberties are somewhat restricted. Mexico is not unique in having these conditions, however, which have been part of a trend in many developing countries.

Books Read Outside of Class

Classroom readings, whether of foreign or national origin, while easier to trace than other books, were not the only source of influence in the field of literature. Respondents from the enlarged sample were asked to identify literature outside of the classroom which had some impact on their generation, not just on themselves. In many cases, some of the books used in classes for several generations of students were equally influential on the formation of other generations of an earlier or later period outside of class. Such outside literature again falls into two broad categories: native and foreign.

Of the native literature, the earliest writers having an impact on those groups graduating after 1920 were Emilio Rabasa and Ignacio Vallarta. Rabasa's historical works were a defense of Mexico and the achievements of the Díaz regime.[70] At the same time, however, his wok leaned toward the social, economic, and political liberalism of Juárez. Later, in the twentieth century, his political views were critical of the revolutionary governments, which he accused of continuing a similar form of dictatorial government.[71] One of his novels, read by many students in the 1920s, was seen as a forerunner of the revolutionary novels, having much social commentary. His works on constitutional law were also important, but his influence there was confined to the students attending the Free Law School. Ignacio Vallarta, also a defender of many of the conditions to be found at the end of the nineteenth century in Mexico, took a position similar to Rabasa on the land issue. He argued that, although it was true that there were cases in which large landholders had defrauded the peasants, they were rare in comparison to cases in which private property had been usurped by the people.[72] Both Rabasa and Vallarta, like Sierra in the classroom, acted as agents of the nineteenth century in the transition to the twentieth century. They were conservative by revolutionary standards, but they carried the liberal ideas of the 1850s to the generations of the 1920s, ideas which were essential to the philosophical formation of those political leaders who emerged as the neo-liberals and moderates of this century.

Slowly, revolutionary novelists began to replace the authors of the nineteenth century. Most important among them were Mariano Azuela and Martín Luis Guzmán. They and other Mexican authors were discussed in a literary history of Mexico by Juan A. Mateos, popular during this period. Furthermore, Agustín and Rafael Loera y Chávez, intellectuals from this period, were responsible for publishing many such authors from 1916 to 1923. Although I had expected revolutionary novels to be most important during these years, in fact the most important native works were political documents or tracts. Of singular importance, as was true in the classroom, was the 1917 Constitution. This document embodies much of the rationale for the Revolution in its articles, which have been described by one student in the following way: "If their hopes could be condensed into one expression, this might be stated as the demand for social justice, a demand for the redemption of the native race from the depths of wretchedness into which it had sunk."[73] But of all the authors writing during the pre-revolutionary and revolutionary period, two—Enrique and Ricardo Flores Magón—were most influential. Although noted by Mexican and North American scholars as precursors of the Mexican Revolution, their political pamphlets and their newspaper, *La Regeneración*, were mentioned frequently by political leaders who were only children during this period. Antonio Armendáriz, typical of this generation of political leaders, although from a rural background, describes their significance:

> During my youth there were only two persons who were of supreme importance in the country in attacking inequities, and these were the Flores Magón brothers. They were the ones who were sacrificed as part of the movement to bring some of their ideas to fruition. The most important of the two in my opinion, was Enrique, who published the paper *La Regeneración*. Even the smallest towns in Mexico received copies of this paper, which protested against the Porfirista government and called for the workers to exercise their rights. In this way, long before Madero arrived on the scene, the country had become indoctrinated.[74]

Again, the early age at which many Mexican political leaders were first interested in political issues probably explains why the works of the Flores

Magón brothers were more important than other writings.[75] It is interesting in this regard that a critical work of this period, as far as the revolutionaries were concerned—*The Presidential Succession of 1910*—was never mentioned by the respondents as a significant book.[76] Lastly, many students mentioned the influence of law theses by several of their brilliant co-students, some of whom themselves became prominent political leaders, as well as the influence of several student newspapers which were responsible for contributing to the climate of change suggested by the Revolution.[77]

Foreign literary influences were equally important in the outside selections read and discussed by these students. As a group, the most frequently mentioned were the world classics published by Vasconcelos, which became available in inexpensive paperback editions throughout Mexico in the 1920s.[78] These books were important because, as Ángel Carvajal has suggested, many of those works provided future Mexican political leaders with examples they might emulate in governing their country.[79]

Future political leaders were also introduced to contemporary literary movements. Alfonso Pulido Islas, who attended school in the provinces during his youth, describes the literary appetites of his companions:

> As eighteen-year-olds we had read the most important of world literature, we were familiar with diverse currents of democratic and socialist thought; we had participated in oratory contests, in critical and social analyses of poetry and other fine arts; . . . and we had studied Greek, Latin, English, German, French, etc. We had read many works in the French language, principally literary works and ones with social themes.[80]

This exposure to classic and contemporary literature appears to have been introduced by the earlier generation of students, who graduated during the mid-1910s.[81] Their literary interests were conditioned by the intellectual battles between positivistic and anti-positivistic groups. Some of the world literature to which they became exposed included poetry and literary works from Latin America. Among the most important authors was José Enrique Rodó, who wrote *Ariel*, a work remembered for its stance against manifest destiny. But this aspect of the work is often exaggerated, and, as Gordon Brotherson has stated, Rodó emphasized a theme more relevant to Mexican political leaders:

> For he was equating Caliban not with the U.S.A., but with the evils of a utilitarian society, and these evils, while particularly apparent at that time in the U.S.A., could equally well afflict any other part of the American continent, and indeed were threaten-

ing to do so in the economically developing River Plate area.
. . . He devoted several paragraphs . . . to the idea that economic development, as in the Italian Renaissance, was a prere-
quisite for refinement and culture. . . .[82]

A more popular group of literary authors came not from South America
or Europe, but from Russia. Among the most commonly mentioned Russian
novelists were Feodor Dostoevsky and Leo Tolstoy. One of the more important political views expressed by Dostoevsky was anti-socialism, which he justified because he believed that Russians might give up freedom for economic
welfare. At the same time, the most dominant theme in his works was his
conception of Russian destiny, an interpretation which emphasized Russian
nationalism.[83] His views of political liberalism and nationalism were appealing to Mexico's post-revolutionary generations, since they were two issues over
which the Revolution was fought and were the crux of concrete events identified earlier as important in the socialization of Mexican political leaders.
A third issue, equally appealing for the same reasons, that of land reform, was
identified by Tolstoy. Although conservative in some respects, he believed
that all land should be given unconditionally to the Russian people.[84] Agrarian reform, seen in the writings of Mexican authors and in the much-studied
Article 27 of the 1917 Constitution, was the subject most widely discussed in
and outside of class. Yet, as will be seen in a following chapter, land reform
was not one of the highest priorities of the post-1946 regimes.

In addition to the Russian novelists, the most frequently discussed literature was Marxist in origin, especially the *Communist Manifesto* and other
works by Karl Marx and Vladimir Lenin. Political leaders remember discussing the impact of Marx's and Lenin's ideas on the world political and economic situation, as well as discussing the relevance of Marxist interpretations
for Mexico.[85] By the mid-1930s the works were well-known to students in the
provinces as well as in Mexico City. Reviews of works by Lenin and Marx
began to appear in student newspapers.[86] Except for students in the School of
Economics, Marxist works were more commonly read and discussed outside of
class than in class.

Two other authors, both European, were read by these generations of
future political leaders: Friedrich W. Nietzsche and José Ortega y Gasset. The
essence of Nietzsche's writings in the realms of politics has been ably summed
up by John Randall:

Almost alone in his age, Nietzsche abandoned, with the Christian scheme of the universe, the Christian scheme of human life
as well. Such a morality is well enough for slaves, content to live

for the present alone; but for the free man who has resolved that the future shall surpass the present, only the utmost assertion against the weak, only the strong self-reliant will to power, will avail to lift man to new heights of nobility.[87]

Nietzsche's ideas were important to the Mexicans because he encouraged strong anti-church beliefs carried over from the radical liberals of nineteenth-century Mexico. Although few post-revolutionaries went so far as to abandon God or Christianity, many gave only a cursory respect to religion and to the Church. Perhaps more important, his stress on the will to power, or, in other words, the struggle for state power regardless of the costs, provided a justification for the seizure of power so that man and society could be transformed.[88] General Obregón certainly justified his return to the presidency of Mexico in similar terms, and those political leaders who followed Obregón, by institutionalizing control of the Mexican political system in the hands of a political elite, have used parallel arguments.

José Ortega y Gasset, one of the great Spanish thinkers of this century, postulated a different philosophy from that of Nietzsche. In a sense, he argued just the opposite, suggesting that the greatest threat to civilization was state intervention in the lives of the masses. His ideas were presented in *The Revolt of the Masses*, a book widely read by future political leaders in the 1920s and 1930s. He further suggested that Spaniards, as well as citizens elsewhere in the world, needed to be politically educated so that they could participate in politics and intelligently and calmly discuss political issues.[89] His influence was amplified by the fact that his works appeared in Spanish, used concrete examples from Spain, and were circulated in an intellectual journal he published called the *Review of the West*.[90]

In summary, books, whether they were read for classes or outside of classes, provided Mexican political leaders with a diversity of social, economic, and political views. The majority of the works seemed to support several general positions. One set of books provided these young Mexicans and their professors with a rationale for rejecting the principles of the Porfiriato. Another set of books advocated a change in goals for the twentieth century, but the means were crudely divided between achieving economic growth and social change at the price of individual political liberties, or attempting moderate economic and social change along with the maintenance of political liberties. Mexican political leaders, in suggesting that they were influenced by a diversity of views, support the scholarly interpretation that their philosophy in governing, whether economic, political or social, is an eclectic, pragmatic approach, borrowed from many philosophies as the century evolved under their leadership.

6

Teachers as Socializers of Mexican Political Leaders

Teachers and university professors have been shown to be one of the influential socializing groups in most societies. In Mexico there are certain structural reasons why educators deserve special attention. As I have argued elsewhere, professors, more than any single group, serve as recruiters of future political leaders in Mexico.[1] This function is important because, in Mexico and elsewhere, the recruiters both socialize the potential recruit and operate to effect several subsequent screening processes.[2] Not only are professors responsible for recruiting the Mexican political leaders under study here, but they seem to be equally responsible for recruiting and socializing leaders of the major opposition party.[3]

Professors who serve as recruiters of political leaders in Mexico have not been appointed to that task by political elites; rather, they themselves are prominent members of that elite. As one author suggests, recruiters in most political systems eliminate potential tension between themselves and the newly recruited through the selection of like-minded individuals.[4] If this statement is true, it implies that a broadly accepted set of values and beliefs is perpetuated from one generation of leadership to the next, and that in Mexico the professor-political leader is instrumental in inculcating those values and beliefs. Since political leaders have often identified professors as both their recruiters and their primary socializers (Table 6.1), it becomes equally important to find out who teaches the professors.[5] As demonstrated pre-

Table 6.1 Primary Agents of Socialization for Mexican Political Leaders

Agent	Response	
	% [a]	No.
Family members [b]	25	12
Events, activities, or social environment	23	11
University environment	8	4
Professors	33	16
Books	10	5

Note: Based on responses elicited from the expanded group. Since some respondents identified two sources of socialization as equally important, the figures are based on a percentage of the total responses to this question. There were forty-eight responses from forty-five individuals.

[a] Does not total 100 due to rounding.

[b] Family members had been defined to include extended family members. However, in identifying individual family members in socialization roles, the Mexicans mentioned only nuclear family members.

viously, professor-politicians who recruit and socialize Mexican political leaders have themselves received the same treatment from a previous group of professor-politicians.[6] In Mexico, educated political leaders tend to be a self-perpetuating political elite.

As socializers, professors have been important for various reasons. In the Mexican case, Rafael Segovia has shown a strong political influence of teachers upon students even in the elementary school. In Mexico, in spite of the contemporary conditions of large classes, Segovia found that a fifth of fifth- and sixth-grade students and a third of the secondary students he surveyed in public schools talked to their teachers about politics.[7] In my interviews with political leaders who identified professors as influential on their formation, particularly those from humble social backgrounds expressed their sense of awe and good fortune in being noticed by and taken under the wing of distinguished professors and public men.[8] In influencing Mexican students, professors almost always competed successfully against peer groups. Antonio Armendáriz has clearly expressed the reason for this superiority: "Professors were more important to me than friends because they had a clearer notion of what needed to be done. My friends were often as perplexed as I."[9] Many of the teachers-public men considered their teaching careers crucial to the recruiting of competent individuals to collaborate with them and to follow public careers. Others, such as Jesús Silva Herzog, believed his most important accomplishment was his role in the formation of young economists in the classroom.[10]

In chapter 4 it was argued that educated political leaders were socialized through their school environment as distinct from being socialized in specific classes or by individual professors. There is additional evidence available that the university experience as distinct from classes in particular does have an impact on substantive values.[11] However, evidence on the influence of *teaching* on values is scanty and less conclusive. The emphasis in most studies has been on the influence of teachers as a group and classroom experiences as a whole, whereas the research for this study leads to the conclusion that what has been important is individual teachers and their unique classes. The state of our knowledge concerning the role of all teachers and the structure of classroom experience has been summarized best by Willis Hawley. He found that the opportunity to discuss controversial issues in class resulted in a greater sense of political efficacy on the part of the student. Further, providing students with opportunities to share in classroom decision-making and responsibilities reduced student alienation from school and others and increased self-esteem and a sense of social responsibility, although the effects of providing students with an opportunity for involvement in school-wide as opposed to classroom decision-making was unclear.[12]

The evidence is inconclusive as to what impact teachers' attitudes and personalities have, but testimonials from students in various studies indicate the importance of professors. In his review of intensive interviews with University of Washington students, Alex Edelstein concluded that "their numerous testimonials to the influence of professors and courses—shows clearly that there are important things to be learned about the emotional, intellectual, and ideological functions served by student-professor relationships."[13]

Mexican political leaders agree with such an assessment of their relationships with teachers, seeing them as important in spite of certain personal predispositions. As one leader wrote: "Although it is possible to have certain innate tendencies which determine your type of activity (in my case, for example, there were in my family four generations of lawyers) . . . , the influence of some professors, and possibly in some cases, some co-students, cannot be doubted."[14] For some Mexicans, teachers at all levels were important in their socialization. The late Martin Luis Guzmán told the author, "If I had to rank the influence of various groups, I would place teachers first. This was true of primary school, preparatory school (which then was secondary), and law school."[15] Or, as put by another Mexican, "The most important were my professors, in particular Antonio Caso, José Vasconcelos, Vicente Lombardo Toledano, and Ezequiel Chávez. They were fundamental in forming my ideas. At a secondary level I would include Manuel Gómez Morín. All of them influenced me through their classes and their writings."[16] Many others, although not greatly influenced by most professors, remarked that one professor was of particular importance.

Professors have been and will continue to be important as socializers in Mexico and elsewhere because they are disseminators of political values and skills, they impart cultural norms with political and economic overtones, and they provide a model of individuals and of society by the way in which they conduct themselves and their classes.[17] Almost all studies of the impact of curricula have ignored an obvious mediating factor: the nature and quality of instruction.[18] Since teachers and professors play an important role in determining the effectiveness of curriculum, in what ways have they influenced various Mexican leaders? Perhaps the most important thing about the general teaching environment was that, contrary to common assumptions, Mexican politicians felt that their professors were highly competent, concerned about their students, and interested in their subject matter.[19] Liebman, Walker, and Glazer contradict themselves by presenting the typical view of part-time professors early in their work (p. 75), but their own survey evidence from the National University of Mexico and the University of Guanajuato showed that 70 percent of the students found their university experience satisfactory or very satisfactory and 50 percent rated their professors as excellent. In addition, the conditions which hinder close teacher-student relationships in the 1980s were much less prevalent in the universities of the 1920s and 1930s.[20]

Why have Mexican professors, in spite of the stereotype of the unprepared, uninterested teacher, had such an influence on future political leaders? Personalities of individual professors have had an important bearing on student-teacher relationships. As will be seen in the discussion of individual teachers who were named as influential socializers, personality traits are foremost in the memories of their students and contemporaries. Naturally, it is generally believed that such "teacher qualities as 'warmth,' 'stimulation,' 'organization,' and 'responsibility' lead to greater ability to communicate information, provoke thinking, and affect the values of students."[21] One Mexican, Salvador Azuela, commented that the fervor of the professor was most decisive in influencing students.[22] Classroom style alone is not significant, but, in combination with other qualities, it may attract certain students.[23] As Willis Hawley suggests:

> The student's readiness to imitate or assimilate aspects of teacher behavior and attitudes depends also on the student's own feelings for the teacher. Teachers who are liked by students or are otherwise respected because they meet student expectations or are seen as helpful are more likely to shape student learning, other things being equal, even though such learning may not be what the teacher thinks he or she is teaching.[24]

Students who identify with a professor often develop personal relationships with him. Mexican political leaders have repeatedly attested to the fact that they had a strong relationship with one or more of their professors. As Jaros has suggested, it is this kind of contact which results in greater exposure to the teacher's values and is also likely to increase the effectiveness of the learning process.[25] Of the educated Mexican leaders I have interviewed, only two men failed to develop a close relationship with one or more of their professors. As one Mexican suggested, some of the professors most important to the formation of generations of political leaders had these qualities in all aspects of their careers: "Manuel Gómez Morín, because of these and many other things he achieved in his life, was a teacher as much in his classes as outside of them, and . . . I consider that he has had a great and favorable influence on my life."[26]

If professors could attract their students because of their personalities, they were often influential in two ways: through the presentation of their own values and as models. Many of the professors, either indirectly or directly, relayed views about the political system, Mexican economic problems, and social development. Those who had served in the Revolution provided examples and made some students more aware of the social realities of the revolutionary and post-revolutionary periods.[27] Some students received an ideological orientation from such professors:

> I think the National School of Economics had the most important impact on the formation of my ideological views. The questioning attitude of my professors directed my ideas toward socialism, ideas which I first had acquired in normal school. I believe normal school had a tremendous impact on our intellectual development. One of my professors was a constitutionalist from Veracruz by the name of Saul Rodilles. He directed my generation toward a liberal ideology. His interpretation of our history was an important element in my own ideological orientation. He taught us how to make interpretations with objectivity, especially for those events pertaining to the nineteenth century. These ideas were first acquired in normal school and matured at the National School of Economics.[28]

Studies of other Latin American universities suggest that professors try not to get involved in political discussions in class. But, as the same study points out, it is difficult not to talk about subjects of contemporary significance, and, furthermore, professors' political inclinations are usually known to the students and seem to have a subtle influence upon them.[29] Because of the university environment in Mexico, discussions of contemporary changes were common in sociology, public law, and economics classes, and in those humanities subjects such as literature in which major changes were taking place in form and content. Although most Mexican political leaders remembered only limited discussions of political topics in class, politics was an important topic outside of class and in the written works of many of their mentors. As Eduardo Bustamante and others suggest, these professors were as important in what they wrote as in what the taught. He believes, for example, that Alfonso Caso, José Vasconcelos, and Alfonso Reyes were positive influences in modernizing students' ideas through their essays.[30]

Other professors who took the initiative or were encouraged by their students formed discussion groups outside of class to debate various intellectual topics. Many of these professors formed regular breakfast or luncheon groups with students and other faculty, often groups which met for years.[31] Many of the friendships which grew out of these intellectual circles remained active for decades.[32] In a more formal way, such contact between students and young professors or would-be professors was enhanced by a structural change in the National Law School. In 1934 in some courses two professors, the regular and an assistant, began to teach. The professors alternated, and the function of the regular professor was to serve as a discussion leader, whereas the assistant was in charge of going over fundamental points treated by the older professor. This increased contact between students and professors introduced many young assistant professors, who were generally the best students of the immediately preceding generations, to students only several years younger than themselves. The rapport which developed often contributed to important and lasting relationships.[33]

Regardless of the values or points of view expressed by various professors, many, because of their behavior and stature as teachers and public men, served as models to their young students. Sealtiel Alatriste wrote to the author, "As a group, our professors, more than imparting knowledge, served as models for us to imitate in real life. The influence which they had on our ideas was decisive."[34] As models, they were important in two broad ways. First, many students tried to follow their example and become competent professors.[35] In imitating their professors, they too placed themselves in a position to both socialize and recruit future generations of political leaders. Second, professors served as models for students interested in public careers. Although Glazer suggests that the majority of professors in Chile did not encourage or discourage political activity, he concludes that students' perceptions of their professors' attitudes were often influenced by the extent those professors were active.[36] Since the overwhelming majority of those professors remembered by political leaders as being decisive in influencing their social, economic, and political views were themselves active in public life, they provided a positive model to be emulated by many of their students with political interests. The political activity of these professors may have had a causal relationship on their attractiveness to students. Massialas found that teachers with expressive classroom behavior, which is more likely to attract students, were more involved in political affairs and most willing to discuss controversial topics.[37] This finding may also explain why professors who were public men were commonly found among those educators most responsible for the philosophical formation of Mexican political leaders.

It should be mentioned that certain professors had negative influences on political leaders. For example, a number of professors, because of their harsh criticisms of the failures of revolutionary leaders and the Revolution itself, disillusioned their students. On the other hand, many political leaders became active in public life primarily because they hoped to change the conditions these same professors criticized.[38] Other Mexicans were disenchanted with the style in which a subject was taught, rather than merely the content. As one respondent commented, "Mexican history did not influence me greatly; in fact, it had a negative influence on my ideas because of the way in which it was taught."[39] Still other respondents believe that for themselves, and for other members of their generations, professors were uninfluential ideologically. One respondent provides the rationale for this view:

> I have the impression that the influence of professors at the National University on the ideological formation of youth was nonexistent. I think that destiny, ideology, and even the interests and ties of the university students of my age were the result of circumstances encountered on abandoning the classroom and looking for a way to earn a living. I remember, for example, that Díaz Soto y Gama, Professor of Agrarian Law, an honest, courageous politician and at heart a *zapatista*, practically never had students who became defenders of Agrarian Reform.[40]

A study based on the attitudes of students in different sections of an American government course who had been exposed to professors with different patterns of advocacy and different personal values showed that students' values were unaffected by the political postures of their professors.[41] However, this study, and all other studies known to the author, make no attempt to classify the teaching effectiveness of the professors. Furthermore, political leaders in the Kornberg study and among my own respondents have definitely and concretely contradicted these conclusions as applied to their own experiences. Some Mexicans have pointed out to the author that students who hold the same ideas as their professors on political questions throughout their careers are rare, but this finding may be the result of political career needs rather than any lack of initial influence.[42]

It should be noted that matching up the political ideologies of students and professors is not an exclusive or necessarily accurate measure of a professor's influence on his student, and suffers from the same qualifications which might be applied to party identification when studying children's and parents' political attitudes. Numerous testimonials from Mexican political leaders indicate quite clearly the influence on the same student of several professors holding well-known but different political views. Furthermore, a student might easily be influenced by a teacher's political views, but not necessarily by his economic views; or by his moral beliefs and behavior, but not by his social philosophy. Any attitude learned or encouraged by a professor, whether ideological or moral in nature, could affect a political leader's career and behavior in public office.

The professors' influence on their students was wide in scope. In the case of many Mexicans, professors were influential on the specific career choices of their students.[43] In addition, professors were responsible for teaching students how to study a problem and examine its implications objectively.[44] In terms of broad values, several leaders attribute their social and political consciousness to the efforts of their professors.[45] This social and political consciousness was given concrete direction among some students, who were encouraged to serve the needs of their country first, and earn a living second.[46] The moral principle of service to country was complemented for a small group of political leaders by the moral position of their professors on the question of personal behavior and respect for the law. In this regard, students often singled out Professor Erasmo Castellaños Quinto, who taught Spanish literature at the Preparatory School.[47]

Lastly, and perhaps most importantly, professors were often primarily or partially responsible for the ideological views of students who entered public life. Regardless of the views they learned, there seems to be an effort on the part of both professors and students to form a mutual understanding among themselves and other graduates for the benefit of Mexico and the middle class.[48] Such an attitude was formally recognized in the First Congress of Mexican University Graduates in 1933, which proclaimed as one of its principles that the interchange between professors and students at the National University was a practical means of establishing ties of unity and mutual understanding among university graduates throughout Mexico.[49]

Regardless of the degree of influence which professors had on the socialization of future public figures, their importance is obvious. For that reason, and because, as pointed out in a previous chapter, so many political leaders who held office from 1946 to 1970 selected professors as primary influences on their formation, it is essential to know more specifically who these professors were and, more importantly, what their ideologies or values were, as reflected in their classroom teachings and written works. The professors who were most important in the socialization of Mexican political leaders at the National Preparatory School and the National University share the following characteristics: 1) homogeneous backgrounds overrepresentative of urban birthplaces and middle and high socio-economic status; 2) long careers in teaching; 3) degrees from the same institutions, that is, the National Preparatory School and the National University; 4) involvement in student political or intellectual activities as students; 5) studies under the same distinguished professors; and 6) among the professional school professors, highly successful public careers.[50]

In naming specific professors who were most influential on their philosophical formation or that of their friends, Mexican political leaders selected forty professors who taught primarily at the National Preparatory School and the National University, the two schools most responsible for the education of Mexico's political leaders in the past and the present (see Table 6.2).[51] This select group of socializers had all of the characteristics mentioned above. Furthermore, unlike the Mexican population in general, their fathers' occupations, when known, were most frequently professional ones.[52]

At the end of the second decade of the twentieth century, the majority of professors at the National Preparatory School and the University could be described as admirers of Porfirio Díaz, or at least suspicious of the Revolution and its leaders.[53] Some of the respondents began their preparatory education during that period. In the 1920s, as suggested in the previous chapter, the Preparatory School and the University were undergoing an important transition characterized by two different sets of professors. As Miguel Alemán suggests, "The professors whom I had were products of a transitional period and of the past century which had just recently come to an end. There was still a presence of the teachings and philosophy of the nineteenth century when we went to school."[54] One of the more important issues which separated the new professors from the traditional groups was their emphasis on scientific or objective presentations of subject material instead of a normative or evaluative analysis.[55]

If one examined the socialization of earlier students at the National University and National Preparatory School on the basis of the ideological preferences of the professors, one would probably have the impression, which would be accurate, of an ideologically conservative faculty. But a more careful examination of only those professors who were seen by their students to have been important in their socialization process reveals quite a different picture. It is important to make such a qualitative evaluation of professors because, after a pro-revolutionary interlude during the 1920s, conservative professors, in the opinion of many students, began to dominate the university again in the 1930s. As one political leader, who graduated in the late 1930s, described it,

> The majority of my professors were conservatives and not defenders of the Revolution, or they tended to teach law as a technical

**Table 6.2 Professors Most Influential on the
Socialization of Mexican Political Leaders**

Professor	Socio-Economic Status[a]	Where Educated		Profession of Father
		Prof.	Prep.	
Enrique Octavio Aragón	—	UNAM	—	—
Narciso Bassols	middle-class	UNAM	ENP	lawyer, judge
Ramon Beteta	middle-class	UNAM	ENP	lawyer
Manuel Borja Soriano	—	UNAM	ENP	—
Rodulfo Brito Foucher	upper-class	UNAM	ENP	lawyer, judge
Luis Cabrera	lower-class	UNAM	ENP	baker
Antonio Carrillo Flores	middle-class	UNAM	ENP	composer
Alfonso Caso	middle-class	UNAM	ENP	engineer
Antonio Caso	middle-class	UNAM	ENP	engineer
Erasmo Castellaños Quinto	—	UNAM	state	—
Ezequiel Chávez	middle-class	UNAM	ENP	doctor, politician
Luis Chico Goerne	middle-class	UNAM	state	lawyer, politician
Mario de la Cueva	middle-class	UNAM	ENP	doctor
Antonio Díaz Soto y Gama	middle-class	state	state	lawyer
Roberto A. Esteva Ruiz	upper-class	UNAM	—	—
Gabino Fraga	—	UNAM	state	—
Julio García	—	—	—	—
Trinidad García Aguirre	middle-class	UNAM	state	lawyer
Eduardo García Máynez	—	UNAM	ENP	—
Jorge Gabriel García Rojas	—	UNAM	—	—
Manuel Gómez Morín	middle-class	UNAM	ENP	small businessman
Enrique González Aparicio	middle-class	UNAM	—	—
Fernando González Roa	—	state	state	—

science rather than a practical skill. There were exceptions to this among the professors I had, including Luis Chico Goerne, Vicente Lombardo Toledano, and Antonio Díaz Soto y Gama."[56]

Conservative professors did, however, have a considerable impact on Mexican political leaders, if not always ideologically. Among the professors selected by the respondents, fourteen of the forty men have been identified through their writings and their students as falling into a conservative ideological framework (Table 6.3).

Table 6.2
(continued)

Professor	Socio-Economic Status[a]	Where Educated		Profession of Father
		Prof.	Prep.	
Julio Guerrero	—	UNAM	—	—
Francisco de P. Herrasti	—	UNAM	—	—
Vicente Lombardo Toledano	upper-class	UNAM	ENP	businessman
Manuel López Aguado	—	UNAM	—	—
Antonio Martínez Báez	middle-class	UNAM	state	doctor, educator
Enrique Martínez Sobral	upper-class	foreign	foreign	lawyer
Miguel Palacios Macedo	middle-class	UNAM	—	doctor, general
Joaquín Ramírez Cabañas	middle-class	none	ENP	—
Samuel Ramos	middle-class	UNAM	state	doctor, educator
Alfonso Reyes	upper-class	UNAM	ENP	general, politician
José Romano Muñoz	—	—	—	—
Andrés Serra Rojas	middle-class	UNAM	ENP	businessman
Jesús Silva Herzog	middle-class	UNAM	none	businessman
Mario Sousa Gordillo	—	UNAM	ENP	—
Eduardo Suárez	middle-class	UNAM	ENP	notary
José Vasconcelos	middle-class	UNAM	ENP	bureaucrat
Alberto Vázquez del Mercado	middle-class	UNAM	ENP	court secretary

KEY: UNAM = National University; ENP = National Preparatory School; — = no information

[a]The designation of middle-class was based upon the profession of the father and the cultural and economic benefits such an occupation would provide for the family. If the economic resources or political influence of the family were known to be substantial, the designation of upper-class was used. The primary concern, however, is with whether a person came from low socio-economic circumstances or better-than-average circumstances, and not whether he was middle- or upper-class in origin.

These conservative professors can be divided into several groups. The first includes the positivists, some of whom were apolitical while others, who in the classroom were objective pedagogues, were believers in the principles which helped to sustain the Díaz regime. The second group, labeled humanists, were important in the destruction of the intellectual underpinnings of the positivist philosophy sustaining the Díaz regime. On the other hand, they were not advocates of the neo-liberal or socialist economic ideas which became well-known after 1920. The third group, the liberals, continued the liberal line of thought from the 1850s into the twentieth century. Generally sup-

Table 6.3 Ideologies and Political Careers of Professors
of Mexican Political Leaders

Professor	Ideology[a]	Level of Public Service
Enrique Octavio Aragón	positivist/apolitical	none
Narciso Bassols	neo-liberal/left/Marxist[b]	high-level
Ramon Beteta	neo-liberal/left	high-level
Manuel Borja Soriano	liberal/apolitical	low-level
Rodulfo Brito Foucher	liberal	high-level[c]
Luis Cabrera	liberal	high-level
Antonio Carrillo Flores	neo-liberal/left	high-level
Alfonso Caso	neo-liberal/left	high-level
Antonio Caso	humanist	middle-level
Erasmo Castellaños Quinto	apolitical	none
Ezequiel Chávez	positivist	high-level
Luis Chico Goerne	neo-liberal/center	high-level
Mario de la Cueva	neo-liberal/left	high-level
Antonio Díaz Soto y Gama	neo-liberal/center	high-level
Roberto A. Esteva Ruiz	liberal	high-level
Gabino Fraga	neo-liberal/center	high-level
Julio García	positivist	high-level
Trinidad García Aguirre	liberal	high-level[d]
Eduardo García Máynez	neo-liberal/center	none
Jorge Gabriel García Rojas	neo-liberal/center	high-level
Manuel Gómez Morín	neo-liberal/center/liberal[b]	high-level
Enrique González Aparicio	Marxist	middle-level
Fernando González Roa	Marxist	high-level
Julio Guerrero	positivist	middle-level
Francisco de P. Herrasti	humanist/apolitical	none
Vicente Lombardo Toledano	neo-liberal/center/Marxist[b]	high-level
Manuel López Aguado	apolitical	none
Antonio Martínez Báez	neo-liberal/left	high-level
Enrique Martínez Sobral	liberal	middle-level

porters of the Revolution, they advocated the political liberties and some of
the moderate social reforms suggested by that movement, but supported a
capitalist economic structure only slightly modified from the nineteenth century. Each of these groups deserves some examination.

Table 6.3
(*continued*)

Professor	Ideology[a]	Level of Public Service
Miguel Palacios Macedo	liberal	high-level[c]
Joaquín Ramírez Cabañas	neo-liberal/left	none
Samuel Ramos	neo-liberal/left	high-level
Alfonso Reyes	humanist	middle-level
José Romano Muñoz	neo-liberal/right	middle-level
Andrés Serra Rojas	neo-liberal/center	high-level
Jesús Silva Herzog	Marxist	high-level
Mario Sousa	Marxist	high-level
Eduardo Suárez	neo-liberal/center	high-level
José Vasconcelos	neo-liberal/right	high-level
Alberto Vázquez del Mercado	neo-liberal/center	high-level

[a] It is always difficult to categorize people ideologically. These definitions are broadly defined, used only in the context of twentieth-century Mexican politics, and refer to a person's ideological views as expressed during the 1920s and 1930s. In this sense, then, positivist refers to those who believed in the principles behind the Díaz regime, if not in Díaz himself, and who saw education as an objective science. The humanists placed more emphasis on abstract, individual rights and less on empirical principles; at the same time, they rarely were advocates of the radical economic and social reforms expressed in the 1917 Constitutional Convention. Liberals did not place any special emphasis on humanism, but, like the humanists, they were sympathetic to individual political liberties and unsympathetic to radical economic and social reforms. The neo-liberals profess the revolutionary ideas espoused by prominent leaders of the 1911–1920 period and codified in the 1917 Constitution. Such ideas have become part of the "official ideology" or philosophy, and, as a broadly defined and eclectic collection of themes, they range along the political and economic spectrum, within revolutionary boundaries, from right to center to left. Marxist refers only to orthodox Marxists.

[b] Two labels have been given to each of three professors: Narciso Bassols, Manuel Gómez Morín, and Vicente Lombardo Toledano. In all three cases, the changes are extreme, and are often forgotten by students of Mexican politics, who are quick to label Gómez Morín as a conservative-clerical ideologue, and Lombardo Toledano and Bassols as Marxists.

[c] Rodulfo Brito Foucher and Miguel Palacios Macedo both held high-level positions in the rebellious de la Huerta government, although Brito Foucher was also Rector of the National University (1942–44), and Palacios Macedo was Subsecretary of Industry and Commerce (1923).

[d] Trinidad García qualifies for this label because of his prominent role in the formation of the National Action Party.

Positivist Professors

The positivists, of which there were only a few selected by the respondents as influential, included Enrique Octavio Aragón, Julio Guerrero, Ezequiel Chávez, and Julio García. The first, Octavio Aragón, taught many Mexican political leaders in his psychology class at the National Preparatory

School for more than three decades before his death in 1942. But, although he was a supporter of experimental psychology, in general he advocated the positivist system. He authored several important books in his field, on three occasions directed the National Preparatory School, and, in 1934, the National University. But his political philosophy, at least to his students, was neutral. A second professor at the National Preparatory School, Julio Guerrero, was well-remembered for his class on world history (although he did teach international public law for some time at the Law School) and for his work *La génesis del crimen en México* (1901), described by students as one of the best sociological studies of his era. The work caused quite a sensation in Mexican and French intellectual circles.[57] It provided generations of students with a detailed description and analysis of Mexican pathological conditions, rather than just a description of the results of other studies. During the revolutionary period Guerrero served until 1914 as a Judge of the Higher Military Court and as a Federal Deputy. Political leaders remembered his friendliness and interest in other people.

Of the professors with positivist philosophies who taught at the National Preparatory School, the most important for future political leaders was Ezequiel A. Chávez, an older contemporary of Guerrero and Aragón. Like Aragón, he taught psychology and was prominent in school administration, having served as director of both the National Preparatory School and the Graduate School of the National University, and as Rector of the University. His teaching career spanned fifty years. During the Porfiriato, he served as *Oficial Mayor* of Justice and Public Education for ten years, and, during the last six years of Díaz's administration, he was Subsecretary of Public Instruction. It would have been difficult for him not to have grown up as a positivist intellectual, both because of his education under positivist teachers and because his father was a federal deputy, senator, and governor of the state of Aguascalientes during the Porfiriato.[58] Although his daughter argues that he was not the positivist which so many of his contemporaries believed him to be, for our purposes it is more significant to know what his students perceived him to be rather than what he may have actually been.[59]

In his classes and particularly in his writings, Chávez dealt with Mexican social problems. One theme in particular, the importance of peace and unity, stands out, a theme which was translated into a strongly held belief by the post-1920s generations. He argued that historically it was peace and the resulting financial situation that made possible the purchase of railroad stock from foreign companies. He saw this growing nationalism and Mexican control in a favorable light. Not content to point this case out as a historical illustration, he urged Mexicans to subordinate their individual desires for the common goal of unity.[60] Although he was part of the generation being rejected politically and intellectually by the revolutionaries and anti-positivists of the Atheneum of Youth, Chávez, like his much younger contemporaries, was a nationalist. This sense of nationalism reappears constantly in the teachings and writings of other influential professors of this era, regardless of their personal ideologies.

The last person included in this positivist group is Julio García, who became known to generations of young law students because he taught the first course in civil law at the National University. Seen by his contemporaries as an eminent jurist, he also helped the fledgling Free Law School establish itself. He typified the man of the nineteenth century who contributed to the transition from one political era to another. Although not a revolutionary, he did serve as Subsecretary of Foreign Relations during Francisco Madero's brief tenure as president. He was extremely well respected by his students, and one, Emilio Portes Gil, who knew him at the Free Law School, appointed him to the Supreme Court when he became President in 1929.[61] García, because of his knowledge and moral uprightness, and not because of any political views, made a lasting impression on his students.

Apolitical Professors

Two teachers who were not members of any political groups, but who deserve some comment, were professors Erasmo Castellaños Quinto and Manuel López Aguado, neither of whom was ever in public office. They were apolitical contemporaries of the previous professors. Castellaños Quinto taught Spanish, classical, and world literature at the National Preparatory School, leaving a favorable impression on political leaders who were his students as early as the 1920s and as late as the 1940s. Originally a lawyer, he left his practice to become a full-time professor at the National University and Preparatory School. Nervous by nature, he had one of the earlier-mentioned qualities of an effective teacher—passion.[62]

The second apolitical professor, López Aguado, had little opportunity to influence his students politically in the clasroom since he taught arithmetic, algebra, geometry, and trigonometry. Like Castellaños, he was a full-time professor at the National University and the Preparatory School. Although López Aguado was non-political, political leaders remarked that he was respected by his students because of his interest in teaching. Political leaders who studied under him during the 1910s were as positively affected by him as those who studied under him in the 1940s, since he had a career which spanned more than fifty years. Like Castellaños Quinto, he was remembered for taking a special interest in students who showed promise.

Humanistic Professors

In addition to being influenced in numerous ways by professors whose ideological orientation was from the nineteenth century, political leaders educated in the 1920s and 1930s came under the influence of anti-positivist intellectuals, the new breed of teachers who were the humanistic critics of the sterile positivist principles. These were men who confined themselves, by and large, to the intellectual world of Mexico and/or Europe and rarely concerned themselves with political matters. Three of these humanists had an impact on future political leaders: Francisco de P. Herrasti, Alfonso Reyes, and Antonio Caso. The latter two men are widely known outside of Mexico; Herrasti, who never left his native country, was considered the first Romanist of Mexico.[63] A lawyer, poet, and author, he became a full-time teacher at the National University, where he taught Roman Law beginning in 1912. He also taught Latin and Greek, and Latin literature,[64] and suggested that the classic past had something to contribute to the formation of a new Mexico and its leaders.

Of the three humanists, only one, Alfonso Reyes, had a career in public service, and that, on the whole, was apolitical since it was confined to a distinguished career in Europe and South America in Mexico's foreign service. The son of General Bernardo Reyes, one of Porfirio Díaz's most feared competitors from within the regime, Alfonso was sensitive to politics and the changes in political fortunes. Like several other compatriots, he went into self-exile in Europe during the Revolution, thus missing much of the sense of what was happening in Mexico during those years. Because he spent much of his life abroad, Reyes served as one of the symbols of Mexico and Latin America's cultural awakening to the world.[65]

Reyes's absence from Mexico reduced the influence he might have had directly as a teacher, since only a very few of the older respondents were taught by him. Instead of coming from teaching, much of Reyes's influence came from his essays. Politically, as Silva Herzog suggests, he supported neither the right nor the left in Mexico, since he saw the right as an accent on the past and realistic, and the left as an emphasis on the future and utopian. To him the solutions would never come from either extreme.[66] He did take a firm and constant position against imperialism. He saw Mexico's greatest post-revolutionary achievement as the expansion of educational opportunities, a policy which he considered Mexico's "highest honor in history."[67] Two of Mexico's most prominent intellectuals of this century, Daniel Cosío Villegas and Jaime Torres Bodet, felt that Reyes's influence was substantial, both on themselves and on their generation.[68]

Although both Herrasti and Reyes were influential on Mexican political leaders, Antonio Caso, both as a humanist and as a professor of many
generations, stands out as supreme above all other teachers in influence, regardless of philosophy. It is therefore essential to understand Caso as a teacher
and a man of ideas, since his influence was superior to any other single individual on the philosophy of Mexican political leaders and provides an important
key to understanding the collective values of contemporary political leaders.
Caso, known to most students of Latin America as one of the brilliant leaders
of the Atheneum of Youth movement in Mexico, was the son of a civil engineer. A graduate of both the National Preparatory School and the National
University during the first decade of the twentieth century, he soon became
active in university administration, serving as the first Secretary of the National University in 1910 and later as a founding teacher and director of the
Graduate School. Later, he became Director of the National Preparatory
School and Rector of the National University. In the 1920s he served the
government as an ambassador to several South American countries. A teacher
of the philosophy of history and of sociology, he was one of those unusual
men who had a definitive influence on his students through his style of teaching, his substance, and his personality.

As an intellectual and anti-positivist, Caso played a crucial role. As his
peer and sometime critic, José Vasconcelos, concluded, "Caso's work was
vastly more important than any militant politician."[69] He helped to lead and
direct the Atheneum of Youth's fight against positivism, a role for which he is
best known. In addition, as one author believes, he used his abilities and influence to achieve the cultural emancipation of Mexico.[70] At the same time,
he exerted a tremendous influence within the University. Most importantly,
unlike many of his distinguished contemporaries, he remained influential up
to the time of his death, shortly after World War II.[71] One of the goals of Caso
and his intellectual collaborators was to give intellectual thought a sense of
direction and discipline by pursuing a moral philosophy, a philosophy which
can best be described as humanism.[72]

As a teacher, Caso was able to attract students to his substantive views
because of other skills he possessed. The first of these skills was his ability as a
speaker, attested to by dozens of Mexican political leaders from various generations and with different ideological views. He was a lively, emotional lec-
turer, as illustrated by the comments of one of his former students: "The class
ended. Nobody moved from his seat. A contracted, emotional silence followed his last words. And afterwards, a bit of emotion, which burst into
applause."[73]

Caso's speaking skill was not the only remarkable quality of his teaching. He was also remembered by many students for his ability to inspire curiosity and for the integrity of his criticism and the thoroughness of his scholarship, not a common tradition in Mexico.[74] The two general values which students seem to have learned from Caso were humanitarianism and the need to create something truly Mexican.[75] One of his more successful students, Antonio Carrillo Flores, explains in a concrete way the importance of humanitarianism:

> Caso's ideas, particularly the one regarding the dignity of each individual as a human being, and the relationship of this idea to economic development, have had an important influence on my philosophy. I believe that this idea is particularly important in the sense that economic development is an improvement or an increase not just in certain statistical indicators but on the quality of human life.[76]

It is for all of the above reasons that Caso has been called the "illuminating guide of Mexican youth" for more than three decades.[77]

As a humanist, Caso was apolitical in the sense that he did not involve himself openly in political disputes or participate in public life. In class, and particularly in his writings, he expressed views which had definite political and social overtones. Perhaps his most consistently expressed view, and one which coincides with that of those professors already analyzed, was his attitude toward things Mexican. The Revolution, which he accepted, showed that the importation of foreign cultures and economic and political systems had done little to resolve the problems of Mexico.[78] Not only was imitation a cause of past problems, but it would create equally unsolvable problems in the future. He was a fervent nationalist, and he encouraged his students to discover themselves and the authentic reality of Mexico first, and then to formulate ideals that could be used to improve this reality.[79]

Related to Caso's sense of nationalism and understanding of the Mexican reality was his philosophical position that no system of philosophy has any integral truth, that no one can offer such a truth.[80] Instead, he suggested that Mexicans must rely on pragmatism to solve their own problems.[81] If one word could be used to describe Mexican political leaders and the evolution of their political system it would be *pragmatic*. Since Caso was a teacher to so many of these political leaders and other professors of those leaders, his support of this value has a special importance. His view that no philosophy had an integral truth and that Mexico needed to look inward for solutions explains, in part, his aversion to both individualism and collectivism. Instead, he advocated a society based on social justice.[82]

Caso believed that no individual, group, or party should see itself as superior to the law.[83] To him, a just society required freedom of conscience, freedom of political association, and freedom to have private property, all of which necessitated a system of laws and an authority to promulgate and enforce those laws.[84] The role of the government was to promote the well-being and happiness of the people through a number of abstract cultural goals.[85] He rarely specified in his writings the concrete economic or social goals of government, but he did criticize in his classes the ills of Mexican bureaucracy. He also excited his students about the possibilities of industrializing their country.[86] And, perhaps most important, although his political and economic views supported neither capitalism nor socialism per se, he believed in an evolutionary system stressing order, but an order unlike that of the Porfiriato, and one which would allow for dynamic and progressive change.[87]

Caso's influence as a teacher and writer were complemented by the fact that his books were not just read by the intellectual community, but served as basic texts in sociology and social sciences at the National University.[88] He also published many essays.[89] Caso was in the mainstream of Mexican ideas in the sense of encouraging pragmatic, Mexican solutions to Mexican problems. But his was a moderating influence on the eclectic revolutionary themes, particularly his emphasis on evolutionary, orderly change and the protection of individual rights. Political leaders' ideas reflect these themes in Caso's thought. Many of his students, as shall be seen in the following chapter, have adopted, in practice and belief, a pragmatic, evolutionary, and Mexican solution to their problems, and their values, on the whole, are an eclectic mixture of conservatism and reformism.

Liberal Professors

Although singly not as influential as Antonio Caso, the liberals, a second group of professors, were also important to the socialization of many political leaders. Seven of the forty professors in Table 6.2 fall into this group: Manuel Borja Soriano, Manuel Palacios Macedo, Enrique Martínez Sobral, Trinidad García, Roberto Esteva Ruiz, Luis Cabrera, and Rodulfo Brito Foucher. The first of these teachers, Borja Soriano, has been described as apolitical by his students. A notary by profession, Borja Soriano received his education before the turn of the century. As a professor of civil law at the National University and the Free Law School, he taught almost all of the presidents and political leaders who were law students attending classes after 1920. As one of his students suggested, he did not influence his classes politically, especially since he was not a revolutionary, but professionally; in short, "he made lawyers."[90] Borja Soriano's textbook, reedited five times between 1939 and 1966, exemplifies his objective classroom philosophy and was oriented toward western, European law, documented with hundreds of citations including numerous Mexican examples.[91]

The other six liberal professors, equally adept in the classroom, were more active politically than Borja Soriano. Of the six, Miguel Palacios Macedo and Enrique Martínez Sobral were important because they taught economics courses at the National University. Miguel Palacios was early on a political activist, a member of the famous "Seven Wise Men" group, which also included two of the professors in the neo-liberal category, Narciso Bassols and Manuel Gómez Morín. Palacios was a student of Antonio Caso's, and, by the time he became a third-year law student, was deeply involved in student politics. He entered public life immediately upon his graduation from Law School in 1920 as private secretary to the then Subsecretary of the Treasury. He stayed in that department, working under Gómez Morín the following year. In 1923 Palacios became one of the many young professors and students to remain loyal to Adolfo de la Huerta in his futile rebellion against the government. Surviving the rebellion, he went into exile in Paris from 1924 to 1928 and studied economics at the Sorbonne. Again expressing his sentiments in favor of political liberty and just elections, he returned to Mexico to become an important collaborator in José Vasconcelos's ill-fated campaign against the government candidate in 1929. Although not holding high-level offices in the following years, he was extremely influential on government financial legislation from 1932 to 1938, especially the demonetization of gold in 1933 and the organic law of the Bank of Mexico in 1936.[92] Although personally "he was inclined toward classical economic ideas," he gave his students "the opportunity to know all economic opinions, including Marxist philosophy."[93]

Enrique Martínez Sobral was also an economist and professor. Although a native of Guatemala, he received part of his education and a degree in Chile, and he went into exile in Mexico in 1902 because of his opposition, as a federal deputy, to the Guatemalan president.[94] Limited by his foreign birth to a certain level in the Mexican bureaucracy, he became an official of the Treasury Department under Díaz's Secretary of the Treasury. His latent political views reappeared in exile, and he accompanied Madero during his campaign, later becoming his general attorney in New York. From 1930 until his death in 1951, he was head of the legal department for American Smelting and Refining in El Paso, Texas. He was described by his peers as an outstanding speaker on political economy, and Alfonso Reyes, who took courses from him, praised him as an extraordinary professor.[95]

Typical of many other intellectuals of his generation, Martínez Sobral could identify with only some of the changes wrought by the Revolution. A political liberal, he was more moderate in his economic views. His immediate impact on economic ideas stemmed from the fact that he produced in 1911 the first economics textbook which used numerous examples from Mexico. His work, which even in the second edition discussed such subjects as socialism and Christian Democracy, also analyzed the influence of various economic schools on the 1917 Constitution.[96] He believed in state intervention in economic life, a progressive position for a man educated in the nineteenth century; for him it was the manner in which the state intervened which caused problems, not state intervention per se. He believed the state should guarantee individual rights so that no group would be tyrannized.[97] There is no evidence, however, from his students or biographers that he advocated the state's taking an aggressive role in the resolution of specific economic and social problems. Like Emilio Rabasa, another lawyer-professor who was his contemporary, Martínez Sobral wrote a number of novels, several of which dealt with social issues. Most notably, in *Su matrimonio*, he wrote that lower-class Guatemalans, and Latin Americans in general, prostituted themselves because of a lack of education. It is doubtful, however, that many Mexican students were familiar with these novels.[98]

The remaining four professors with liberal ideologies all taught law courses. The first of them, Roberto Esteva Ruiz, graduated from the National University at the turn of the century. During the Porfiriato he taught at the National Preparatory School and the Law School, and at the same time began to hold numerous posts in the Mexican judiciary and justice department. His public career ended abruptly in 1914 after he served as Subsecretary in charge of Foreign Relations during the last year of Victoriano Huerta's reactionary regime. He spent the next seven years in exile in Spain, returning to his teaching at the National Law School in 1921 along with other discredited professors-public men of the previous decade. He remained a professor at the Law School until 1957, during which time he earned a reputation as an eminent jurist, serving as a Justice on the International Court of Justice and as Dean of the Law School. As a teacher he was influential because he taught three of the last five courses required of most students during those years.[99] Although he had held a position in the Huerta government, he also had served in the foreign relations ministry under Madero. He was receptive to the political changes wrought by the Revolution and to the changes occurring in law concerning the relationship between collective interests and individual interests.[100] However, his influence on political leaders was apparently professional rather than political.

A contemporary of Esteva Ruiz's at the National Law School, and one of the most important ideological thinkers of the Revolution, was Luis Cabrera, a man largely forgotten by political leaders and Mexicans in general. An organizer of the Anti-Reelectionist Party, he became a federal deputy under Madero in 1912, where, as a brilliant speaker, he began to advocate changes in the agrarian laws. After the murder of Madero, he supported Venustiano Carranza, serving him in a number of positions, particularly in the United States. In 1918 he became Carranza's Treasury Secretary, and, when Carranza fled the capital pursued by General Obregón's troops in 1920, Cabrera accompanied him. He retired to private life but continued a prolific writing career which he had begun in the 1890s. Cabrera taught during the first two decades of the twentieth century and even became Dean of the Law School in 1912, but he was most influential through his political essays published under the pseudonym of Blas Urrea and his speeches at numerous conferences at the National Library.

In the area of agrarian policy, Cabrera advocated expropriation with indemnification for the public good. He neglected none of the various aspects of the agrarian problem, including the division of large properties, the development of small properties, adequate irrigation and credit, and the dotation of *ejidos*.[101] In other areas, he echoed the nationalist sentiments of many of the other professors. His political ideas, however, were a carryover from nineteenth-century liberalism as espoused by both Madero and Carranza. He was a constant critic of the failures of the Revolution in the post-revolutionary period and continued to represent "an outmoded liberalism that openly proclaimed its goal of a nation built on political democracy, initiative, and private property rather than on drastic social change."[102] His biting criticism sometimes brought him into conflict with the government, and in 1931 he was deported to Guatemala because of his writings. As an independent voice of criticism and an early advocate of organized agrarian reform, he had some influence on the thinking of Mexican political leaders.[103]

The last two liberal professors, Rodulfo Brito Foucher and Trinidad García, were members of the younger generation of professors born at the turn of the century. The first of these men, Brito Foucher, had several similarities with other liberals. He was the grandson of the governor of his home state, Tabasco, where his family had considerable land holdings; his father was the right-hand man to the Governor of Tabasco during the last years of the Porfiriato and was assassinated in retirement in 1912.[104] Brito Foucher was active in student politics at the National Preparatory School and the National Law School, where he eventually became president of the student federation.[105] Almost immediately after graduating in 1923, he became an active and prominent supporter of the de la Huerta rebellion, serving as Subsecretary of Foreign Relations and of Government. When de la Huerta was defeated, Brito Foucher fled into exile to the United States. On his return to Mexico in 1927, he became professor of general theory at the Law School and Dean in 1933. In 1942 he was appointed Rector of the National University. Always politically inclined, he was well-liked by his students, and in class he constantly related law to political realities.[106] Though he was politically liberal, his economic views were typical of the nineteenth century. He was constantly involved in political intrigues of one sort or another. His attractiveness to students, even political leaders, stemmed from his efforts to relate law to concrete cases in Mexico and from his political activism. Ideologically, his influence was minimal.

Trinidad García, the last of the liberals in this study, was a contemporary of Narciso Bassols, Miguel Palacios, and Manuel Gómez Morín at the National Law School. Upon his graduation in 1919, he became a professor of civil law at the National University. In 1934 he became Dean of the Law School. García was a private man in his political views, and his impact as a teacher was professional, since he taught several courses in the civil law curriculum.[107] An author of one of the basic introductory texts in civil law, his work discusses the relationship between law and economic policy as well as the impact of sociology on contemporary law. He devoted considerable attention to Mexican law and Mexican cases. His neutral ideological view, similar in this regard to Antonio Caso's, can be seen in his summary of the purpose of law: "The true purpose of Law should be to protect and harmonize all of the interests, whether collective or individual, and to assign to each one its own role; the collective interest cannot be explained without the individual, and the protection of one is no more important than the other."[108]

Leftist Neo-liberal Professors

The largest group of professors, in terms of broad, ideological views, is made up of neo-liberals. Subdivided, they fall into three neo-liberal categories: left, center, and right. The neo-liberals with leftist views, one of the larger subgroups, include Narciso Bassols, Ramón Beteta, Antonio Carrillo Flores, Alfonso Caso, Antonio Martínez Baéz, Joaquín Ramírez Cabañas, and Samuel Ramos. Of these professors, two were primarily remembered as teachers because of their classes at the National Preparatory School: Joaquín Ramírez Cabañas and Samuel Ramos. Unknown to most foreign students of Mexico, Ramírez Cabañas, a native of Veracruz, moved to Mexico City to live with his uncle, a general during the Porfiriato. Although he attended the National Preparatory School, he had to leave due to a lack of finances, never completing professional school. However, by 1918 he began to publish poetry, then a novel, followed by numerous sociological and historical studies. He collaborated on many important historical collections and edited a series of works. Because of his personal accomplishments, he was appointed as professor of Mexican history at the National Preparatory School and at the School of Philosophy and Letters. An excellent teacher up to his death in 1943, he taught Mexican history so that students would not forget the contributions of nineteenth-century history and its historians.[109] A multi-faceted intellectual, he was a close friend of Jesús Silva Herzog and worked under him at the Secretary of the Treasury. Ramírez Cabañas's main influence on students was his strong sense of nationalism and emphasis on Mexican solutions to Mexican problems. He was also responsible for helping to prevent the early demise of the National School of Economics in 1934.

Like Ramírez Cabañas in his emphasis on Mexico's past, Samuel Ramos became much more well known for his interpretations of Mexican culture. The son of a prominent Michoacán educator and intellectual, Ramos came to Mexico City to study medicine but changed his mind in 1919 and switched to philosophy. Later he studied at the Sorbonne and the University of Rome, ultimately earning a Ph.D. from the National University. In 1922 he began to teach philosophy at the National Preparatory School. He considered himself, as far as his philosophic thought was concerned, a student of Antonio Caso. Another mentor was José Vasconcelos, and, like both of his teachers, Ramos "continued their method of studying Mexico's present situation in the light of the historical past."[110] His major contribution to the socialization of Mexican political leaders resulted from his critical attempt to get Mexicans to see themselves, to analyze their problems realistically, and to solve their problems by examining their own history.[111]

The other professors with leftist neo-liberal ideas fall into two groups, those who were remembered by their students for their professional knowledge, and those who were remembered for their political or economic views as well as knowledge of their subject matter. The first group included Antonio Martínez Báez, Alfonso Caso, and Mario de la Cueva. Martínez Báez and de la Cueva were contemporaries, having attended the National Law School together. Both were members of the first prominent, post-revolutionary law-school generation, a group which was to have a tremendous influence in the University and in public life.[112] Martínez Báez's father was a prominent Michoacán intellectual and educator in Morelia who served as a constitutional deputy in 1916–17. Martínez Báez began his studies in Morelia but left the second year to complete his law degree at the National University, where in 1925 he became an assistant to Narciso Bassols in his law class, substituting completely for him in constitutional law by 1929. At the National Prepara-tory School, he substituted for Samuel Ramos in ethics in 1927. His impact on his students resulted from his erudition in the field of public law and from his exploration of how law could be used to promote development and define the relationship between public and private interests in Mexico. His interpre-tations in the latter realm evolved through years of experience in the federal government, beginning with his position as director of the legal department of one of the federal banks in 1935 and culminating with his appointment as Secretary of Industry and Commerce from 1948 to 1952.

Martínez Báez's co-student, Mario de la Cueva, a native of Mexico City, generally remained within academic life. He studied under Manuel Gómez Morín, Narciso Bassols, and Alberto Vásquez del Mercado and served as a professor of the general theory of law from the 1920s through the 1970s.[113] In 1938 he became Secretary General of the National University and, two years later, Rector. He wrote a classic textbook on labor law in Mexico. Al-though his classes introduced students to many European ideas, his impact was largely professional. He had an important influence on graduates of the 1940s and 1950s, particularly, including President Miguel de la Madrid.

Alfonso Caso, the remaining neo-liberal prominent for his erudition, was the younger brother of Antonio Caso. Overshadowed by the stature of his brother, he was really a member of a different generation, the same group to which Manuel Gómez Morín, Narciso Bassols and Miguel Palacios be-longed. In 1919, the year he graduated, he began to teach philosophy and later sociology at the Law School. Although better known for his work in Mexican archaeology and his explorations of Monte Alban, he also distin-guished himself within the University, serving as Director of the National Preparatory School from 1938 to 1944 and afterward as interim Rector of the National University during a serious crisis. His political leanings expressed themselves early, and he joined the Mexican Labor Party, founded by his classmate and brother-in-law, Vicente Lombardo Toledano, in 1919. Like Mar-tínez Báez, he taught Miguel Alemán at the National Law School; as president, Alemán appointed Caso as his first Secretary of National Properties.

In general, Caso believed that both he and his generation were more sympathetic to the left than to the right and that they believed in the justice of the revolutionary activities.[114] In class he was an excellent critic of the shortcomings of the Revolution and the government. Morally he stood as an example of integrity, and, when he could not maintain that integrity in pub-lic life for reasons beyond his control, he resigned as Secretary of National Properties.[115] His emphasis on personal service to his country was a value which served as a model for many of his students.

The other neo-liberal professors with leftist leanings, Narciso Bassols, Ramón Beteta, and Antonio Carrillo Flores, were influential on the formation of political leaders not so much because of their scholarly achievements, but because of their economic and political views and their considerable involvement in public life (all three served as Secretary of Treasury). These men represented the three most important university generations of their era: the 1919–20, the 1925–26, and the 1928–29. Bassols, who was the oldest of the three, was one of the most influential professors among political leaders in Mexico and had a significant influence on Antonio Carrillo Flores, Antonio Martínez Báez, and, later, Hugo B. Margáin, Secretary of Treasury during the first years of the Echeverría administration.

A graduate of the National Preparatory School and the National University, Bassols descended from opposing heritages. As Enrique Krauze notes, Bassols inherited the radicalism of his great-uncle, President Sebastian Lerdo de Tejada, and the Catholicism of his grandfather, who established a religious press and wrote several religious works.[116] After graduation in 1921, he became professor of logic at the National Preparatory School, and two years later he took on the subjects of guarantees and *amparo* as well as constitutional law at the Law School. Before he stopped teaching in 1931, he had served as Secretary General of Government of the State of Mexico, Chief of the Legal Department of the National Agrarian Commission, Dean of the Law School, and head of the government committee in charge of liquidating old banks.

The ideas he presented as a professor came almost totally from Mexico and occasionally from Latin America. In particular he was influenced by the Revolution, the Constitutional Convention, and the ideas of Luis Cabrera.[117] As a student, he had also been greatly influenced by José Enrique Rodó's *Ariel*, a work which surely contributed to his sense of nationalism.[118] In his class on guarantees and *amparo*, he generally presented his material in a purely juridical fashion.[119] However, he did not think of law as a sterile and objective subject, for he debated one of the prominent positivist professors of his era that the law should be classified ideologically and that its ideological function should be discussed in class.[120] In his other classes, he constantly talked about Mexico and its problems, the misery of the masses and the need to assist them and to create laws to protect Indians and peasants.[121]

In spite of his dissatisfaction with some of the methods used by the government to achieve the goals of the Revolution, Bassols did not discourage students from serving Mexico; in fact, just the opposite. Setting his own example in the decade following 1930, he served as Secretary of Public Education, Government, Treasury, and then consecutively as Ambassador to London and to Paris.[122] Even outside the government he remained politically active, forming the League of Political Action with numerous former students to criticize the regime of Manuel Ávila Comacho. In 1943 he ran and lost as a federal deputy, and in 1947 he became a founding member and vice-president of the Popular Party (later the Popular Socialist Party). His students remembered that above all else he stimulated and encouraged them to identify and define clear means by which they could work to help Mexico.[123] He also provided his students with a moral model worthy of emulating. Scrupulously honest, he donated his salary as Secretary of Public Education to Mexican peasants, and, when he died in 1959, he was poor.

His views on society changed over time, from a moderate neo-liberal view to a Marxist interpretation in the late 1930s. Even in the 1930s his view on the agrarian problem was clear: he believed that land should be distributed to those who worked it, and that it should be given out quickly. To equivocate would, in his opinion, serve the interest of large landholders and North American capitalists and betray the Indians.[124] He was largely responsible for the new Land Restitution and Donation Law of April, 1927, an attempt to create a juridical and administrative structure for agrarian problems.[125] Bassols, unlike his co-student Gómez Morín, believed that some violence would still be necessary to achieve a solution to the agrarian problem.[126]

Bassols's economic views were formed around his belief that modern man could rebuild society and destroy existing forms or structures not contributing to society's benefit.[127] He opposed capitalism and argued that the large part of material goods should belong to society. He moved gradually in the early 1920s from a social liberal view influenced by the Mexican Revolution to one of socialism.[128] His later views were influenced by Keynes, Marshall, and Marx.[129] In 1937 he translated the work of John Strachey, *Theory and Practice of Socialism*, for Mexican readers. Ultimately, for Bassols, Mexico's economic development required a rapid renovation of economic structures.[130]

Ramón Beteta, one of the students who studied under Bassols's generation, spent most of his youth in Mexico City. After attending the National Preparatory School, he followed the typical pattern of continuing at the National Law School. However, he temporarily left the National University to earn a degree in economics from the University of Texas.[131] Graduating with honors in just two and a half years, he returned to Mexico City in 1924 to complete his law degree, studying under Manuel Gómez Morín. As a student he worked as a waiter in Austin and as a low-level employee of the Secretariat of the Treasury in Mexico City. Even before completing his law degree, he began to teach fellow students as a professor of political economy at the National Law School, a course which he continued to teach until the 1940s.

Ramón Beteta had a crucial role in the socialization of many Mexican political leaders because for many generations he represented their only exposure to a formally taught course in economics at the Law School. In fact, he was the first Mexican with an economics degree to teach that subject in his country. Beteta emphasized three themes: agrarianism, the labor movement, and nationalism. On the agrarian question he was anti-bourgeoisie, favoring the policy of communal land holdings. He further argued that "to stop with the distribution of the land, and not to take advantage of the opportunity for its complete socialization, is not only a weakness, but a danger, the danger that in its agrarian aspect the Revolution, having triumphed, will die through not having been carried to its logical conclusion."[132] His attitude toward the role of labor in Mexican society was equally favorable, and he believed that the workers should acquire increased power.[133] For Beteta, Mexico's growth and greatness could be achieved not through agricultural self-sufficiency alone, but through the process of industrialization as well. In the view of one of his students, Beteta believed that such a process had to be shared with and guided by the state.[134]

The third theme which Beteta emphasized, that of nationalism, constantly reappears in his writings. Culturally, he stressed the importance of understanding the influence of the Indian in Mexican life.[135] Economically, his views on nationalism and the role of the state were intertwined: "We want Mexico to be Mexican, and Mexico's wealth to be produced for the benefit of the country at large, and in particular for those engaged in the productive process."[136]

Beteta was an engaging teacher[137] whose economic ideas covered examples from both North America and Mexico. Furthermore, he gave much practical advice on the basis of his public career, which spanned more than twenty-five years and included such positions as Subsecretary of Foreign Relations, Subsecretary of Treasury, and Secretary of Treasury.

Like Beteta, Antonio Carrillo Flores, who succeeded him as Secretary of the Treasury in 1952, attended school in the United States and became fluent in English. He received his advanced education at the National Preparatory School and the National Law School. Like Beteta, he started his public career as a low-level employee of the Secretariat of the Treasury when he graduated in 1929. Two years later he became a professor of general theory, later switching to administrative law, which he taught until 1952. Most influenced in law school by Narciso Bassols, and later by Eduardo Suárez, Carrillo Flores worked under Suárez in the Treasury. He left this position in 1944 to become Dean of the Law School, returning to government the following year as Director of the National Finance Bank. From then until 1970 he held cabinet-level positions and in 1957 was considered as a pre-candidate for President of Mexico.[138]

One of the most successful political leaders in Mexico after 1946, Carrillo Flores influenced his students through his role in public life and the experiences he could bring to the classroom. His political and economic views had certain similarities with the ideas of Beteta. Carrillo Flores took the view that the Constitution in no way limited the Mexican state from intervening in economic affairs.[139] But his view of state intervention was not one-sided, and, although he criticized the excesses of private initiative, he commented favorably on the contributions it could make to Mexican development.[140] He was a nationalist in the sense that he saw as the most important achievement of the Revolution the turning of Mexico back to the reality of its own situation and problems.[141] While maintaining this view, he was not averse to the use of foreign capital to assist in Mexico's growth. Perhaps reflecting the earlier views of his professor Narciso Bassols, Carrillo Flores insisted on the need to improve the distribution of wealth in Mexico.[142]

Moderate Neo-liberal Professors

The middle-of-the-road neo-liberals were a sizable group among the most influential professors of Mexican political leaders. Those who were more renowned for their knowledge of their subject matter than for their political views were Gabriel García Rojas, Gabino Fraga, Andrés Serra Rojas, Eduardo García Máynez, and Alberto Vásquez del Mercado. Gabriel García Rojas, who attended the National University, was a supporter of the Revolution as a student, and helped to found the Local Student Congress of the Federal District.[143] He graduated in the early 1920s and soon became professor of general theory and of obligations and contracts at the Law School. In the 1920s and 1930s he was, in the words of one of his students, "one of the few professors who, with great brilliance and solid arguments, presented the thesis of natural law (law based on innate moral sense), which had been thrust aside by the prevailing legal positivism."[144] Although García Rojas did embark upon a public career, first as a federal deputy and later as a Supreme Court justice, he is most remembered by his students as a knowledgeable and congenial professor.

Gabino Fraga, who was a co-student of García Rojas, came from Morelia to attend the National Law School. A student of Manuel Gómez Morín and Antonio Caso, he was most influenced by Caso.[145] Like so many of the other professors in this study, he very quickly entered public life in 1920, the year he graduated, first serving as a consulting lawyer, then the head of the Department of Advisers, and finally as *Oficial Mayor* of Treasury at age twenty-one. In 1925 he became a professor of administrative law at the National University, a course which he continued to teach into the 1960s. That same year, the government promulgated a new ejido law for which he was largely responsible.[146] In 1934 he established his reputation as a jurist by publishing a book, *Derecho Administrativo*, which became the standard text in its field. The work provides a lucid discussion of the role of the state and the importance of contemporary socialist doctrines, and it argues for the need to place administrative power under the control of law or a regime legitimized by law.[147] Fraga's reputation as a jurist was recognized by his nomination to the Supreme Court in 1941.

Andrés Serra Rojas, a brilliant student, graduated from the Law School some eight years after Fraga. As a member of the important 1928–29 generation, Serra Rojas was a student activist who participated in the National Student Congress. Like his co-student Antonio Carrillo Flores, he was quickly recruited into government service; he began working his way up in the Attorney General's office and reached the post of Assistant Attorney General in 1933. He began teaching at the School of Law, writing various works on administrative law. Both his friends and his students remember him as a lyrical speaker and kind individual.[148] He had many student disciples, not because of his philosophical ideas, but because he had considerable contact with his students and was helpful to them.[149] He continued his public career, serving as a federal deputy from his home state of Chiapas and as an orator for his friend and co-student, Miguel Alemán. In 1946 he became Alemán's Secretary of Labor, and in 1964 he served as a senator.

Another member of this group of moderate neo-liberals, Eduardo García Máynez, became one of Mexico's most prominent intellectuals. A graduate of the National University in 1930, and later of the University of Berlin, he became a professor at the Law School and the School of Philosophy, teaching ethics and the philosophy of law, among other courses. He studied with both Antonio and Alfonso Caso, and taught at the University for more than forty years, receiving an LL.D. in 1950. García Máynez's achievements are confined solely to the intellectual and academic world. The author of many books and essays, and a former Dean of the School of Philosophy, he is remembered by the younger generation of political leaders as an individual of great erudition.

Equally limited in his political influence was Alberto Vázquez del Mercado, a co-student and friend of Manuel Gómez Morín and Narciso Bassols. Considered one of the members of the "Seven Wise Men" generation, he grew up in the provinces in Chilpancingo. As a first-year law student, he founded the publishing house Cultura, which produced many fine works during the following years. Before graduating from the Law School in 1919, he tried his hand at politics, running and losing as a federal deputy from Guerrero, his home state. He opened a law office and taught literature at the National Preparatory School, where he was described as an erudite, critical, and sarcastic professor. He taught mercantile law for only a short while at the Law School, and in 1921 again entered public life as Secretary of the Department of the Federal District, a position through which he used his influence to help Lombardo Toledano and Alfonso Caso obtain important positions in the same department. When Vasconcelos entered the presidential race in 1929, Vázquez del Mercado became an active and close supporter. Although he was a Vasconcelista, he was appointed to the Supreme Court in 1929. In 1931, in a celebrated example of moral integrity, he resigned from the Supreme Court because of the government's deportation of Luis Cabrera. His influence as a teacher appears to have been the result of his expertise in mercantile law and his willingness to defy the government on a moral principle. Unfortunately, like the man he defended, Luis Cabrera, Vázquez del Mercado's abilities were never made use of by the government nor was he remembered by generations after 1930, although he practiced law in Mexico City until his death in 1980.

The other neo-liberals in this category, Antonio Díaz Soto y Gama, Eduardo Suárez, Luis Chico Goerne, Manuel Gómez Morín, and Vicente Lombardo Toledano, were important to the socialization of political leaders because of their political and economic views. Of the many professors selected as important by Mexican political leaders, only a few actually participated in or were notable in the Mexican Revolution. Díaz Soto y Gama, one of the active precursors of the 1910 Revolution, was one. Díaz Soto y Gama graduated with a law degree from the Scientific and Literary Institute of San Luis Potosí in 1901, and in his home state he helped other notable precursors found a Liberal Club. In exile from 1902 to 1904 because of his anti-Díaz activities, he returned to Mexico and fought for his agrarian views·before the 1912 federal congress. When Victoriano Huerta came to power, Díaz Soto y Gama joined Emiliano Zapata, becoming one of the important forces behind the agrarian movement.[150]

In 1933 Díaz Soto y Gama began teaching Mexican history at the National Preparatory School and agrarian law at the Law School. Known as an outstanding debater in Congress, he brought the themes of the Revolution into his classes and emphasized revolutionary events, such as the Convention of Aguascalientes.[151] Although he became more conservative over the years, his original radical position focused strongly on one issue: land reform. He wrote during this period that the fundamental problem of Mexico in the past had not been education, but race relations, and that this problem indirectly explained, in his opinion, the agrarian problem in the post-revolutionary years. His solution was to give the peasants, especially the Indians, land.[152]

The next three professors, Eduardo Suárez, Manuel Gómez Morín, and Vicente Lombardo Toledano, were all contemporaries who led significant public lives in Mexico. Eduardo Suárez received his law degree in 1917 and immediately began to practice law. In the 1920s and early 1930s he served as a technical adviser to numerous international committees, traveling to the United States, Europe, and South America. In the 1920s he began to teach courses in civil procedures, administrative law, labor law, and international public law at the Law School. In 1935 he became Cárdenas's appointee for Secretary of the Treasury, a position he held until 1946. Suárez influenced his students both inside and outside of class. Antonio Carrillo Flores, who followed his footsteps professionally, felt that Suárez was the most important teacher in his professional life and one of the most influential men in modern Mexico.[153] Carrillo Flores was more progressive in his view of Mexican financial policies than his mentor. He notes that Suárez did not believe the state could justly distribute income and that it was necessary to have inequality to create growth. Suárez believed that the capitalization of the economy would eventually defeat poverty and that inequality was only a short-run condition. At the time he was also favorable toward the Keynesian interpretation, which was not the prevailing view in 1935, that the government should use deficit spending to promote economic development and to expand the productive capacity of Mexico's economy.[154]

One of the most influential professors of Mexican political leaders, second only to Antonio Caso, was Manuel Gómez Morín, a man who is commonly referred to as the leading opponent and critic of the post-1930s governments in Mexico rather than as a mentor of its political leaders. In reality he was both, achieving this paradoxical position because of his outstanding critical and administrative abilities and a sharp turn in his ideological views. A brilliant student at the National Law School, he became identified as one of the members of the "Seven Wise Men" generation. Upon his graduation in 1918, he became a professor of public law, and later of political economy and monetary law. He continued to teach until 1939.

Gómez Morín quickly advanced in his public and academic career. Remarkably, in 1919, at the age of twenty-two, he became Subsecretary of the Treasury under Luis Cabrera. In 1921 he traveled to the United States for three months as Mexico's financial agent, to study the Federal Reserve System. On his return from the United States he wrote the 1921 law reforming the Mexican banking system. The following year he became Dean of the Law School at age twenty-six. Following his tenure there he reentered public service and wrote, with two other Mexicans, the 1925 law establishing the Bank of Mexico; he became its first chairman and served until 1929.[155] During this same period he contributed another fundamental law to the Mexican financial system, the 1926 Agricultural Credit Law, which, in the opinion of Ricardo Zevada and others, still serves as the basis of today's law.[156]

Like so many of the professors discussed above, Gómez Morín left the government fold to support an opposition candidate, in this case José Vasconcelos, in 1929. After Vasconcelos's defeat, Gómez Morín went into exile.[157]

Without a doubt, during the 1920s Gómez Morín might more accurately have been placed on the neo-liberal left. His students, whether in the early or late 1920s, felt that his classes were filled with critical, revolutionary ideas, and identified him with the revolutionary left, not the conservative right, as was true from the mid 1930s forward.[158]

During the 1920s Gómez Morín was influential on students because of the career orientation he gave them and because of his political and economic beliefs. His practical contributions were threefold: he recruited students to politics, he argued for the necessity to participate in politics, and he gave a great emphasis to the study of economics in Mexico. Gómez Morín argued for the necessity of his generation and its students to organize political groups to influence government policy. It was Gómez Morín who, after Vasconcelos's failure, urged Vasconcelos to start a permanent opposition party in the hopes of attaining power in the future.[159] And, of course, it was Gómez Morín, who, seeing the failure of others to do so, organized the opposition National Action Party in 1939, serving as its president for the first ten years.

In the opinion of Daniel Cosío Villegas, Gómez Morín was the only Mexican up to the mid 1920s who had been interested in economic questions and who had tried to induce various students to study this subject.[160] Many of these students worked in the first technical tax department in Mexico, which was organized under Gómez Morín's influence.[161]

Ideologically, his emphasis during this period was on nationalism, honesty and democracy in politics, and technical pragmatism. Although he was very interested in and familiar with Russia's experiments, Gómez Morín never suggested that any model, including Russia or the United States, was appropriate for Mexico.[162] Instead, he had a pragmatic, eclectic philosophy, of which one element was that the municipality would serve as a basis for Mexico's new political organization. He believed the municipality should be led by a number of commissioners selected through a system of proportional voting.[163] But his most important ideological emphasis during this period was his insistence that Mexicans be instructed in the concept of a technical, modern state. While he believed the functions of the central government should be limited, he argued for technicians to serve as directors of the administrative functions of government. Furthermore, he believed in a mixed economy and a fiscal system responsive to the social function of taxation. He went so far as to propose a fourth governmental body, a technical committee or council having considerable powers, with representation from various professional groups.[164] As Krauze suggests, he was obsessed with the need for competence or technical expertise, a value which Ortega y Gasset discussed in his works.[165] Unlike José Vasconcelos, one of his mentors, Gómez Morín thought the solution to Mexico's problem was through organization.[166]

In the early 1930s, after his experience in the Vasconcelos campaign, Gómez Morín's views began to change.[167] During this period he began to place even greater faith in Catholicism.[168] When he left the rectorship of the National University in 1934, he became quite disillusioned with the path of Mexican development, and his disenchantment increased substantially during the Cárdenas era. By the time he declared himself head of the opposition in Mexico, he had left his professorship to become, once again, a political activist. Although he ran for federal deputy in 1946 and 1958, he was defeated on both occasions, and for the last thirty years of his life he held no public offices. In spite of his role in Mexican politics, he joins the select triumvirate of Narciso Bassols, Vicente Lombardo Toledano, and Antonio Caso as the professors who most influenced Mexico's political leaders since 1946.

The remaining member of this group is Lombardo Toledano, a contemporary and lifelong friend of Gómez Morín. He left his home in Puebla to attend the National Preparatory School at the beginning of the Revolution and graduated from the National University the same year as Gómez Morín, after first trying his hand in engineering and medicine. After earning a master's degree, he began to practice law and became Secretary of the Law School. His career in public life followed as quickly as Gómez Morín's. In 1921 he became *Oficial Mayor* of the Department of the Federal District. The following year he was appointed Director of the National Preparatory School through the efforts of his professor, José Vasconcelos. In 1923 he became actively involved in politics, serving as interim governor of Puebla. After a brief and disillusioning experience, he returned to the Federal District to serve as a member of the city council, until he ran successfully for federal deputy in 1926. In 1918 he became a professor at the National Preparatory School, and, later, a professor of social sciences and industrial law at the Law School.

During the 1920s Lombardo Toledano wrote a work in defense of agrarian reform, arguing that it was a Christian rather than an anti-Christian policy.[169] As one of his students suggested, Lombardo Toledano was influenced by the Christianity of Antonio Caso.[170] Although attempting to turn socialism into a Christian philosophy, an early forerunner of Christian democracy in Latin America, Lombardo Toledano also emphasized as part of his values the need to serve Mexico.

Lombardo Toledano's philosophy, like that of his friend Gómez Morín, can be divided into two eras. About the time Gómez Morín began his ideological move rightward, Lombardo Toledano moved leftward, embracing Marxism.[171] In 1932 he argued for the socialization of industry for the benefit of the public.[172] During this same period he began to write extensively in the newspapers, and his articles were widely read. In his class on industrial law he constantly returned to a major theme, the contradiction between collective bargaining and forced arbitration.[173] He saw a revived labor movement and the political party as means for opposing individualism in society.[174] He attempted to put his political ideas into practice, first by organizing and directing Mexico's largest labor union, the Federation of Mexican Labor in 1936, and then in 1947 by leading an opposition party to the left, which he called the Popular Party.[175] In the field of education he favored direct political socialization, and, when he was expelled from the University in 1933 for his radical views, he founded and directed the Gabino Barreda University and the Workers University of Mexico. He became a leading exponent of Marxism in Mexico, but most of the political leaders who studied in his classes were influenced by his Christian socialism.

The last of the moderate neo-liberals, Luis Chico Goerne, was a contemporary of Vicente Lombardo Toledano. A native of Guanajuato and a descendant of Miguel Hidalgo, Chico Goerne graduated with a law degree in 1918, first teaching at the Colegio de Guanajuato. In 1923 he traveled to Paris, where he studied sociology. On his return he became a professor of sociology, and later penal law, at the National University. He served briefly as a judge in the 1920s, and he helped to produce the Mexican penal codes from 1929 to 1931. In 1929 he became Dean of the Law School. Opposed to the concept of elitist university education in Mexico, he gave a speech in 1930 which advanced the thesis that the University had a political role in the great national and international problems; this opinion was the antithesis to the prevailing view of the University at the time.[176]

An objective evaluator of Mexico's problems, Chico Goerne was not a teacher who readily accepted any political philosophy. He saw the postrevolutionary generations as divided into three groups. The first group was attracted to communism, which he saw as unappealing to most Mexicans because of their nationalism and the universalism of the communist doctrine. The moderate second group, in his opinion, hoped to apply the classical democratic principles in Mexico, but he saw difficulties in maintaining these liberties because of the necessity of the state to intervene to distribute land to the peasants. The third group was conservative, and he believed it would attempt to use totalitarian methods to defend the interests of religion and capitalism, a technique which he felt would be unappealing in Mexico because of the democratic sentiments expressed in the Revolution.[177] In 1935, in spite of his views favoring mass access to the University, he was appointed rector, and his tenure coincided with the attempts of Cárdenas to broaden the base of the University's population. In 1947 a former student, President Miguel Alemán, appointed him to the Supreme Court, where he remained until his death in 1960.

Conservative
Neo-liberal Professors

The smallest group of neo-liberal professors of Mexican political leaders were those on the right. One of these, José Romano Muñoz, taught ethics and civics for at least thirty years at the preparatory school. Students from various generations described him as a highly respected, popular professor who influenced young people to think about their values and philosophical views. Although his career was confined to academic life, he did serve on several educational planning commissions, and in the 1940s he was the Director of Higher Education for the Secretariat of Public Education. His influence was largely on students' general values and the meaning of those values rather than on their specific political or social views.

The most influential member of this group, but one whose teaching career was limited, was José Vasconcelos, the person considered by most Mexicans to have done more for education in the post-revolutionary period than any individual. Born in the provincial capital of Oaxaca, Vasconcelos left his family to attend the National Preparatory School and the Law School, from which he graduated in 1907. He soon became sympathetic to the precursor movement in Mexico, becoming vice-president of the Progressive Constitutional Party and an active participant in the Madero campaign.[178] A member of the Atheneum of Youth with Antonio Caso, he became, in the words of Henry Schmidt, "the archetypal Revolutionary intellectual, fusing esthetic, political, and educational ideals and presiding over a Mexican rebirth into innocence and utopia through a flight from the sophistication and corruption of the old regime."[179] During the 1910s, Vasconcelos's political and philosophical influence reached its zenith, but, as Alonso Portuondo suggests, his unique role as the leading Mexican intellectual in Latin America and a crucial actor in his country's politics was short-lived because, after 1916, "his thought ceased to be part of the mainstream of Mexican political and social evolution and his fiery voice became part of the right-wing reaction."[180] Yet his influence on student generations was to begin after 1920, when he became

Rector of the National University and a year later Secretary of Public Education. As a classroom teacher he was not very influential, largely because he did not have the interest or ability to teach well.[181] Instead, he became known as the "Teacher of the Youth" during the 1920s because of his works as Secretary and because of his writings. During these years he wrote a monthly column for *El Universal*, which was read religiously and which influenced the ideas of these student generations.[182]

During the 1920s Vasconcelos became the chief spokesman for "Americanism" in the sense of a Mexican and Latin American culture.[183] He was a strong nationalist, inheriting this belief from his parents.[184] But he was not a nationalist in the narrow sense; rather, he wanted to use nationalism to "defeat Anglo-Saxon Protestant imperialism in order to bring about a Latin American union."[185] In addition to his emphasis on native solutions to Mexican problems, he clearly believed that it was a duty to work for a better Mexico, a duty which he instilled in many of his followers.[186] In 1924, disillusioned with the direction of General Obregón's government, he resigned as Secretary of Education; he went into exile during President Calles's regime, which he criticized in his writings. In 1928, when President-Elect Obregón was assassinated after breaking the revolutionary tradition of no reelection, Vasconcelos decided to oppose the official party's candidate, Pascual Ortiz Rubio. He returned from exile and rallied many of his peers—co-professors and students from the 1920s—behind his cause. His views in this campaign emphasized his belief in the need to reestablish moral integrity, the dignity of the individual, and the protection of basic political liberties.[187]

As an educator and university administrator, Vasconcelos argued strongly for the view that the federal government should take the responsibility for a universal education. Although, like Caso, he believed that the University should be the source of spiritual knowledge and the forum for philosophical enquiry, he did not believe in autonomy for the University, only intellectual isolation.[188] As time passed, Vasconcelos's views grew more conservative, and his influence waned except in sympathetic intellectual circles. Why did this man, who had such influence on so many generations, lose control over his power? One reason, alluded to earlier, is that his views no longer represented the mainstream of post-revolutionary thought. Perhaps more important, as one of his early followers suggested, he did not know how to use his intellectual influence politically.[189] This weakness was not confined to Vasconcelos, and, like so many other influential teachers of Mexican political leaders, he was too uncompromising, too ambitious, or too selfish to remain in public office.

Marxist Professors

The remaining professors in our select group have been classified as Marxists, a classification based more heavily on the perception of their students than on whether or not they were actually orthodox believers in Marxism. As suggested above, since it is the students we are concerned with, particularly those who became political leaders after 1946, it is their perceptions of teachers, more so than the reality, which is most important. One of these men was Fernando González Roa, a contemporary of José Vasconcelos from Guanajuato. Although he graduated from the University of Guanajuato in 1904, he came to Mexico City to serve as a judge and to practice law. He served as Secretary of the Justice Department under President Madero and later became Madero's Subsecretary of Government. He began to teach at the National Law School and the Free Law School after publishing several major works, among them *El aspecto agrario de la revolución mexicana* (1919) and *El problema rural en México* (1917). His students remember him as a notable teacher in the field of international law, in which he had considerable experience as a negotiator for Mexico under President Carranza, but it was his writings which were more influential on future political leaders.[190]

Although he was not a Marxist per se, he was very familiar with Marxist ideas, and they appear throughout his early writings.[191] In his writings in the 1920s he recognized the difficulties Mexico would have if some of her reformist policies were interpreted by her neighbors as the application of Bolshevik principles.[192] One of his constant concerns was that Mexico should retain control over her own national destiny and continue to preserve it. Even well after the Revolution he believed that foreigners constituted a state within a state in Mexico.[193] He felt that if too much land fell into the hands of foreigners, Mexico's nationality would be lost.[194]

González Roa, like Díaz Soto y Gama, considered the agrarian problem the key solution to Mexico's problems. For him there were only two classes of societies, those who had resolved the land question to benefit the largest number, and those who protected the privileged.[195] The importance of property, in his view, related to its social function, that is, the collective service it could provide to the Mexican population. Although he preferred the collective benefits of land, he viewed the small individual farmer who might receive such land as contributing to the growth of citizenship and the maintenance of a democratic political regime, similar to the philosophy of Jeffersonian agrarian democracy.[196] Lastly, he believed that the underground mineral resources, particularly oil, had an international importance, and that powerful countries would attempt to perpetuate imperialism by using agents to acquire such resources in Mexico.[197]

Jesús Silva Herzog, a younger contemporary of González Roa's, has been highly influential on the ideas of political leaders who studied economics. A native of San Luis Potosí, he spent nearly two years studying in New York. After his return, he became a reporter for a new revolutionary paper in San Luis Potosí. In 1919 he began to study at the graduate school at the National University, where a German professor of economic policy, Alfonso Goldschmidt, interested him in Marxist philosophy.[198] In 1924 Silva Herzog began to teach at the National School of Agriculture and at the National University. In 1931 he became a professor at the still incipient economics section in the National Law School. He continued his public career during the 1930s, eventually becoming Director of Revenues. After the petroleum conflict emerged in 1937 he became an expert on the subject and later wrote an excellent critical analysis of that problem. Because of his expertise, he was asked by President Cárdenas to direct the government company in charge of petroleum. In the 1940s he continued his public career, working under Eduardo Suárez as Subscretary of Treasury in 1945–1946.

Silva Herzog is readily identified by his students from this period as a Marxist, but he is not an orthodox Marxist. In his own words, he is a "heterodox Marxist. I do not accept everything from Marx. It seems to me that it is not certain that the entirety of the history of humanity has been a class struggle."[199] As several writers suggest, Silva Herzog mixed classical Marxist interpretations with humanism and rationalism to create a democratic socialism in the Mexican sense. He believed that Mexico could create its own solutions and that the maintenance of individual liberty was essential.[200] Like Bassols, Silva Herzog set an example of moral integrity, personal honesty, and frankness throughout his years of public service. A fervent nationalist, he saw the petroleum expropriation of 1938 as a basis for Mexico's economic independence, to be preserved at all costs.[201] Both in his writings and his teachings he had a tremendous influence on the graduates of the National Economics School, many of whom were later cabinet secretaries and public officials.

Two remaining Marxist professors were Enrique González Aparicio and Mario Sousa, close friends and natives of Veracruz. González Aparicio, who graduated from the National Law School in the early 1920s, became interested in the study of economics. Like Ramón Beteta, he had to go abroad to obtain extensive courses in this field, and he received a diploma in economics from the University of London. He also studied at the Anglo-American School in Moscow. An orthodox Marxist, he returned to Mexico City, teaching at the Normal School and the Law School. He soon began to teach economics courses in the new section at the Law School, and, when the economics division became a full-fledged school in 1935, he became its first dean. A student of Manuel Gómez Morín, González Aparicio entered public life as a technician for the Secretariat of the Treasury. He later served as Director of the Economics Department of the National Ejido Credit Bank. In 1929 he joined Gómez Morín and other classmates to support Vasconcelos's presidential campaign.

As a professor and writer, González Aparicio stressed historical materialism in his classes.[202] In 1938 he wrote an important pamphlet on the petroleum question, setting forth a thesis which blamed foreign control for Mexico's slow economic growth.[203] Under Cárdenas, his ideas received a sympathetic ear, and he became one of the President's agrarian theorists.[204] He had an important influence on the nationalist sentiments of students in the 1930s, but his career was cut short in 1940 when he died at the age of thirty-six.

Equally influential on students who studied economics was Mario Sousa, who graduated from the Law School in 1925, earning an economics degree in 1940 and a law degree ten years later. Like his friend González Aparicio, he began teaching economics immediately after his graduation in 1925, and taught at the National Normal School, the Law School, and later the Economic School. His public career was somewhat similar to González Aparicio's, and they crossed paths several times at the National Ejido Credit Bank and the National Bank of Labor and Industrial Development. With González Aparicio and others, he helped to found the National School of Economics, replacing his friend as the second dean in 1938. In 1940 he became Subsecretary of Industry and Commerce, and, six years later, head of the Department of Agrarian Affairs.

During the 1930s, due to his early conversion to Marxism, Sousa was one of the most important Marxists in Mexico.[205] In 1938 he gave a conference on the petroleum issue with González Aparicio at the National Preparatory School. He severely criticized capitalism and blamed its growth during the imperialist stage for creating many of the problems Mexico and other countries would face.[206] He was also highly critical of the inequalities present in Mexican society.

This brief inventory of the careers and ideologies of this influential group of professors is indicative of much diversity in their thought and experiences. Yet, in spite of the range of ideological preferences, certain distinct patterns stand out. In terms of their own education, most of the professors and political leaders graduated from the same institutions and studied under a previous generation of students. This explains why professors can and do have a continuous influence on generation after generation of political leaders, if only indirectly. A professor like Antonio Caso, who taught many of these professors as students, was able to influence students even after his death, when his own students became teachers. This is not to suggest that students absorbed all of the ideas of their professors and became exact ideological reproductions of their mentors. Such is obviously not the case, but what is important is that a small group of educators, whose careers and friendships were intertwined, had a substantial influence on the formation of students who entered politics.

Ideologically, the most consistent theme represented in all of these groups is a combination of nationalism and pragmatism, most commonly expressed in the sense of finding realistic Mexican solutions for Mexican problems, followed by the need to protect Mexican sovereignty from foreign infringements and influence. The state is seen as an institution capable of resolving and correcting many of these problems. Furthermore, humanism and concern for the individual becomes an ever-present value affecting the social and political ideologies of many of these teachers and their students. The liberalism of the nineteenth century continues to be important in the ideological formation of the new generations, as illustrated in the idea of the protection of individual political liberties and the emphasis on the social implications of economic and political problems—most specifically, the land question.

Further, as models for their students, professors offer a variety of experiences and values to be considered. First, there is an overwhelming emphasis on public service, illustrated by the careers of most of these professors. Second, a remarkable percentage of professors who were political activists supported groups *opposed to* the government, generally on the basis of moral principles concerned with the protection of political liberties. Lastly, several of the politically active professors and many of the non-activists were characterized by strong moral principles and integrity. It is interesting to speculate on the political careers of the most influential professors, Antonio Caso, Manuel Gómez Morín, Narciso Bassols, and Vicente Lombardo Toledano. Caso, of course, did not participate in public life. But the other three, who were major public figures of their times, all participated in opposition movements and were founders or co-founders of opposition parties in Mexico. This fact may be due to their willingness to practice their ideological views; in some cases, their morality made personal compromise, essential to a successful public career, too difficult. Whatever the case, it has been the professors who were politically active both within and outside the official system who have most influenced political leaders in Mexico. The contribution of Mexican professors to the socialization of their students can be described as an eclectic philosophy stressing nationalism, nativism, humanism, pragmatism, statism, and political libertarianism, or a melding of nineteenth- and twentieth-century interpretations, a mixture which has contributed to the peculiar substance and structure of Mexican development in the post-revolutionary era.

7

Political Leaders and Their Values

Values can be described as "highly generalized attitudes that define a person's orientation to life in terms of the things he deems most important."[1] Ideological beliefs consist of a person's preference for social, economic, and political philosophies. Both values and ideological beliefs have some effect on a politician's behavior. There has not been extensive research on the interrelationship between the two, but it is evident that personal values, under various conditions, do affect a person's views on political or economic issues.[2] Furthermore, the patterns of political action are themselves a reflection of "deeply ingrained values and understandings which are part of the [Mexican] political culture."[3]

Certain relationships exist among background variables, personal values, and ideological beliefs, but it cannot be suggested that elite preferences will accurately predict behavior patterns or performance in office. One study of French political elite preferences showed that they coincided with French government policy only about half the time.[4] There may be numerous reasons for the discrepancy between values and behavior. In the case of Mexico, the political culture inhibits personal attachments to the substance of public policies among political leaders.[5] Not only do political leaders fail to be identified with controversial policy positions, but they fail to be innovative in policy areas. Furthermore, the degree of personalism within the system and the centralization of policy formulation in the name of the president pressures top leaders to identify with the president and his policies.[6] Further, in addition to curbing their own impulses for long-range personal goals, politicians do so for the purpose of political compromise as well. But, as Donald Searing argues, although political behavior is not always a reflection of values, there are "no convincing reasons to dismiss values *a priori* as symbolic flags with little relevance for behavior. They deserve serious investigation as significant components of political belief systems."[7]

In determining the personal values and ideological beliefs of Mexican political leaders, I intend to present the representative views of a generation. In general, political elites hold personal and ideological views more intensely and more stably over time than does the average citizen.[8] Still, the reader should expect the responses to be tempered by age and experience, even though many of the leaders insisted that their ideas at the end of their careers accurately reflected their beliefs at the beginning of their careers.

When one is describing values and beliefs held by these various leaders, it is important to know whether or not these individuals see themselves as members of representative generations. Many who were members of the "Revolutionary Generation" saw themselves as a special group drawn together by a singular experience, that of the Mexican Revolution.[9] But not all members of a generation have similar values or beliefs; rather, as defined by Samuel Ramos, "the unity which converts a group of individuals into a 'generation' comes from a mutual concept of life, even though life is expressed in many different forms and activities. . . . To deserve the name, a generation must be united by strong spiritual bonds, not simply by motives of expediency."[10]

For members of the early revolutionary generations, many of whom were mentors and professors to the political leaders under study, the guiding principle seemed to be best expressed as a vision of a new Mexican society which would be just, a principle which Cosío Villegas describes as akin to a religious faith.[11] Two members of this earlier group, Martín Luis Guzmán and Javier Gaxiola, however, believe that the universal values of their generation were reflected in intellectual, literary, and artistic works, but that their attitudes on how to achieve a just society were quite diverse.[12]

Observers of contemporary Mexican political development believe that among the immediate post-revolutionary generations there was a "common identity and a shared ideological perspective regarding the direction of future change and the goals to be pursued."[13] Members of the early 1920s generations saw the eclectic ideology of the Mexican Revolution as forming a significant part of the attitudes of student generations in this period.[14] Although individual members believed that they held a set of common beliefs, those

beliefs became more diverse as time went on.[15] One member of this generation summed up the beliefs which characterized the early post-revolutionary
groups: they believed, first, that the acts of public figures should benefit the
masses; second, that much more emphasis should be placed on the human
rather than the technical aspect of programs; third, that they should be concerned with the poor; fourth, that democracy was an extremely important
value; and, fifth, that a well-prepared person should be able to improve his
position in life.[16] The views of the generations from 1920 to 1925 are of special importance because they were the first of the post-revolutionary generations to dominate the National University and to enter public careers. As
Eduardo Bustamente suggested in 1976, "This was a group which poured its
entire life into the most creative period of growth for Mexico, from 1925 to
the present. For better or worse we participated very heavily in the development of governmental power."[17]

   The generations which followed centered on the Alemán generation of
1925–29 and were responsible for the changes in political administration and
government policy from 1946 until 1964.[18] Their underlying goal changed,
but it was related to that of the previous generation: the creation of a new
state. What inspired this belief? As a general cause, some members of these
groups point to the social climate. For others, it was a personal incentive to
develop Mexico economically and to benefit from that growth, or it was the
desire to see Mexico accomplish great works for the benefit of all Mexicans.
Still other political leaders saw the unity of these individuals stemming from a
sort of spiritual solidarity among most of the families who were survivors of
people who had fought in the Revolution and had maintained liberal ideas
from the 1850s and 1860s.[19] Again, most of the members of this generation
believed in similar goals and in identifying the same problems. But, like earlier groups, they differed largely in the criteria by which they evaluated the
achievement of these goals. For example, one respondent noted that Miguel
Alemán, Antonio Ortiz Mena, and Antonio Carrillo Flores, all from the
1925–29 generation, and all of whom very much determined Mexican financial policy from 1946–70, had the same ideas concerning problems and goals,
but different views regarding the procedures for solving those problems and
achieving the goals.[20] Despite their differing views on procedures, this generation, above all others, saw itself as a collective group whose combined efforts
were significant. Furthermore, the informal leader of that generation, Miguel
Alemán, believed that it initially had a great sense of unity and has retained a
remarkable degree of unity over the years.[21]

   Beginning in the early 1930s and continuing through 1940, members of
various generations continued to describe universal ethical values and similarities in goals. Among the various responses as to what these generations'

goals were is an amorphous concept of the need for change, that is, to change everything. Again, however, the solutions were different and followed clearly defined ideological paths, particularly democratic versus socialist. Many believed that what distinguished their generation from those following was a definite concept of what they wanted to do, even if they disagreed on the method. The disparities among needs and goals versus means appear to be typical of political elites everywhere. Frank Bonilla, in his perceptive analysis of Venezuelan leaders, found that, while there was surface agreement about needs and goals among this elite, there was considerable difference in the level of commitment to the pace of reforms, the volume of investment needed in redressing inequalities, the causes of the problems, and the capacity of people to change or continue to endure deprivation.[22]

The 1930s generations, larger and more diverse than previous groups, did not form broad, unified, and cohesive friendships.[23] Each generation sees itself as different to some degree from those who came before or after it, but it is remarkable that the general views of political leaders from 1915 to 1945 are similar, and that the need for change, whether referring to social injustice, the state, or the status quo, has been a key principle over time, in spite of the significant environmental changes taking place during the Revolution and the period immediately following. This continuous thread among the political leadership's thinking in Mexico parallels an analysis by political scientists of two North American generations spanning the dynamic changes of the late 1960s which concluded that "the net result of life-space changes among the young and of historical forces operating on each generation is a smoothing out of intergenerational antagonism, a smoothing out accomplished even over the eight turbulent years covered by our observations."[24]

Personal Values

We know that there are some broad universal principles underlying the unity of various generations of Mexican political leaders, but what, specifically, are their personal and ideological beliefs? When asked to identify personal values most important to them and what they looked for in others, Mexican political leaders agreed on five points: individual freedom, service for others, hard work, knowledge, and honesty. In a comparative context, these personal values are not surprising. A study of local leaders in India, Poland, the United States, and Yugoslavia concluded that the following were what leaders valued most about each other: honesty, selflessness and dedication to public service, intelligence, education and professional knowledge, good relationship with people, and general leadership ability.[25] The personal value missing among Mexican responses is that which refers to getting along with others. Perhaps Mexicans automatically assumed the importance of this quality, since personal relationships, as already suggested, are an important part of the political culture and essential to career mobility. A value mentioned by many Mexicans but which does not appear in the list from local leaders from other countries (due to the difference in the phrasing of the question) is the emphasis placed on personal liberty. Some Mexicans considered liberty to be their most important value. Most of them defined it in terms of respect for personal dignity, which, not surprisingly, is a conceptualization of the humanistic philosophy so important in the education of most of the respondents. As one leader suggested, liberty, like any other personal value, requires limitations.[26] In some ways the high priority given to liberty and individual dignity among Mexican political leaders is surprising in view of the degree to which authoritarianism is present in the Mexican culture.[27] On the other hand, the emphasis on political liberty among political leaders may explain the eclectic nature of authoritarian politics in Mexico and the low degree to which it actually infringes on individual liberties of speech and press.

Of equal importance to Mexican political leaders (and politicians everywhere) is the emphasis given to social service. As one public figure expressed this value, "Man is morally obligated to serve others in whatever profession he may make for himself. After the Revolution the majority of students had the idea of serving their country."[28] Another prominent leader expressed this value in terms of personal satisfaction when he stated that "gratitude should be the greatest reward to a public man, and that a public man should always be most interested in the good of the general population."[29] However, not all political leaders suggested a selfless motive for themselves or others. Julián Garza Tijerina, a party leader and senator under Cárdenas, believed that among his generation of students at the Military Medical School in 1925 most wanted better economic conditions than their parents had had. He felt that service had come second to self-improvement.[30] As is true in interviews with all politicians, it may well be that the value of social service is emphasized for the benefit of the interviewer. However, a good case could be made for differences experienced by Garza Tijerina at the Military Medical School, which recruited from very humble families during the 1920s, and the students at the National University, who came generally from better economic circumstances.

Another value frequently mentioned by Mexicans was the importance of hard work for personal success. For example, José Hernández Terán, who spent more than thirty years in the field of irrigation, ultimately serving as Secretary of Hydraulic Resources, felt the value most important in his personal philosophy was to work diligently and take on responsibility. "When I first started to work for the National Irrigation Commission, they did not have hours, which meant that the person who wanted to improve himself had to be self-disciplined."[31] Another leader received his personal philosophy of hard work from one of his professors, expressed in the phrase that "in work there is gold and the riches of nations."[32]

A fourth personal value chosen as important by Mexicans was knowledge and experience. Some saw this in terms of preparation for a task. Others viewed it as being important only when an individual was willing to see that a plan was carried out as well as being the intellectual author of it. Still others saw knowledge as an abstract equivalent of truth or the willingness to determine it. This conceptualization was best expressed by Antonio Armendáriz:

> The highest value for me as a young man was that man should choose truth, pure truth, but that truth is a very difficult tunic to wear. Each person is limited in what he can know. I remember that Antonio Caso once said that, "If you could choose, would you want to be able to know all the truths or always want to have the passion to attempt an answer to any question?" If I had to choose one or the other I would choose to have the passion to answer.[33]

Lastly, similar to politicians elsewhere, Mexicans admired honesty, morality, and frankness. Some, such as Angel Carvajal, saw personal morality as essential to defeating corruption in Mexican public life.[34] For others, it was a question of personal behavior and moral honor not to benefit from a public position.[35] This statement of belief does not mean, of course, that politicians, including some of those interviewed, necessarily practiced what they valued —corruption in Mexican political life is well known. The fact that honesty is not a prominent symbol of Mexican public life may make it of greater importance to political leaders as something to be attained. Others saw personal sincerity, in terms of saying what they really thought, as a prestigious value.[36]

Ideological Beliefs

Personal values, as suggested above, have some relationship to ideological beliefs. Such relationships are not constant, but the interviews with Mexican political leaders concerning their ideological beliefs suggest that these values do indeed overlap with one another, and, in fact, strongly held personal values become integral parts of political, economic, and social ideologies. Respondents were asked a series of open-ended questions to determine important political and economic beliefs.[37]

The economic-political belief most commonly referred to by Mexicans and often by other politicians is the large degree to which the state should play a role in economic development. This finding is not surprising among Mexican leaders, first because statism was a theme so strongly emphasized among their professors and political mentors, and second because the 1917 Constitution made an early commitment among developing nations to the state's involvement in the economy. Most Mexican leaders advocated a balanced role between the state and the private sector, a position characteristic of the neo-liberals in Mexico. Rubén Vargas Austin describes this position, which is both moderate and pragmatic:

> The modern Mexican liberals [neo-liberals in this study's terminology], typified by such economic policy statesmen as Secretary of Finance Antonio Carrillo Flores, characterize their philosophy as one that aims to promote political stability and economic growth by using all forces available, public or private, through the coordination of the State.[38]

This balanced view, representing the philosophy of the majority of political leaders, has also been described by Eduardo Bustamante:

> Private enterprise should not spend its time debating the role of the government in the economy; rather, once the government decides to follow a policy, the private sector should encourage it to do an effective job. The government is not justified in intervening in an area in which private enterprise is failing just to save jobs, because it does not have the expertise to operate such failing industries. The basic error of the government is that it does not have a well-defined program. On the other hand, government intervention in some areas such as petroleum, electricity, and railroads has probably achieved more success than the private sector.[39]

However, it cannot be said that professors were largely responsible for conveying the view that the state should intervene in the economy, since one formulator of economic policy stated that his professors had not conceptualized a concrete substitute for laissez faire policies in the early 1920s.[40] Some politicians favored state intervention as a result of their own reading and believed that the government should implement policies in favor of broad masses of Mexicans rather than small groups. Not only was their economic philosophy influenced by the number of the people to be benefited by economic growth, but others saw government, reflected in the changing emphasis in law texts during the period, as directly involved in dispensing social benefits to the people. By the 1930s, the role of the state had become a highly controversial issue and was strongly debated among various professors. In spite of this controversy, the 1917 Constitution, of considerable influence on political leaders, continued to provide definite support to the mixed economy.[41] Because of its legitimacy, the Constitution continues to be important in the formation of the views of political leaders. Hugo Margáin, Secretary of Finance in the early 1970s, acknowledges this influence in his statement that, "I am a man of the Constitution of 1917, a constitution which favors a mixed economy."[42]

The view that the state should have control over large areas of the economy is a philosophy supported by young educated Mexicans. In a survey of Mexican university students in 1970, Rosalio Wences Reza found, first, that the majority of students believed that the people and the state should control a large part or some part of the national wealth, and, second, that a large minority believed that the government should have nearly complete control. Only 5 percent of the students believed that the state should have almost no control.[43] This minority view is also represented, to the same degree, among Mexican political leaders. For example, one respondent suggested that "Mexico has developed in spite of the role of the government. Governmental administrations are too contrary and personal from one administration to the next."[44] A larger group of political leaders, like students, take the opposing view that state intervention should be more substantial. Again, the differences within the political leadership in Mexico stem from the continuous debate over means, divided largely between a socialist and a mixed capitalist-socialist approach. One of the keys to understanding this difference about means is the argument over whether economic well-being promotes individual liberties, or whether individual freedoms provide an incentive for improving personal standards of living. This conflict has been described by one of the respondents:

> I think that for my generation the main goal was to achieve a better standard of living and a higher level of education while at the same time improving the quality of political life through greater freedoms. I think my generation was unified in these aspirations. But there were two different means: one was through a socialized economy, the other was through a combination of socialism and private enterprise. My personal opinion is that socialism has played a very important role in Mexican development in such activities as energy and transportation. We need to control these types of activities, but other areas should remain in the hands of private enterprise.[45]

Another theme which ran through the process of professorial socialization of political leaders was pragmatism. This concept is a substantial part of the philosophy of Mexican political leaders. Ideological beliefs, as long as they are contained within the broad boundaries of the revolutionary ideology, have not been of primary significance to the careers of Mexican political leaders, unless those individuals have publicly espoused extreme nineteenth-century liberal ideas or orthodox Marxist beliefs. Pragmatism has become an essential part of the belief structure of Mexican political leaders because of the nature of politics. As one respondent describes it, "Politics is real life. A politician's ideology cannot be some theory borrowed from the United States or Europe. It has to be something which results from your practical life."[46] Pragmatism is a practice essential to all political activists. This attitude begins very early in the lives of Mexican and Latin American student leaders, many of whom enter national politics. In his description of student political activists in Latin America, Kenneth Walker says that "political involvement presumably leads to a commitment to the rules of the political game, and to an awareness that what looks like corruption from the outside may often be the consequence of the necessary compromise, or give and take, which elected representatives must engage in."[47]

Pragmatism is not only an ideological tenet of Mexican leaders, but a professional value, too. As Antonio Carrillo Flores mentioned, his golden rule in politics is to open his eyes to reality before doing anything.[48] That advice has served him well; few men can claim careers as successful as his in public life.[49] Lastly, pragmatism seems to have a special importance to the students who entered politics through their participation in or on the fringes of the José Vasconcelos presidential campaign in 1929. Many of the participants of this campaign, and of the earlier 1927 opposition campaign, turned to a pragmatic approach to take political control of the official apparatus from within, rather than becoming disillusioned or permanently participating in the ranks of the opposition. One of the respondents describes this phenomenon:

> What was important about this generation was its participation in the Vasconcelos campaign. The participants were the most brilliant members of our generation. After Vasconcelos was defeated and abandoned the country, many were dispersed throughout Mexico. The impact on some was to emerge in local and state politics. For example, Miguel Alemán became a senator from Veracruz, and, of course, when the governor-elect was assassinated, this opened the door for him to become governor. He began forming a group, but one inside the official party, not a group with an ideological emphasis or goal, but a group which would emerge in control of the political system.[50]

Mexican politicians are also pragmatists because their personal ideological beliefs are eclectic, again following the pattern set by their mentors and professors. Several respondents made the following comments:

> I do not like to classify myself as having any label, because my philosophy is one which centers on improving the welfare of my country regardless of the source of the idea. I want to remove the ignorance from my country, but, at the same time, I recognize the difficulties which Mexico faces.[51]

> I do not have a fixed political ideology because I am in agreement with any policy which benefits Mexico, and I disagree with those that do not benefit her.[52]

> I would describe myself as a populist, that is, I am interested in all ideas which promote human equality. I am more inclined to the methods of the left. I would describe my philosophy as a humanistic political ideology.[53]

These views, as has been demonstrated in previous sections, come from a variety of sources—historical, personal, and literary. One prominent member of the 1928–32 generation, an important transitional group among student generations and political leaders in the 1950s and 1960s, describes, in part, the eclectic combination of intellectual sources:

> I do not believe I am much different from most of the other members of my generation. I am a democrat with a liberal strain from the nineteenth century. I also have been influenced in my political views by the Spanish anarchists and, of course, by the Flores Magón brothers, who, as you know, were also a bit anarchistical. My political views were also influenced by the Russian Revolution, but not in the sense of the communist solutions; rather by the problems which were brought to the forefront in the revolution.[54]

Other political leaders, especially those who were educated before and immediately after 1920, often describe themselves as revolutionary liberals, who, by any definition, hold a mixture of transitional beliefs from the nineteenth and twentieth centuries.

The most striking universal belief among the Mexican political leaders, a belief which refers to means rather than ends, is an almost universal emphasis on peace and order, a theme prominent in the pre-1910 era in Mexico.[55] Although the Mexican Revolution seems to have shared its influence with many other sources of socialization on the post-revolutionary generation, when it comes to peace and order, the environment created by the Revolution is preeminent. Furthermore, this belief, rationalized in only slightly varying terms, is expressed consistently from the oldest down to the youngest generations. The views of leaders from different age groups clearly illustrate the continuity of this belief:

> My generation [1921] had a great desire for peace and order because of their experiences with the Revolution. My generation was one which emphasized organization, to create order out of chaos. I believe that this desire was much greater than was true of other and later generations. Lawyers were very occupied with formulating new laws which the country needed for some semblance of order. Doctors were giving service to towns which had not had it for many years. Public accountants had to put order in the accounts of large firms and in government finances. Bank laws were reorganized. A very open environment allowing for great changes in the future prevailed at this time.[56]

> I believe my generation [1925] had a very strong desire for order and peace because of the revolutionary experience, and that this belief was much stronger than in later generations.[57]

> I believe that all of my educational generation [1932] had a very strong desire for peace and stability because of their experience of proximity to the Revolution and because of the ideals of their parents, many of whom had fought in the Revolution itself. I recall numerous conversations among parents of my generation commenting on the suffering they had encountered, especially the farmers and workers.[58]

> We were living within a political structure undergoing great renovation [1939], and there was a feeling among many of us that care needed to be taken to avoid another revolution.[59]

The transfer of this value from one generation to another is not surprising, since North American scholars have suggested that dispositions toward either peaceful or nonpeaceful means of political change can be passed on from one generation to the next.[60] This transition would be particularly easy among a political elite united by a continuous educational environment and a long-term teacher-mentor relationship, and the value has been transferred to the youth of the 1980s in spite of their lack of contact with the social dynamics of the Revolution. Although the large majority of students interviewed by

Wences Reza, unlike political leaders, believed major changes in the political system were necessary, 78 percent thought violence was not necessary to achieve these changes.[61] This nonviolent view is equally true of Latin American students in countries not experiencing a major social revolution in the twentieth century. In his study of Panamanian and Costa Rican elite students, Daniel Goldrich concluded that "75 percent agreed or strongly agreed that violence should never be used to resolve political questions."[62]

As an integral element in the political beliefs of our respondents, the desire for peace and order encouraged the development of subsidiary ideas important to promoting tranquility. According to many of the political leaders interviewed, this stability required collaboration among the various political factions within the governing political elite. Antonio Carrillo Flores, often a spokesman for his generation, states this view pragmatically:

> I believe that friendship and cooperation were very important qualities believed in by my generation, and that this kind of cooperation and friendship has made the Mexican system work. We have to look for things that unify Mexicans rather than things that divide us. Everything is possible in peace, and violence is not really necessary to achieve social justice and economic development.[63]

Not only has collaboration become a means of achieving social peace, but, in the words of one perceptive observer, it has encouraged the moderate ideological view espoused by the majority of our respondents, or what he describes as "a philosophy of doing things very harmoniously, never taking an extreme position either to the left or to the right, but developing a sense of balance or equilibrium that is the ideal of a conciliatory position."[64]

Mexican political leaders emphasized the need for unity and political stability not only because of the Revolution itself, but also because of the conflict between socialism and fascism which struck Europe and Latin America during the early 1930s. Mexico found its economy shattered and its social norms uprooted by the Revolution, just as Europe was devastated intellectually and physically by the Great War. The pattern adopted by Mexican political leaders seems to be shared, to some extent, by post-revolutionary leaders elsewhere. William Quandt, in his analysis of the Algerian leadership, concluded that "the dislike for political controversy and the threatening nature of political opposition have led many Algerian leaders to the belief that only by creating 'homogeneous' ruling groups can one insure political stability."[65] Although Mexican political leaders adopted political order as a primary belief, it did not become an overriding goal to the exclusion of change.[66] Instead, most of them viewed change within the context of political stability, and peace became an end as well as a means.[67]

Another value important to Mexican leaders was personal liberty and democracy, widely sought among Mexican political leaders and reflected in other political concepts of this group.[68] Furthermore, the importance of personal freedoms tends to explain the limited role of the state most political leaders advocate in Mexico. Like the concept of peace and unity, democracy and political liberty are ideological beliefs emphasized among all generations beginning during the revolutionary decade. One leader suggests that his generation (1920) advocated democracy and "a wide range of self-expression, limited by respect for those ethical and social precepts which give inner strength to freedom, discipline to fulfill one's duty, which collectively permit and explain the exercise of the rights of the individual."[69] To Mexican leaders, democracy not only included the typical political liberties but the concept of no reelection, a theme introduced during the precursor era prior to 1910, and a central political issue in the 1927 reelection of General Obregón.[70] Miguel Alemán discussed his generation's (1929) view:

We debated and discussed many Revolutionary ideas as students. One of the ideas most prominent in our ideology was that of no reelection, which we strongly supported. We also had a strong belief in the principle of democracy and the necessity of its growth in Mexico. As students we participated in many political activities and student groups. When the PNR was founded in 1929, we formed the first professional group to exist within the official party.[71]

Other leaders stressed the importance of individual liberties:

The most important value I learned from my student days and which I have always felt obliged to support is that of the preservation of personal liberty.[72]

There were a number of similar values among the members of my generation, despite the fact that we were divided into those with Catholic, liberal, and socialist tendencies. The most important value of my generation [1939] centered on liberty and the belief that the individual should be important.[73]

I cannot conceive of or believe in a system in which man becomes an instrument of the state. Man should have considerable freedom to express himself.[74]

The importance of individual liberty in the political beliefs of Mexican politicians stems both from the legitimacy of the individual guarantees in the 1917 Constitution and from the humanistic teachings common to many of their notable teachers, as well as from the political liberalism of the 1850s, which characterized the beliefs of many of their parents and grandparents.

Some political leaders, whether or not they consider the role of the state and individual liberties to be important, define their political and social beliefs in terms of the concrete implementation of the provisions of the 1917 Constitution, or what Frank Brandenburg labeled Constitutionalism.[75] As Hugo Margáin suggested, "Our most prominent idea was to implement the Constitution of 1917."[76] The difficulty with identifying constitutionalism as an element in political beliefs is that most individuals stress some principles but ignore others. For example, Antonio Carrillo Flores, in talking about Narciso Bassols's early teaching career, notes that he "was a supporter of the political provisions of the 1917 Constitution but was not yet concerned with its social aspects."[77]

A belief of lesser importance to all political leaders, but consistently held from one generation to the next, is anti-militarism. Most of the leaders who grew up during the early 1920s soon adopted this view, which explains why so many of them supported Vasconcelos in 1929, since he was the first civilian post-revolutionary candidate of any significance. For some, professors were the source of this belief.[78] Among the generations of the 1920s and 1930s, a feeling of anti-militarism contributed to their political activism and pragmatic approach to dominating the official party from within. It was Miguel Alemán, the son of a revolutionary general, who became the first civilian president in 1946. But Alemán was something more than a symbol of civilian political control, and early in his campaign he attracted many intellectuals and young people with political interests because of his civilian background and because of his choice of civilian intellectuals and lawyers as his closest campaign collaborators. When he became president, he instituted a significant change in the percentage of military officers holding high offices in his administration.[79] This change was quickly perceived by political leaders:

> In the post-revolutionary period lawyers were in positions inferior to that of generals. Psychologically, it was very important when Alemán brought many lawyers and professors into his ministries. This surprised us and had a serious impact; in fact, I would describe it as a political change of extraordinary proportions.[80]

That this attitude is still strongly held among civilian political leaders was reflected in an interview with a high official of the Echeverría administration who expressed visible disgust and dismay that the resignation of the Governor of Oaxaca in March 1977 had resulted in a general's becoming the new interim governor.[81]

A belief of Mexican politicians typical of leaders of developing nations everywhere is their strong sense of nationalism, especially in relation to the United States. The historical and geographical reasons for Mexico's antagonism to the United States are well-known.[82] Mexican leaders, like those elsewhere, see their northern neighbor from two perspectives: "on the one side is admiration for the North America that stands for freedom; on the other is repudiation for the North America that incites and supports those who impede freedom in Latin America."[83]

As measured by events alone, this sense of nationalism and antagonism toward the United States was particularly strong among the generation of leaders who graduated from professional schools before the mid-1920s, since, to them, the occupation of Veracruz and the Pershing expedition were events intruding on their own territory.[84] As a result of the Revolution, foreigners, but particularly United States citizens, brought many claims against the Mexican government. This subject, as one Mexican recalls, was of great interest to the young generations: "The United States was a subject of great concern to us and was constantly discussed. I thought the Secretary of Foreign Relations should achieve a resolution to Mexican-North American claims. This question was extremely important then."[85]

Nationalism, in the sense of economic independence, received a substantial boost with Lázaro Cárdenas's expropriation of foreign oil interests in 1938, an event second only to the Revolution in its socialization effect on Mexican political leaders. A sense of economic nationalism was particularly strong among the student generations at the National School of Engineering during the late 1930s and early 1940s. As one graduate told the author, "My political ideas are really affected by an exacerbated sense of nationalism. I have always believed that my country should be equal to other countries and develop its own industries. I have always had a certain anti-imperialist attitude."[86]

The most important economic and social belief of Mexican leaders, following their commitment to a strong role for the state in the economy, is a belief in the importance of social mobility and an improvement in the standard of living for all Mexicans. For many, especially those from humble backgrounds, mobility was found in the ability of individuals like themselves to govern their own country. This view has been best expressed by Antonio Armendáriz, who came from campesino parents and was fatherless as an infant:

> I believe that the university provided people from rural backgrounds with an opportunity to achieve a better position in life. This, however, has been true only for certain individuals, but has

not been a general condition. As a result of the Russian Revolution, I saw that many young people could achieve positions of power in their government. This event pushed my generation into being more perceptive about what was happening in Mexico. In short, it indicated to me that people from humble backgrounds could govern their country.[87]

For others, social justice, or improved social welfare for all Mexicans, became the primary goal of their generation. This theme became attached to the belief that the state should play an important role in the economy, because to many the state was the primary means by which wealth could be redistributed to the masses.[88] Not surprisingly, the dual goals of an improved welfare and a higher standard of living were those most important to political leaders everywhere, whereas the political forms for achieving those goals had a much lower priority.[89]

Lastly, closely tied to the concept of social justice for all Mexicans is the belief that political leaders and others with advantages should serve their country and their people. Although public service seemed more important to Mexican political leaders as a personal value than as a social ideology, several expressed this concept in the latter context. Angel Carvajal, for example, attempted to put this philosophy into practice as a student and young professional:

> I helped organize a society called the Vasco de Quiroga Association. We had classes for workers during the evening hours at the National Preparatory School. After a year we promulgated a manifesto published throughout Mexico suggesting that students and educated people had the obligation to help less fortunate people. We recruited students everywhere to support our efforts. In a year's time we had earned the confidence of the workers and had taught several thousand of them.[90]

For some leaders service to others went beyond their fellow Mexicans: "I believe that we have to help each other, whether rich or poor within my country or among rich and poor countries."[91]

Achievements and Failures of the Revolution

The beliefs described above reveal a great deal about how Mexican political leaders might perceive both problems and solutions. It is more difficult, however, to know how their personal values and ideological beliefs affect their interpretations of various policies in public life. One of the most widely discussed issues in Mexico in the 1970s and 1980s, as was true a generation ago, is the Revolution of 1910, and whether its influence has failed, made great achievements, continued to propel government policy, or just faded away.[92] Because the achievements of the Revolution form part of the rhetoric of the official party and the government, and because political leaders are constantly called upon to defend its principles, it was believed that if political leaders were asked to evaluate the failures and achievements of the Revolution, their responses might reveal the intensity and extent of their personal and ideological beliefs.

Although I have not categorized the collective evaluations of the Revolution by these leaders according to their beliefs, it is quite clear that their appraisals of the Revolution are very much related to their values and beliefs as they described them. Furthermore, these appraisals have a certain consistency among the majority of the political leaders. What they originally hoped the Revolution would accomplish in identifying problems and goals has been expressed by Ramón Beteta, a representative of the early 1920s generations and a mentor to many later political leaders.[93]

> With the Revolution, our greatest force, we have discovered ourselves; analyzing the Revolution, we have understood our heterogeneity, our lack of unity; studying its causes, we have found at the base of our society a system of injustice and oppression; investigating its results, we have found a movement of integration, a desire for mutual understanding and a realization of better economic conditions for our lowest classes. All the various sides of the Revolution point toward the same goal. . . . In all of these, as well as in many other phases of the Revolution, we perceive the attainment of our great hope; that Mexico may become a great nation.[94]

Mexican leaders expressed pride in some of the achievements of the Revolution, but not one had completely uncritical praise. Furthermore, they seemed to focus on the question of property, either in terms of agrarian reform or nationalization of resources, and on economic development. Favorable comments on political and social achievements of the Revolution were few. A selection of responses commenting on the achievements included the following:

> The most important achievement of the Revolution was to rescue basic industries and natural resources necessary to provide us with the ability to achieve a growing economy. If this had not happened, we would have been left behind.[95]

The most important achievement has been the establishment of some goals concerning property and natural resources. There are concepts which establish social property. There has been the development of protections and limitations of public resources, exemplified in the nationalization of these resources and the intervention of the state in regulating the economy and as a factor in economic democratization.[96]

The achievement with all of its effects has been the agrarian reform, followed by changes in the labor movement, the multiplication of schools and universities, and, lastly, the material infrastructure necessary for economic production.[97]

These positive assessments were tempered by critical appraisals:

Without a doubt, the pre-revolutionary regime was changed. There has been economic progress since 1920, such as the degree of industrialization, the application of the agrarian reform, the technification of agriculture, and the development of great hydroelectric dams. But the technification of agriculture has been limited to very few farmers. The agricultural bank, for example, has been a failure. The demographic explosion and urban migration are serious problems. We need to organize agricultural production—we have lost a lot of time. The liberation of the farmer will improve his production.[98]

The goals of the Revolution have not been achieved. One of the important achievements was the distribution of land, but this has not been satisfactorily completed, since today many people hold lands outside of the law. The small farmers do not have the investment or the technology to produce a satisfactory living.[99]

I think all of our governments are obligated to implement the principles of the Revolution. Our greatest failure is that the government has not protected public resources, allowing the wealth to leave the country. This has been a major fault and is the origin of the present situation in Mexico.[100]

Turning to an analysis of the failures of the Revolution, Mexican leaders, in addition to their criticisms of the agrarian reform, centered their comments on political goals, followed to a much lesser extent by social failures. The political failures most commonly noted by these leaders were centralization of power, lack of democratic participation, bureaucratization, and corruption. Centralization of decision-making was criticized because it makes federalization of power in Mexico a theory, not a reality.[101] Lack of participation, the most common political failure identified by political leaders, was attributed to atrophy, apathy, and ignorance. The last of these problems arose, in the opinion of several leaders, from the failure to implement widespread education throughout Mexico. The other political failures, as well as the failure of the Revolution in general to achieve its goals, was blamed on the "lack of methods and goals. Political life is like a pendulum in Mexico, from one extreme to another. This is due in part to a lack of definition and planning."[102] In fact, for some Mexicans the lack of definition within the revolutionary program was so great, and the emphasis among various presidents so diverse, that they found it impossible to identify specific achievements.[103] Lastly, in addition to the failure of widespread education, it was felt that another social problem still requiring considerable effort is the disparity between middle and lower classes in Mexico.

In talking about the failures of the post-revolutionary governments to implement completely and effectively the principles of the Mexican Revolution, Mexican leaders have criticized their own leadership and that of their collaborators. Their private views are not far away from those of a group which often is the government's severest critic—university students. When asked their opinion of post-revolutionary governments, 85 percent of the Mexican students interviewed by one author thought those regimes had benefited the country some of the time.[104]

Views of Contemporary Problems

Another way of determining the importance of ideological beliefs and personal values on the perceptions of political leaders is to attempt to determine their priorities concerning contemporary problems. Mexican political leaders, when asked to identify the most important issue facing their country at the time of the interviews, listed seven major problems (Table 7.1). Their interpretations and preferences reflect both the objective conditions in Mexico and their own personal experiences and ideological predilections. A comparison of Mexican and Venezuelan leaders show that both see economic problems as most crucial. In the case of Mexicans this finding is not surprising, since ideologically they advocate an important role for the state in resolving economic problems. Furthermore, emphasis on reducing unemployment can also be related positively to their personal views of the work ethic and opportunities for improvement. Some leaders believe that if the economy is properly managed, Mexico, using its own resources, can produce the necessary changes. Others believe that, in addition to hard work by each individual, the government needs to ensure that the national resources will be

Table 7.1 Problems Identified by Mexican and
Venezuelan Political Leaders as Most Important

Problem	Mexican Responses (%)	Venezuelan Responses (%)
Economy[a]	39	110
Agrarian reform[b]	17	52
Population growth[c]	17	23
Leadership[d]	13	—
Education	10	65
Participation[e]	10	—
Youth[f]	10	27

NOTE: The responses are from the core sample of Mexican political leaders and from Frank Bonilla's analysis of Venezuelan elite views, as reported on page 254. Both groups gave multiple responses, and I have included only those problems of greatest importance. Those problems of great importance to Venezuelans, but not mentioned by Mexicans, were substandard living conditions (39 percent) and family disorganization (38 percent).

[a] *Economy* for Mexicans included unemployment, housing, foreign control, slow growth; for Venezuelans, poverty and unemployment.

[b] *Agrarian reform* for Mexicans was defined in terms of the land-distribution problem; for Venezuelans, the concept of rural backwardness was used.

[c] *Population growth* in the Venezuelan survey included excessive city migration.

[d] *Leadership* referred to experience, morality, and independent thinking.

[e] *Participation* referred exclusively to the need for increased political participation.

[f] *Youth* for Mexicans meant lack of integration; for Venezuelans, social disorganization and delinquency.

used for the benefit of Mexico, not for foreigners.[105] Still others believe that the economic problems stem from inefficient management of resources, improper budgeting, or lack of planning. Furthermore, one leader stressed the importance of time in dealing with this problem, fearing that slow growth might well increase the possibility of a military government in Mexico.

Mexicans, like Venezuelans, place a high priority on solving the agrarian problem. The agrarian reform, of special interest to their professors, a part of the revolutionary environment, and an integral article of the 1917 Constitution, has, in the opinion of most of these leaders, been characterized by many failures.[106] One view of these agrarian problems has been described by Miguel Alemán:

> To me the most important problem in Mexico today is that of the rural area. If the demands of the world for food increase, and they surely will, then Mexico cannot be left behind in the area of food production. The Mexican Revolution was really an agrarian Revo-

lution. In dealing with the agrarian problem we cannot forget that there are laws and institutions which we must enforce and use to solve the problem. But to solve the agrarian problem, our farmer needs to obtain a better education so that he will be totally responsible for his land and for the production of crops. [107]

Another view, which stresses the abuses, both economic and political, of social property, has been suggested by Manuel Hinojosa Ortiz, a leader who has written widely on agrarian questions:

> The agrarian problem today is very serious. We have expropriated *ejidos* and turned social property into private property. The most important characteristic which deserves to be corrected is the agrarian bossism which exists in the *ejido*. [108]

Although the Mexican government has been slow to recognize publicly the problems of demographic growth, political leaders from past regimes were quick to identify them. [109] Mexicans, like observers of this problem elsewhere, point to the demographic problem as critical because of the increased pressure it places on other problem areas. The late Martín Luis Guzmán aptly expressed this view:

> The most important problem is to prevent a demographic explosion which prevents a fast rate of economic growth in Mexico. We are headed toward a situation in which the problems will never be resolved in any kind of regime regardless of whether it is mixed, capitalist, or socialist. For example, the agrarian reform program is confronted with too many people who still do not have lands after forty years. Also, the immediate consequence of population growth is an inability to educate everyone. [110]

In addition to the economic, agrarian, and demographic problems, Mexicans, unlike their Venezuelan counterparts, stressed two important political problems, the need for greater political participation and organization and the need for more experienced, honest, and innovative leadership. Perhaps this finding stems from the Mexicans' personal values and from their ideological emphasis on individual liberties, principles which they described as still not having been fulfilled by the Revolution. Furthermore, their emphasis on political order and pragmatism and the failures of the political system since 1929 have probably made them sensitive to criticisms of the lack of participation and the centralization of decision-making. But in analyzing the political system, leaders stress different problems, as illustrated by the following interpretations:

The most important problem of the country is its political organization. The people do not know how to express themselves politically or how to organize themselves. We have advanced greatly in getting the people to vote, to participate in our system, and things are calmer today. For example, women vote, even nuns, a group which I saw in the last election. There is not the same danger involved in abusing voting privileges in the Federal District as there might have been in the past.[111]

Today in Mexico students are not taught; they are indoctrinated. We need people and leaders who can think for themselves. People are not intellectually informed in the true meaning of the word.[112]

The most important problem is that the people who govern must develop a consciousness that power cannot be absolute or unlimited. Their illusions should not be converted into political devices. They also need to realize that public funds should not be spent in a capricious way, but must be used carefully for the future growth of all Mexicans. We cannot tolerate the misspending of scarce public resources. Honesty and responsibility in government today are more urgent than ever before.[113]

I believe that this government [Echeverría's] wanted to give younger people a chance to run things in Mexico. But I believe they made the mistake of giving too many important positions to young people who had no experience. Many of the mistakes they have made have been a result of this lack of experience. Mexico cannot afford such errors during this period of its development.[114]

Lastly, Mexicans felt that several social problems were important. In mentioning the problem of youth, they saw the need to achieve a greater integration of views between older and younger generations, and for young people to achieve a greater maturity in attempting to implement their goals. Education was deemed necessary to provide larger numbers of Mexicans with the knowledge and self-discipline necessary for solving political and cultural problems.

Public Policy for the Future

The primary purpose of this chapter has been to shed some light on the values and beliefs of political leaders in relation to developmental patterns in Mexico from 1946 to 1970. However, of equal interest is Mexico's future. Because Mexican public policy has always been incremental in nature, and because the political leaders interviewed in this study are themselves among the more important mentors and professors of the new generation of political leaders of the 1970s and 1980s, two politically loaded questions were asked the interviewees relating to Mexico's future and the ideological beliefs of these public figures. First, is the extent of the role of the government in the economic sector adequate? And, second, should the extent of political participation be increased? These two questions were chosen because they deal with issues which have often been used in other studies to separate liberal and socialist views.[115] Furthermore, in Mexico in 1976–77, these two issues were under intensive discussion after Luis Echeverría's criticism of the private sector and the devaluation of the peso in the fall of 1976, and José López Portillo's commitment in 1977 to increase participation and democratization in the choice of local candidates.[116]

The responses to the question of whether or not the role of the government in the economy was sufficient were evenly divided between those who thought it sufficient and those who thought it should be increased. No leader thought it excessive. Those who thought it should be stronger, however, qualified their answers with serious reservations. Alfonso Pulido Islas suggested the Marxist view:

> I think planning is necessary in all phases of life to achieve the goals of our country. This is the only road which we can follow. It needs to be coercive and obligatory for everyone. We must follow a given path. I believe that the government should be more involved in the economy, but there needs to be much better planning and greater responsibility for what is happening. Executive control needs to be more definite and precise.[117]

The non-Marxist view supporting greater state involvement was equally critical:

> Government does not exist to eliminate private property because all of the useful objects of life would be gone. A great bureaucracy is worse than private property because it has all of the power and abuses it. The criticisms of capitalism are valid but the proposed solutions are not.[118]

Another view advocated government intervention but doubted those in leadership positions:

> The government should have a more important role in the economy today. The government needs to take a moral role in leading

the country. Many leaders do not have the experience or sensitivity to understand the problems in Mexico.[119]

Other respondents believed that the government's role was already sufficient and felt there was little need to increase it. Their answers usually suggested reasons why that role should not be increased:

> I believe that the role of the state as a stimulant in improving economic conditions in Mexico should not disappear. A person should be able to earn wealth for himself; in other words, the profit motive should remain a part of the Mexican system. If this right disappears, the economic system will fail. The state should not become a dictator over the economy, but it should have an important role in it, without absorbing it. In effect, it should serve as a coordinator of the economy.[120]

> The role of the government in the economy is one designed to maintain social equilibrium. If it exceeds this role, it will bring about a disequilibrium in the system. If the state does not desist from intervening in the economy, it will produce a socialist economic system in Mexico.[121]

Perhaps the Mexican political system has been most criticized for the lack of effective participation and suffrage among the masses. As in their responses about the role of government in the economy, political leaders fell into two large groups: those who thought Mexicans were not yet ready for increased participation, and those who thought they were ready (though the implementation of such increases required considerable forethought and planning). Only one leader was convinced that Mexicans already had sufficient participation in the system. These views have been echoed by leaders in other developing countries. Quandt has suggested that

> while it is widely believed that the establishment of effective state authority and the beginnings of satisfactory economic growth must precede any moves toward greater citizen participation or decentralization, there is nonetheless a strong belief among many members of the political elite that eventually the masses should play a greater political role.[122]

Mexican responses to the question about increased participation in the future seem to reflect their realism and pragmatism regarding the ability of the masses to handle such privileges and, at the same time, their personal and political beliefs stressing the importance of individual liberties. Some thought increased political participation would come naturally through the redistribution of income: "I think the best way to achieve democracy is not by pushing a button or developing a formal conception, but rather through the democratization of economic resources."[123] Others thought that liberty should be the principle guiding all public policy: "Above all, the most important principle which needs to be maintained and achieved in any solution to our problems is the development of democratic principles and individual freedoms. We must continue to grow in this area so that our solutions are justified."[124] Those who thought Mexicans were ready for greater participation most commonly identified, as obstacles to its implementation, problems related to education:

> We should not let the obstacles or difficulties of promoting more democracy serve as an excuse for not implementing it in Mexico. Without a doubt Mexico is not a very homogeneous country; for example, look at the differences in our language. In Spain all groups understand Spanish, even the Basques, who speak another language. A universally understood language is a necessity for public reaction to government policies. This condition does not exist in Mexico. This problem has always produced difficulties in communication and in implementing policies. Communication is necessary for unity. When voting occurs in places where Spanish is not spoken, the people have no idea of who or what they are voting for. We have to achieve a degree of comprehension among all people before they can vote with a sense of consciousness.[125]

> The population should participate politically in great numbers, but this participation is also related to education. It is very difficult to say whether democracy would be possible in Mexico because of cultural factors, the lack of communication, and the lack of education. The population is easily deceived by politicians who promise certain programs. It might be possible. Greater importance needs to be given to the politicization of the people because they are a mirror of our country.[126]

An equally sizable group of leaders, for generally the same reasons, thought Mexicans were not yet ready for increased participation. Luis de la Peña best expresses the more pessimistic view:

> I do not believe that Mexico is really ready for increased participation because the people are not ready to take on the responsibility. Although I think more participation is necessary, we first have to achieve broader education and a cultural education designed to prepare people for participation in political affairs. The solution, however, is difficult to achieve.[127]

Mexican political leaders, whether describing their own values and beliefs, evaluating the failures and achievements of the Mexican Revolution, or discussing current problems and future solutions to those problems, show an obvious consistency in their views, a consistency which is typical of the recent past and most likely will be true in the future. Ideologically their views approximate quite closely the views of their most philosophically influential teachers; statism, pragmatism, nationalism, and libertarianism again form an eclectic mold. The pragmatic nature of their views explains how they can support the essential need for orderly transition, even if that means the use of authoritarian methods, while also subscribing to the importance of individual liberties. Furthermore, although their views vary widely on certain issues and beliefs, there is a certain universality in goals, if not in means. It can be argued that, if ideological beliefs have any influence on the pragmatic nature of the Mexican politician, they surely help to explain the development of Mexico's peculiar political structure as described by most observers. The universality of certain beliefs, particularly views on violence, also helps explain the success which Mexican leaders have had in unifying, retaining, and evolving their control over the political system.

8

Implications for the Future

Mexican political leaders have been influenced by many sources of political socialization, and the degree to which they have been influenced by each source varies from one individual to another. In spite of this diversity in source and intensity, however, there are certain common patterns which run through the backgrounds of these individuals. Four characteristics are most important: the degree to which parents or grandparents were actively involved in or discussed political matters; the dynamic post-revolutionary environment in which they grew up; the early age at which Mexican leaders became interested in politics; and the substantial influence of professors, particularly at the National Preparatory School and National University, on their beliefs.

Before analyzing the significance of these four characteristics, it is worth reintroducing a question discussed in the first chapter: what is the validity of these statements by political leaders, and how should they be interpreted? The answer to this question relies heavily on three conditions: the relationship between the interviewer and interviewee, the intensity with which a respondent holds such a view, and the ability of the interviewer to assess the degree of intensity with which a view is held. As Richard Sennet has argued, the differences in class background, education, and experience, among other factors, between interviewer and interviewee has an effect on how the person responds to a question.[1] Furthermore, how the answer will be used will also affect the response.

To begin with, my relationship with each interviewee varies from one individual to the next. My correspondence and interviews with Mexican political leaders began in 1968. Since then, I have had more than one hundred and fifty interviews with Mexican political leaders of all backgrounds and generations. Many of those individuals have responded to several interviews over a period of years. The results of this periodic contact is that it has given me a better opportunity to assess the degree to which certain beliefs are held by an individual, if only on the basis of the repetition of certain responses during various visits or in letters. Furthermore, repeated contact has created a feeling of trust between myself and many respondents to the extent that an individual is willing to criticize the political system, individual political leaders, or a presidential administration he collaborated with, and to show considerable emotion in reacting angrily, sadly, or humorously to a specific question. Therefore, the interview material presented throughout the text of the book has been selected because it is representative of various groups of leaders, and equally important, although not readily visible from the reading of these responses, because these beliefs were strongly held.

This assessment, however, does not mean that each statement made by every political leader is "true" in the sense of accurately reflecting either what actually contributed to the politician's choice of career or the source of his values and beliefs; rather, these responses suggest what political leaders themselves *believe* to have been true. Those responses which I believed were for my benefit as an interviewer have been discarded. In other words, what is most accurate about these responses is that in most cases the respondents themselves believe what they said to be true.

The degree to which Mexican politicians gave self-deprecating, modest answers, or answers verging on self-interest, in and of itself can be valuable in studying the collective personality of the political leader. Therefore, for example, when an individual suggests "for the public good" as a reason for choosing a public career, rather than "it was the best opportunity to achieve fortune and fame," "public good" may become the justification for seeking "fortune and fame." However, even so, the "public good" rationale may eventually become the primary reason in the mind of the politician.

Knowledge about the above-mentioned common patterns of socialization experiences of political leaders is important for several reasons. First, as suggested by Kenneth Prewitt,

> whether socialized or mobilized into politics, persons entering the
> active stratum are influenced by an identifiable and differentiat-

ing set of social experiences. By establishing what these social experiences are, we can take a step in explaining the process which
narrows the entire citizenry to the few who govern.[2]

But how people become leaders is only one important aspect of this knowledge. Equally valuable is that it might provide some insight into why the political structure itself has evolved in its particular direction.

Furthermore, knowing something about the beliefs and values of political leaders and their recruitment patterns in Mexico has certain implications
for change. As Putnam concludes, "If generations of political leaders moved
rapidly onto and off the politcal stage, the collective culture of the elite
should respond quickly to social change. If, on the other hand, a given generation of leaders monopolized positions of power for a long period, the lag
between social and attitudinal change would be greater."[3] Although some
studies suggest that certain generations of political leaders in Mexico are replaced after fairly short periods in office, continuity can be accomplished in a
somewhat different manner.[4] Instead of actually controlling government positions, as was typical under Porfirio Díaz, Mexican political leaders have controlled the recruitment process, and, more importantly, a large share of the
socialization process, in their roles as fathers and professors of future leaders.
It is crucial to understand this role in order to see how the Mexican political
system works and why it has followed its own peculiar development.

Of the four common socialization patterns mentioned above, perhaps
the two most important are the social environment of the Revolution and the
preparatory school and university experiences. The first of these shared experiences has contributed to a sense of unity. Extremely important to this revolutionary experience was the resulting emphasis placed on nonviolence and
the need to promote cooperation among the members of these generations in
order to achieve peaceful transition and growth in Mexico. The preparatory
school and university experience, universal to so many public figures, only
added to the sense of unity already established. Again, this is not to suggest
that these individuals agreed on ideological means as a result of these experiences; rather, they gradually developed an elite culture characterized by certain unwritten rules or beliefs. Among these beliefs was one agreed-upon
means: orderly transition without large-scale violence. But several other patterns developed out of these socializing experiences, and they seem to have
been duplicated, interestingly enough, in the experiences of British political
leaders from the public schools and from Oxford and Cambridge, as described
in chapter 4. Political leaders in Mexico, regardless of personal or ideological
faction within the official family, have demonstrated their ability to communicate with each other and to make the transition from one administration to

the next, even in cases in which there is considerable opposition to the chosen pre-candidate.

This cultural pattern has some important implications for the Mexican political system. Not only does it imply certain ground rules to which the players must agree in order to stay in the game, but, as one scholar has suggested, it may well influence the content of the political process:

> Underlying this process are sets of beliefs, values and procedures which stipulate that such a process is a "good" thing, that it fits the actor's expectations, and that it is "the way to do things." In this very limited sense, this deeper set of shared understandings is super-organic in that it defines the very content of the processes which are contained in events in Mexican political culture.[5]

It is also likely that the common socialization experience, the relationship between the recruiters and the socializers, and the closed nature of the Mexican political system have helped to perpetuate similar beliefs and behavior patterns. In his longitudinal study of Bennington graduates, Theodore Newcomb reached two major conclusions that may be applied to the Mexican political scene: that individual beliefs remained startlingly constant over a period of years, and that an existing belief could be maintained by creating an environment in which either new information could be avoided or other individuals support one's own information.[6] Mexico's political leaders have created a supportive environment by accepting the informal rules of political behavior and by playing an important role in socializing new political recruits.[7]

Another important conclusion of this study is that Mexican leaders, whether one looks at how they developed an interest in politics, how they became involved in politics, or how they were politically socialized, have certain similarities with political leaders of other, rather distinct cultures. The more closely cultures approximate each other in their development and their social and political structures, the more likely it is that similarities among political leaders will occur. For example, large numbers of political elites everywhere become interested in politics at an early age. But in a culture like Mexico, where politics is a full-time vocation and the political system is competitive only in an internal sense, involvement in political activities must start early. In contrast, North American political leaders can create a political following and catapult themselves into successful political careers on the basis of their ability to appeal to the public. This phenomenon can occur just as easily when they are in their thirties and forties as when they are in their teens or twenties. In Mexico, early contact with public officials, whether they are teachers, administrators, or party leaders, is essential to most successful careers.

Universal among political leaders is the high percentage who have parents from professional backgrounds and who were also in politics. Data is hard to come by for this variable in studies of political leaders in any culture. It is estimated that in Mexico, if more information were known, confirmed figures for all political leaders would shift upward from 30 percent having politically active families to a figure approximating 50 percent. For political leaders in Latin America, it is predicted that comparable figures could be found. The more open the system and the greater the social mobility, the more likely it is that politicians from political families will occur in smaller numbers. Politicians in general, as is the case of Mexicans, will be less likely to follow the views of their parents than the average citizen, since the political leader, by nature, develops a sense of intellectual independence at an earlier age than his peers. The fact that many Mexican politicians came from political families, and that many did not adhere to their parents' beliefs about the Revolution, illustrates the importance of a major political and social event as a competitor against more traditional socializing agents. However, it is also important to note that many parents were favorable to the Revolution, and that many grandparents who were politically active were supporters of Benito Juárez and Miguel Lerdo de Tejada, important contributors to nineteenth-century liberalism in Mexico. Although Peter Smith's study shows that the Revolution opened up political positions to a group of leaders different from that in the Porfirian era, the post-revolutionary group which took office after 1946 often had historical ties, through parents and grandparents, to the liberal traditions of the nineteenth century.[8]

Unlike North American and Canadian leaders, Mexican leaders have been substantially socialized by their professors. Again, as has been shown earlier, this fact is due to the social structure in Mexico, where few persons have access to an education, where few good preparatory schools and universities existed during the period in which these political leaders were educated, and where most prominent leaders received a higher education. Furthermore, the educational system itself contributed to this situation, first because the majority of students left home to attend preparatory school and the university, leaving their families at an earlier age than their North American counterparts. Second, because of inadequate salaries, the majority of educators were professional people with other careers, and many of them, especially those professors chosen by Mexican politicians as having the greatest influence on their philosophies, were themselves political leaders. Lastly, educators who are public figures are largely responsible for the recruitment of educated political leaders into the Mexican political system, and they often serve as models to be emulated by younger generations. There are certain similarities with the British or European educational systems. But students in Mexico, at least in the post-1910 years, were recruited from more diverse class backgrounds than were British students at the major public schools and Oxford and Cambridge. Therefore, it is less likely that the National Preparatory School and the National University provided as cohesive a culture as characterized the British counterparts during a similar era.

Because Mexican teachers are important recruiters and socializers of Mexican political leaders, who in turn follow in their footsteps, much of the socialization process is confined to a small and in many ways homogeneous group of men. Furthermore, given the educational pattern in Latin American countries, and evidence from several studies of Venezuela, Argentina, and Guatemala that the education of political leaders in those countries is also confined to a small number of institutions, it would be fair to speculate that the same pattern exists to some degree in those cultures. This established pattern in Mexico is not only important in understanding the recruitment process, but, perhaps more importantly, explains to a large degree how Mexicans have maintained a sense of unity and political order since the 1940s. This pattern also suggests another element in the centralization of Mexican politics.

The beliefs of Mexican politicians, the least studied of all aspects of elite socialization, again suggest certain universal patterns, however speculative, in their personal values. In analyzing their ideologies, one may well find similarities among political leaders who have governed their countries in the aftermath of a revolutionary period. In this regard, the most important concept, as demonstrated in the Algerian study cited earlier, is the belief that order and unity are essential to the governing process and that political liberties and increased participation have a much lower value.

The traditional sources of influence on the values and beliefs of Mexican political leaders may well shed some light on the future ability of Mexico's political system to change. Interviews with political leaders in the José López Portillo administration suggest that younger individuals are equally influenced by three of the four sources mentioned at the beginning of this chapter, excluding the dynamic post-revolutionary environment, which by their youth had dissipated in intensity and scope.[9]

What makes these sources most important for understanding Mexico's political leadership and the structure of the political system is the strong intertwining between the recruiters and those who provide the sources of socialization. To begin with, recruitment practices in Mexico have evolved over a long period of time and have not yet changed.[10] As I suggested in chapter 6, the university has been the most important institution in the recruitment function.[11] Because this continues to be the case for younger political leaders who govern in the 1980s and will continue to guide Mexico in the next decades, it implies that future leaders will have been both recruited and influenced in their values and beliefs by the same individuals. Furthermore, figures for those leaders who come from politically active families have not declined, and, since family ties too are known to be important in the recruitment process as well as in the intellectual formation of children, the success of many future leaders will no doubt be related to their family background.

When characterizing the Mexican political system, care must be taken in assessing the importance of turnover in political leadership and the degree to which the recruitment process is closed. While the turnover in actual individuals does occur in sizable numbers from one administration to the next, the question of measuring continuity and turnover may not be clearly revealed by numbers of new individuals, but rather by the heterogeneity or homogeneity of their experiences, and that of their parents and grandparents.[12] The continued importance of politically active families from one generation of leadership to the next suggests that the recruitment structure selects from a narrower pool of future leaders than appears to be true on the surface. A major structural change could affect, to some degree, the ability of parents and professors of a specific generation to influence future leaders or recruit them, as happened to many of the respondents because of the Revolution, but since this is not a forseeable event in Mexico's immediate future, it is unlikely that the typical pattern will change.

Ultimately, one can only speculate on the effect which the learning and recruitment patterns of political leaders will have on Mexico's future. It would be fair to conclude that there is little that can be found in the values and beliefs which imply that future leaders will significantly change the structure of the political system or governmental policies. Although such a change might occur, it would probably come from a different source of political beliefs and from leaders recruited outside the traditional recruitment structure.

APPENDIX

The Respondents

Mexico's national leadership has followed three basic career patterns: administrative-judicial, party-electoral, and mixed. By far the most common has been the first type, in which public figures have worked their way up through the state and federal bureaucracies. Among this study's general population of political leaders from 1935 to 1977, approximately 55 percent of the 900 office-holders emerged through the administrative route. Sixty-one percent of the expanded group followed solely administrative-judicial careers. This pattern has gradually been on the increase since the early 1940s and is more pronounced among those 204 persons holding the cabinet-level positions from which the core group was selected (Table A.1).

Cabinet-level positions include the directorship and, where appropriate, the sub-directorship of the following agencies between 1946 and 1970: Attorney General of Mexico (11 office-holders), Bank of Mexico (3), Department of Agrarian Affairs and Colonization (9), Department of Tourism (4), Federal Electric Commission (4), Mexican Institute of Social Security (4), Mexican Petroleum Company (8), National Bank of Foreign Commerce (4), National Company of Public Commodities (8), National Finance Bank (2), National Railroads of Mexico (4), National Steel Industry (3), Secretariat of Agriculture (14), Secretariat of Communications and Transportation (4),

Table A.1 Core Group of Respondents

Name	Dates Positions Held
Salvador Aceves	1964–70
Sealtiel Alatriste	1964–66
Miguel Alemán	1946–52, 1960–70
Antonio Armendáriz	1952–58, 1960–70
Praxedis Balboa Gojón	1952–62
Eduardo Bustamante	1946–49, 1958–64
Enrique Beltrán Castillo	1958–64
Antonio Carrillo Flores	1946–70
Angel Carvajal	1946–58
José Castro Estrada	1951–52
Ernesto Enríquez Coyro	1952–64
Manuel Franco López	1964–70
Francisco González de la Vega	1946–52, 1961–64
José Hernández Terán	1964–70
Manuel Hinojosa Ortiz	1952–57
Hugo B. Margáin	1961–70
Pedro Daniel Martínez	1964–70
Antonio Martínez Báez	1948–52
Manuel R. Palacios	1946–52
Alfonso Pulido Islas	1964–65
Agustín Salvat	1964–70
Andrés Serra Rojas	1946–48
Víctor Manuel Villaseñor	1952–69
Ricardo José Zevada	1952–65

Secretariat of Foreign Relations (12), Secretariat of Government (10), Secretariat of Government Properties (15), Secretariat of Health (12), Secretariat of Hydraulic Resources (10), Secretariat of Industry and Commerce (10), Secretariat of Labor (8), Secretariat of the Presidency (11), Secretariat of Public Education (10), Secretariat of Public Works (8), Secretariat of the Treasury (13), and Ambassador to the United States (5).

The second most common pattern among all high-level political office-holders is a mixed administrative-electoral career, although, for most, the number of years in administrative positions has exceeded that in electoral-party positions. This has been the pattern followed by all Mexican presidents during the years included in the population of general political elites, with the exception of José López Portillo, who followed a strictly bureaucratic career. Nearly 35 percent of Mexico's high-level office-holders followed a mixed pattern. The expanded group contains 28 percent from this category. Lastly, and least important, have been purely electoral-party careers, in which a person shifts from one electoral position to another, oftentimes alternating with a position in the party bureaucracy. About 10 percent of the expanded group, equal to its national representation, has been included. The sample is weighted somewhat in favor of the administrative career type, because the core group is representative of national policy-making office-holders, the majority of whom from 1946 to 1970 emerged from administrative-judicial careers.

I have purposely omitted military officers with political careers from the figures. At the highest levels, such officers have generally held only two positions: Secretary of National Defense and Secretary of the Navy, both of which have not been included as positions represented by the core or expanded group. The top three positions in each of these agencies have always been held by a career officer and have been excluded from consideration in this study because military officers have experiences quite distinct from those with strictly civilian political careers. Officers who qualify, however, are part of the general population of political leaders.

The individuals who formed the expanded group of interviewees for this study (Table A.2) include all of the individuals in the core group plus an additional group of office-holders who often held positions before 1946 and after 1970, who might have graduated before 1920 or after 1939, who might have come from some of the other important public or private universities in Mexico, or who held high electoral office. Furthermore, I have included several individuals who have held important public academic positions, often politically involved, but who have generally had careers on the fringes of Mexican politics. Like members of the core group, each has been purposefully chosen because he is representative both of a certain type of career pattern in Mexican politics and of the political ideologies of Mexican political leaders.

The 900 individuals who form the general population are a nearly complete population of political leaders in Mexico who have held the highest offices from 1935 through January 1977. There is nearly complete data on fifty-nine variables for approximately 85 percent of the office-holders who have held office at certain levels in Mexico. This population will serve as a basis for comparison with the small core and enlarged samples used throughout the book. Unless indicated, all figures referring to Mexico's general political leadership are based on this data. Individuals holding the following positions during the years specified above have been included:

Table A.2 **Expanded Group of Respondents**

Name	Dates Positions Held
Salvador Azuela[a]	1933
Efraín Brito Rosado	1946–52
Ezequiel Burguete	1966–70, 1970–75
Raúl Cardiel Reyes[a]	1962–64, 1964–70
Ignacio Chávez Sánchez[a]	1933–34, 1961–66
Mario Colín Sánchez	1970–73
José Angel Conchello[b]	1972–75
Víctor Correa Racho[b]	1969–70
Daniel Cosío Villegas[a]	1932
Luis de la Peña Porth	1970–73
José Juan de Olloqui	1970–76, 1976–82, 1982–
Julio Faesler	1970–76
Julian Garza Tijerna	1934–40
F. Javier Gaxiola	1940–44
Alejandro Gómez Arias[c]	1947
Hugo Pedro González Lugo	1945–47
Manuel González Ramírez[a]	
Martin Luis Guzmán	1970–76
Roberto Mantilla Molina[a]	1954–58, 1961–66
Miguel Palacios Macedo	1923
Emilio Portes Gil	1928–34, 1934–35
Alfonso Francisco Ramírez	1941–59

1. President of Mexico.
2. Secretaries (and Sub-secretaries and *Oficiales Mayores*, where applicable) of the following cabinet agencies: Agrarian Reform, Agriculture and Livestock, Attorney General, Attorney General of the Federal District and Federal Territories, Communication and Transportation, Defense, Federal District, Foreign Relations, Government, Health and Public Welfare, Hydraulic Resources, Industry and Commerce, Labor, National Properties, Navy, Presidency, Public Education, Public Works, Tourism, Treasury.
3. Directors and Sub-directors of the following decentralized federal agencies: Import-Export Paper Company (PIPSA), Institute of

Table A.2
(*continued*)

Name	Dates Positions Held
Pedro Ramírez Vázquez	1975–76, 1976–82
Raúl Rángel Frias	1955–61
Jesús Reyes Heroles	1964–76, 1976–82, 1982–
Ricardo Rivera Pérez[a]	
Gonzalo Robles	1935
Roberto Robles Martínez	1965–76
César Sepulveda[a]	1962–66
Leopoldo Solís Mánjarrez	1976–82
María Emilia Tellez	1970–76
Jaime Torres Bodet	1940–48, 1958–64
Manuel Ulloa Ortiz[b]	1939
Alberto Vázquez del Mercado	1921–23, 1929–31
Eduardo Villaseñor Angeles	1939–40, 1940–46
Agustín Yáñez	1953–58, 1962–70
Fernando Zertuche Muñoz	1970–76, 1976–82, 1982–

[a] These individuals were rectors, secretaries general, or deans of the National University, or directors of the National Preparatory School No. 1. As I have suggested elsewhere, the rectorship of the National University might be considered a political office. However, it has its own idiosyncracies, and I do not wish to confuse that career type with others which are the focus of this study.

[b] These are members of the National Action Party who were included to present some experiences from representatives of this group.

[c] Alejandro Gómez Arias was Vice President of the Popular Party in 1947.

Social Services and Security for Federal Employees (ISSSTE), National Coffee Company, National Company of Public Commodities (CONASUPO), National Railroads of Mexico, National Sugar Finance Company, National Steel Industry, and Petroleos Mexicanos (Pemex).

4. Directors and Sub-directors of the following federal banks or financial institutions: Agricultural Credit Bank, Bank of Mexico, Foreign Trade Bank, and the National Finance Bank.

5. President and Justices of the Supreme Court.

6. President and Justices of the Superior Court of the Federal District.

7. Ambassadors to France, Great Britain, the Soviet Union, the United States, the Organization of American States, and the United Nations.
8. Senators, repeating Federal Deputies. (To give better representation to female political leaders, women federal deputies, even if they served for only one term, were included.)
9. Presidents, Secretaries General, and Secretaries of the Institutional Revolutionary Party (PRI) and its antecedents, and of the Authentic Party of the Mexican Revolution (PARM), the National Action Party (PAN), and the Popular Socialist Party (PPS).
10. State Governors.
11. Sector leaders and union leaders of such organizations as the National Federation of Popular Organizations (CNOP), the National Peasant Federation (CNC), the National Federation of Labor (CTM), the Federation of Government Employees' Unions (FSTSE), and the National Union of Educational Workers (SNTE).
12. Rectors of the National University and the National Polytechnic Institute.

Notes to the Chapters

Chapter 1

1. James W. Wilkie, *Elitelore* (Los Angeles: Latin American Center, UCLA, 1973), pp. 31ff.

2. Roderic A. Camp, "Review of James W. Wilkie, *Elitelore*," *The New Scholar*, Vol. 5 (Fall, 1975), pp. 198–200.

3. Jack Dennis, "Major Problems of Political Socialization Research," in Jack Dennis, ed., *Socialization to Politics* (New York: John Wiley, 1973), p. 24.

4. Donald J. Mabry, "Changing Models of Mexican Politics, A Review Essay," *The New Scholar*, Vol. 5 (Fall, 1975), p. 36.

5. Donald D. Searing, "The Comparative Study of Elite Socialization," *Comparative Political Studies*, Vol. 1 (January, 1969), pp. 471–500.

6. Heinz Eulau, "Recollections," in John C. Wahlke, Heinz Eulau, William Buchanan, and Leroy Ferguson, *The Legislative System* (New York: John Wiley, 1962), p. 94.

7. Richard Dawson and Kenneth Prewitt, *Political Socialization* (Boston: Little Brown, 1969), p. 43.

8. Robert A. Dahl, *Polyarchy: Participation and Opposition* (New Haven: Yale University Press, 1971), p. 167.

9. "The Problem of Generations," in Karl Mannheim, ed., *Essays on the Sociology of Knowledge* (London: Routledge and Kegan, 1952), p. 297.

10. Allan Kornberg and Norman Thomas, "The Political Socialization of National Legislative Elites in the United States and Canada," *Journal of Politics*, Vol. 27 (November, 1965), p. 766.

11. Donald Searing, "The Comparative Study of Elite Socialization," pp. 475, 484.

12. See Frank Bonilla, *The Failure of Elites* (Cambridge: MIT Press, 1970), p. 107; and William Hamilton, "Venezuela," in Donald K. Emmerson, ed., *Students and Politics in Developing Nations* (New York: Praeger, 1968), p. 370ff.

13. Richard Dawson and Kenneth Prewitt, *Political Socialization*, p. 161.

14. Daniel Goldrich, *Sons of the Establishment: Elite Youth in Panama and Costa Rica* (Chicago: Rand-McNally, 1966), pp. 19, 106.

15. Rafael Segovia, *La politización del niño mexicano* (Mexico: El Colegio de México, 1975), pp. 12, 40.

Chapter 2

1. Kenneth Prewitt suggests three ways in which an individual's political activity may begin: it may come after many years of preoccupation with public affairs and political happenings; it may be a sudden decision after a short history of political interest; or it may be simultaneous with taking a political office. *The Recruitment of Political Leaders: A Study of Citizen-Politicians* (Indianapolis: Bobbs-Merrill Co., 1970), p. 58.

2. Kenneth Prewitt, Heinz Eulau, and Betty H. Zisk, "Political Socialization and Political Roles," *Public Opinion Quarterly*, Vol. 30 (Winter, 1966–67), p. 575.

3. See Allan Kornberg and Norman Thomas, "The Political Socialization of National Legislative Elites in the United States and Canada," *Journal of Politics*, Vol. 27 (November, 1965), p. 765. The earliest study analyzing the time of initial interest in politics among political leaders is that by Heinz Eulau, who found a similar pattern among state legislators in the United States. See his "Recollections," in John C. Wahlke, Heinz Eulau, William Buchanan, and Leroy Ferguson, *The Legislative System* (New York: John Wiley and Sons, 1962), pp. 77–95.

4. For further evidence of this apprenticeship of political leaders in Mexico since 1900, see Peter H. Smith, *Labyrinths of Power: Political Recruitment in Twentieth-Century Mexico* (Princeton: Princeton University Press, 1979); for the interchange among North Americans, see Thomas R. Dye and John W. Pickering, "Governmental and Corporate Elites: Convergence and Differentiation," *Journal of Politics*, Vol. 36 (November, 1974), pp. 900–925.

5. Prewitt gives no breakdown by education for his sample.

6. See the author's "Parents, the Revolution and the Social Environment as Socializers of Mexican Political Leaders," paper presented at the Rocky Mountain States Latin American Conference, April 7–9, 1977, Tucson, Arizona.

7. For example, since 1935 45 percent of Mexico's political leaders have graduated from the National University in the Federal District. Yet only 13 percent of Mexico's political elite during the same period were born in the Federal District. See Roderic A. Camp, *Mexico's Leaders: Their Education and Recruitment* (Tucson: University of Arizona Press, 1980), p. 39ff.

8. See Kent M. Jennings and Richard G. Niemi, *The Political Character of Adolescence, The Influence of Families and Schools* (Princeton: Princeton University Press, 1974), pp. 247–48.

9. *La politización del niño mexicano* (México: El Colegio de México, 1975), p. 12.

10. *Psychology of the Mexican* (Austin: University of Texas, 1975), p. 26.

11. Kenneth Prewitt et al., p. 573. Kornberg and Thomas found an even more exaggerated relationship, in which 88 percent of those who remembered their first interest in childhood believed family members were responsible, whereas 100 percent of those who initiated their interest as adults remembered external events and conditions (p. 766). Family political activity also affects the likelihood of an individual going into politics. In summarizing some of this literature, Prewitt noted that "the major socialization proposition reviewed states that those most likely to select themselves (and be selected) for public office are those overexposed to politics as youths or adults." See his "Political Socialization and Leadership Selection," *The Annals of the American Academy of Political and Social Science*, Vol. 361 (September, 1965), p. 109.

12. Personal interview with Ernesto Enríquez Coyro, Mexico City, October 26, 1976.

13. Personal interview with Miguel Alemán, Mexico City, October 27, 1976. Alemán later became President of Mexico from 1946–52, and in the early 1980s was still one of the most politically influential figures in Mexico. His father, a prominent general in the Revolution, was killed leading an uprising against the government in 1929.

14. See Roderic A. Camp, "El Sistema Mexicano y las decisiones sobre el personal político," *Foro Internacional*, Vol. XVII, No. 1 (julio–septiembre), p. 79, note 39.

15. Personal interview with Martin Luis Guzmán, Mexico City, October 21, 1976. Guzmán became a prominent publicist, head of the controversial Free Textbook Commission, and a senator in the 1970–76 administration.

16. Personal interview with F. Javier Gaxiola, Mexico City, October 22, 1976, and his *Memorias* (Mexico: Editorial Porrúa, 1975), p. 39ff.

17. Personal interview with Alfonso Pulido Islas, October 28, 1976, Mexico City.

18. Personal interview, Mexico City, October 20, 1976.

19. See Roderic A. Camp, *Mexico's Leaders*.

20. See Peter H. Smith, *Labyrinths*, Chapter 4.

21. Personal interview with a graduate of the National School of Engineering, Mexico City, October 29, 1976.

22. Personal interview, October 28, 1976.

23. Personal interview, Mexico City, October 22, 1976.

24. Personal interview, Mexico City, October 24, 1976. The "Seven Wise Men" was the name given to an important generation of graduates from the National University.

25. Personal interview, Mexico City, October 22, 1976.

26. Kenneth Prewitt et al., p. 574.

27. Roderic A. Camp, "Education and Political Recruitment in Mexico: the Alemán Generation," *Journal of Inter-American Studies and World Affairs*, Vol. 18 (August, 1976), pp. 295–321.

28. Heinz Eulau, "Recollections," p. 80.

29. Hugo Pedro González, a prominent Tamaulipan politician, has expressed the impact of the national university on a provincial student: "The provincial who arrives at the great capital feels very undervalued in the first few months. Not only does he admire his teachers, but also his co-students from the capital. . . . The student environment, customs, and the capital absorb our ideas, . . . but little by little

we distinguish ourselves in our studies, others in sports, and still others by their character, their friendly attitude or through the public offices which they have been lucky to obtain." Personal letter, Ciudad Victoria, Mexico, August 15, 1974.

30. Personal interview, Mexico City, October 27, 1976. Years later, de la Peña became Sub-Secretary of Nonrenewable Resources of the Secretariat of National Properties.

31. Personal interview, Mexico City, October 27, 1976, and his memoirs, *Memorias de un hombre de izquierda*, Vol. 1 (Mexico: Editorial Grijalbo, 1976).

32. The most important event during the 1920s which stimulated an *interest* in politics on the part of future Mexican political leaders appears to have been the re-election campaign of General Alvaro Obregón for president.

33. Personal interview, October 28, 1976, Mexico City.

34. Personal interview, Mexico City, October 26, 1976.

35. Robert D. Putnam, *The Comparative Study of Political Elites* (Englewood Cliffs: Prentice-Hall, 1976), p. 76. See also Mark Kesselman, "Recruitment of Rival Party Activists in France: Party Cleavages and Cultural Differentiation," *Journal of Politics*, Vol. 35 (February, 1973), pp. 2–44; and Allan Kornberg and Norman Thomas, pp. 761–775.

36. In fact, indignation seemed to be a reason for political novices repelled by a bad experience to continue in politics and perhaps even participate more intensely than before. The cause of such indignation occurred among many of the youthful supporters of José Vasconcelos during his presidential campaign in 1929. After he was defeated by the official candidate amidst much electoral fraud, his supporters left politics, formed opposition movements, or began serious careers in the official party or bureaucracy. Some of the respondents commented on this event. Indignation turned Antonio Armendáriz temporarily away from a public career: ". . . after the Vasconcelos affair, I was so disgusted that I retired completely from Mexican politics to such a degree that for two or three years I did not read any Mexican newspapers." (Personal interview, Mexico City, October 25, 1976.)

37. Personal interview with Roberto Robles Martínez, Mexico City, October 29, 1976.

38. Personal interview with José Castro Estrada, Mexico City, August 4, 1974.

39. Personal interview, Mexico City, October 27, 1976.

40. Personal interview, Mexico City, October 26, 1976.

41. Personal interview with Alfonso Pulido Islas, October 28, 1976, Mexico City.

42. Personal interview, Mexico City, July 23, 1975; Sousa was appointed director of a cabinet-level agency.

43. This finding was particularly mentioned by graduates of the law school during the early 1920s. Personal interview with Antonio Martínez Báez, Mexico City, June 27, 1975, and with Antonio Taracena, June 21, 1975.

44. For evidence of this influence on many prominent political leaders, see the author's "La campaña presidencial de 1929 y el liderazgo político en México," *Historia Mexicana* Vol. 26 (September–December, 1977), pp. 231–259.

45. Personal interview, Mexico City, October 28, 1976.

46. For an excellent hypothetical description of such a career, but one which, in the opinion of the author, represents only a single type, see Kenneth F. Johnson, *Mexican Democracy: A Critical View* (Boston: Allyn and Bacon, 1971).

47. Personal interview, Mexico City, October 22, 1976.

48. See his *The Recruitment*, p. 111.

49. Personal interview, Mexico City, October 25, 1976. This individual later had great success in Mexican public life, holding high offices continuously from 1936 to 1973, including that of Minister of Government. He was the major unsuccessful pre-candidate for president.

50. Personal interview, Mexico City, July 28, 1976; for other examples, see the published memoirs of Jorge Prieto Laurens, *Cincuenta años de política mexicana* (Mexico, 1968).

51. Robert D. Putnam, p. 76.

52. This idea originates with a study by Lucille Iremonger, entitled *The Fiery Chariot: A Study of British Prime Ministers and the Search for Love* (London: Secker and Warburg, 1970).

53. Many prominent politicians, as a result of a parent's death, usually the father's, were greatly influenced by the surviving parent. A number of political leaders have mentioned the impact of their mothers on their lives, while others searched for substitute fathers. For example, the late Emilio Portes Gil, president of Mexico and one of its most astute politicians, has paid tribute to his mother and to a teacher who replaced the lost affection of his father. See his revealing account in *Raigambre de la revolución en Tamaulipas, autobiografía en acción* (Mexico, 1972), p. 20ff and p. 41. Other prominent Mexican public men strongly influenced by their mothers include Manuel Gómez Morín and Jaime Torres Bodet. For evidence of this influence, see Enrique Krauze, *Caudillos culturales en la revolución mexicana* (Mexico: Siglo Veintiuno, 1976), p. 39ff, for Gómez Morín; and for Jaime Torres Bodet see his early autobiographical essay entitled "Tiempo de arena," in his *Obras escogidas* (Mexico: Fondo de Cultura Económica, 1961), pp. 191–386.

54. Personal letter, August 15, 1974.

55. "A Study of One Hundred and Sixty-three Outstanding Communist Leaders," in Glenn Paige, ed. *Political Leadership* (New York: Free Press, 1972), p. 271.

56. For a good example, see Alberto Bremauntz, *Setenta años de mi vida* (Mexico: Ediciones Jurídico Sociales, 1968).

57. For an explanation, see Joseph A. Schlesinger, "Lawyers and American Politics: A Clarified View," *The Midwest Journal of Political Science*, Vol. 1 (May, 1957), pp. 26–39; and Allan Kornberg and Norman Thomas, p. 770 ff.

58. Personal interview, Mexico City, October 20, 1976.

59. Personal interview, Mexico City, August 15, 1975.

60. Personal interview, Mexico City, June 24, 1975.

61. See Gordon S. Black, "A Theory of Political Ambition: Career Choices and the Role of Structure Incentive," *American Political Science Review*, Vol. 66 (March, 1972), p. 158.

Chapter 3

1. Richard Dawson and Kenneth Prewitt, *Political Socialization* (Boston: Little-Brown, 1969), p. 111.

2. *Politics of the Migrant Poor in Mexico City* (Stanford: Stanford University Press, 1975), pp. 12–13.

3. Heinz Eulau, "Recollections," in John C. Wahlke, Heinz Eulau, William Buchanan, and LeRoy Ferguson, *The Legislative System* (New York: John Wiley and Sons, 1962), p. 82.

4. Respondents were asked two questions: 1) Who or what was most impor-

tant in the formation of your political, social, and economic ideas? 2) How would you rank the most important socializers in order of importance? Nine of these twelve respondents described one or both of their parents as primary socializing agents.

5. Heinz Eulau, p. 80.

6. For examples of this uprooting, see the following memoirs or novels descriptive of the period: Augustín Yáñez, *The Edge of the Storm* (Austin: University of Texas Press, 1963), for rural Jalisco; Luis González, *San José de Gracia, Mexican Village in Transition* (Austin: University of Texas Press, 1975), for rural Michoacán; Andrés Iduarte, *Niño, Child of the Mexican Revolution*, for provincial Tabasco; Manuel Maples Arce, *Soberana Juventud* (Madrid: Editorial Plenitud, 1967), for provincial Veracruz; Ramón Beteta, *Járano* (Austin: University of Texas Press, 1970), for Mexico City; Pindaro Urióstegui Miranda, *Testimonios del proceso revolucionario de México* (Mexico: Argrin, 1970); and Alberto Bremauntz, *Setenta años de mi vida* (Mexico: Ediciones Jurídico Sociales, 1968), for provincial Michoacán.

7. For a comment on this situation, see Sidney Verba, in Leonard Binder et al., *Crises and Sequences in Political Development* (Princeton: Princeton University Press, 1971), p. 241.

8. Personal interview, Mexico City, October 25, 1976.

9. This figure includes sons and nephews, too.

10. See Philip Abrams and Alan Little, "The Young Activists in British Politics," *British Journal of Sociology*, Vol. XVI (1965), pp. 315–32. Also, Kenneth Prewitt concluded that "a review of all available studies of family background of political actives in American politics suggests that the proportion of the active stratum tracing their involvement to parental influence ranges between 30 and 40 percent, depending on the type of political active studied and the way the question is worded." *The Recruitment of Political Leaders: A Study of Citizen-Politicians* (Indianapolis: Bobbs-Merrill Co., 1970), p. 66.

11. Heinz Eulau, p. 82. Political activism among the parents seems to have always been typical among North American leaders. Sidney Aronson, in his revealing study of political leadership under John Adams, Thomas Jefferson, and Andrew Jackson, concluded that a person's best chance of becoming a member of the political elite was to have been born into it. He found that 52 percent of the office-holders under Adams, 43 percent under Jefferson, and 44 percent under Jackson had fathers who had held political office. See his *Status and Kinship in the Higher Civil Service* (Cambridge: Harvard University Press, 1964), pp. 76–77.

12. Alfred Clubok et al., "Family Relationships, Congressional Recruitment, and Political Modernization," *Journal of Politics*, Vol. 31 (November, 1969), p. 1036. K. L. Tedin suggests that parents have an inherent potential for successful transmission of ideas and beliefs, but that their success depends on how important the issue is judged to be, how often it is discussed, and the accuracy with which a child perceives the parent's attitude. "The Influence of Parents on the Political Attitudes of Adolescents," *American Political Science Review*, Vol. 68 (December, 1974), p. 1592.

13. Heinz Eulau, p. 83.

14. Francisco Javier Gaxiola, *Memorias* (Mexico: Editorial Porrúa, 1975), p. 34ff.

15. Personal interview, Mexico City, October 24, 1976.

16. *The Political Character of Adolescence, The Influence of Families and Schools*, (Princeton: Princeton University Press, 1974), pp. 39–40. Dawson and Prewitt also noted that in a "study of 1,440 college students, it was found that students who re-

ported 'not being very close,' or actually 'hostile,' to their parents were more likely to deviate from parental political positions than were students who reported being 'fairly close,' or 'very close' to their parents" (p. 117).

17. Personal interview, Mexico City, October 27, 1976.

18. Personal interview, Mexico City, October 27, 1976; for an interesting example of a mother's influence on a Latin American activist, see Daniel James' biography, *Ché Guevara* (New York: Stein and Day, 1969), particularly the chapter entitled "The Making of Quixote." Paul Beck and Kent Jennings also believe that "the father is, on the average, more influential only when the mother is a neutral. When the mother is a partisan, the children are more likely to adopt her orientations." "Parents as 'Middlepersons' in Political Socialization," *Journal of Politics*, Vol. 37 (February, 1975), p. 95. The case of Villaseñor also suggests that during a period of dynamic change in political views, the beliefs as well as the intensity with which they are held are important.

19. For some findings about the impact of a fatherless environment on children in general, see the discussion by Dean Jaros, *Socialization to Politics* (New York: Praeger, 1973), p. 84ff. For black children without fathers see the study by J. W. Clarke, "Family Structure and Political Socialization Among Urban Black Children," *American Journal of Political Science*, Vol. 17 (May, 1973), p. 315.

20. Personal interviews, Mexico City, July 29, 1974; June 24, 1975; and October 25, 1976.

21. See Peter H. Smith, whose figures show that 54 and 34 percent of the political leaders from 1900 to 1911 were in the middle and upper classes, respectively. *Labyrinths of Power: Political Recruitment in Twentieth-Century Mexico* (Princeton: Princeton University Press, 1979), Table 3-3. Aronson's study showed that, in the formative years of the United States after the revolution, the parents of political elites came disproportionately from the middle-class professions. Under Adams and Jefferson, fathers of political elites from the professions and commercial occupations accounted for 54 percent of those elites, whereas only 4 to 5 percent of the general population was engaged in such occupations. These figures improved during the Jacksonian period, but were still highly skewed in favor of those two occupational groups (pp. 58–59). Even in the Soviet Union, among the tiny elite which occupied the Politburo from 1917 to 1951, 36 percent of those members whose fathers' occupations were known were from the middle class, hardly representative of the general occupational structure during those years. See George K. Scheuller, "The Politburo," in Harold D. Lasswell and Daniel Lerner, eds., *World Revolutionary Elites* (Cambridge: MIT Press, 1966), pp. 104–105.

22. Allan Kornberg and Norman Thomas, "The Political Socialization of National Legislative Elites in the United States and Canada," *Journal of Politics*, Vol. 27 (November, 1965), p. 772; Richard Centers also found a striking difference in children's attitudes toward collectivism and individualism based on parents' occupation. See his "Children of the New Deal: Social Stratification and Adolescent Attitudes," in Reinhard Bendix and Seymour M. Lipset, eds., *Class, Status and Power* (New York: Free Press, 1953), p. 361.

23. Kent Jennings and Richard Neimi, p. 97; Dean Jarros, p. 80.

24. Rafael Segovia, *La politicización del niño mexicano* (Mexico: El Colegio de México, 1975), p. 16; Jerome Davis, in his study of outstanding Russian revolutionary leaders in 1929, found that professional parents were also disproportionately represented. Although his study is not on the socialization of these leaders, some of the

background data provide for interesting comparisons with Mexicans. See his "A Study of One Hundred and Sixty-three Outstanding Communist Leaders," in Glenn Paige, ed. *Political Leadership* (New York: Free Press, 1972), p. 267.

25. Rafael Segovia, pp. 36–37.

26. Personal letter, Mexico City, July 29, 1974.

27. Obviously, this definition would exclude office-holders under Victoriano Huerta, a reactionary President responsible for the seizure of power from and assassination of Madero.

28. Personal letter, Mexico City, August 7, 1974.

29. Personal interview with Manuel R. Palacios, Mexico City, July 1, 1975.

30. Dean Jaros, p. 81.

31. Personal interview, Mexico City, October 25, 1976.

32. Personal letter from Daniel Pedro Martínez, Mexico City, February 13, 1974.

33. Interview with a former cabinet officer, Mexico City, October 29, 1976.

34. *San José de Gracia*, pp. 94–95.

35. Personal letter from Mario Colin Sánchez, Mexico City, September 11, 1974.

36. Dean Jaros, p. 133.

37. Alex S. Edelstein, "Since Bennington: Evidence of Change in Student Political Behavior," in Roberta S. Sigel, ed., *Learning About Politics* (New York: Random House, 1970), p. 393.

38. Arthur Liebman et al., *Latin American University Students: A Six Nation Study* (Cambridge: Harvard University Press, 1972).

39. Jennings and Neimi have noted that "students and their friends are more alike than unlike in political terms" (p. 248).

40. Kenneth P. Langton, "Peer Group and School and the Political Socialization Process," *American Political Science Review*, Vol. 61 (September, 1967), p. 754.

41. Personal interview, Mexico City, October 25, 1976; similar comments were made by the late Martín Luis Guzmán and Miguel Alemán.

42. Theodore Newcomb, "Persistence and Regression of Changed Attitudes: Long-Range Studies," in Jack Dennis, ed., *Socialization to Politics* (New York: Wiley, 1973), p. 414.

43. Roderic A. Camp, *Mexico's Leaders: Their Education and Recruitment* (Tucson: University of Arizona Press, 1980). Note that President Echeverría appointed several companions from his secondary school to prominent administrative positions. *Excélsior*, June 16, 1976. Echeverría's successor, José López Portillo, attended primary school with his predecessor.

44. Only one respondent mentioned a woman other than his mother as important to his political views and career. Víctor Manuel Villaseñor, one of the few Mexican leaders to have attended college in the United States during the 1920s, gave credit to a remarkable North American woman at the University of Michigan for starting him on a newspaper-writing career. This profession encouraged him to become more interested in political affairs after his graduation.

45. Langton, p. 754.

46. For an analysis of student behavior at a Mexican university, and for a description of how politically active Mexican students moderate their views to conform to the realities of their professional future, see William Tuohy and Barry Ames, *Mexican University Students in Politics: Rebels Without Allies?* (Denver: University of Denver, 1970).

47. Kent Jennings and Richard Niemi, p. 39. A study of the Japanese family found that it does play an important role in the transmission of party identification to children. On the other hand, the role of the family in issue areas seemed to be marginal. Akira Kubota and Robert E. Ward, "Family Influence and Political Socialization in Japan," in Jack Dennis and Kent Jennings, eds., *Comparative Political Socialization* (Beverly Hills: Sage, 1970), p. 38.

48. Arthur Liebman argues that while social class is not a major factor differentiating the students politically, higher-status students do tend to be more oriented toward conservatism (p. 152).

49. See the introduction to his *Psychology of the Mexican* (Austin: University of Texas, 1975), p. xvi.

50. Samuel H. Barnes, "The Legacy of Fascism: Generational Differences in Italian Political Attitudes and Behavior," *Comparative Political Studies*, Vol. V (April, 1972), p. 54.

51. Personal letter from Ramiro Támez Cavazos, former Governor and Senator from Nuevo León, who abandoned his third year of medical school to serve revolutionary troops as a doctor in 1911, Monterrey, Nuevo León, February 26, 1974.

52. Personal letter, Mexico City, April 3, 1974.

53. Manuel Gómez Morín, *1915 y otros ensayos* (Mexico: Editorial Jus, 1973), p. 28. Also, Gómez Morín believed that those individuals from his generation who lived outside of Mexico in 1915, particularly José Vasconcelos and Alfonso Reyes, did not understand certain characteristics of Mexico's development. See Enrique Krauze's comments on Narciso Bassol's view of his generation's being a revolutionary generation, in his *Caudillos culturales en la revolución mexicana* (Mexico: Siglo XXI, 1976), p. 211. The late Daniel Cosío Villegas, in his published memoirs, argued that the "youth of today (I am speaking of those who were born after 1920) do not have the slightest idea of the difficult realities which the Revolution brought, and because of this they talk about it rhetorically." *Memorias* (Mexico: Joaquín Mortíz, 1976), p. 57.

54. For some particularly revealing comments about the influence of the Revolution on ideas and behavior in rural Michoacán, see Luis González, pp. 99–116; and for an older generation of Mexican political leaders, comparable to the men cited above, see James Wilkie and Edna Monzón de Wilkie's detailed interviews in *México visto en el siglo xx* (Mexico: Instituto Mexicano de Investigaciones Económicas, 1969).

55. I have omitted people who chose their preparatory or university environment as most important to their socialization because I found this response to be of particular importance to Mexican political leaders, and it will be discussed in the next chapter.

56. Personal interview, Mexico City, October 21, 1976.

57. *Soberana Juventud*, p. 144.

58. See, for example, the memoirs of Manuel Rivera Silva, later a Supreme Court Justice, who graduated in the 1930s. *Perspectivas de un vida, biografía de una generación* (Mexico: Porrúa, 1974), p. 34.

59. Personal interview, Mexico City, July 25, 1974.

60. "Antecedents to Samuel Ramos, Mexicanist Thought in the 1920's," *Journal of Inter-American Studies and World Affairs*, Vol. 18 (May, 1976), p. 180.

61. Personal interview, Mexico City, October 27, 1976.

62. Personal letter, Mexico City, February 13, 1974.

63. See Wayne Cornelius's comment that people can be influenced by their community even if they are unaware of or are antagonistic to its norms. *Politics of the Migrant Poor in Mexico City* (Stanford: Stanford University Press, 1975), p. 117. One

clear reflection of how values and institutions changed during this period appears in Charles Crosby's analysis of Mexican political cartoons. See his "The Mexican Political Cartoon From 1867 to 1920: A Reflection of Unrest and Revolt," unpublished Ph.D. dissertation, New York University, 1976.

64. Personal interview, Mexico City, June 18, 1975.

65. For example, Manuel González Ramírez remarked that, "I first became interested in Mexican politics in 1922–23 as a result of the discussions I heard concerning the Mexican Revolution. All of the questions and comments concerning the Revolution, whether for or against, interested me from this time forward." Personal interview, Mexico City, October 23, 1976.

66. Personal letter, Mexico City, July 10, 1974.

67. Personal interview with Alfonso Pulido Islas, Mexico City, October 28, 1976.

68. Personal interview, Mexico City, October 27, 1976.

69. Personal interview, Mexico City, July 1, 1975.

70. See, for example, Manuel Maples Arce's comments on the sinking of the *Lusitania* in his memoirs, pp. 28–29.

71. See Richard Centers, p. 361ff. Further evidence of the impact of the 1929 Depression on young people in the United States is provided by the conclusion of Seymour M. Lipset and Everett Ladd, in their large-scale survey of college professors, that "those who were in college in the Depression and immediate post-Depression years report having been somewhat more 'left' in their student days than any other college-age cohort, earlier or later." *The Divided Academy: Professors and Politics* (New York: W. W. Norton, 1976), p. 195. Mexico's political leaders who grew up during this post-revolutionary period might have attitudes substantially different from adults of the post-1940s, similar to children of the New Deal in the United States. However, since I did not interview a substantial group from the latter period, a comparable study was not possible. Heinz Eulau found, however, that North American legislators were least influenced by the Depression or by wars (p. 89).

72. Slow economic growth, poverty, and unemployment were already present in Mexico during the years after the Revolution. The Depression added to Mexico's economic burdens, rather than creating a sharp contrast with the past. But it is remarkable how few authors more than mention the Depression in talking about Mexico's social and economic history in the twentieth century. For exceptions, see James W. Wilkie, *The Mexican Revolution: Federal Expenditures and Social Change Since 1910* (Berkeley: University of California Press, 1970), p. 266; and John W. F. Dulles, *Yesterday in Mexico* (Austin: University of Texas, 1961), p. 500ff.

73. Personal interview, Mexico City, October 27, 1976.

74. Personal interview, Mexico City, October 28, 1976.

75. For a discussion of the careers of those who supported Vasconcelos, and the multifaceted role of the campaign on their political beliefs, see "La campaña presidencial de 1929 y el liderazgo político en México," *Historia Mexicana*, Vol. 23 (No. 2, 1977), pp. 231–259.

76. Personal letter, Mexico City, July 18, 1974.

77. Personal interview, Mexico City, October 25, 1976. Vasconcelos's campaign affected even generations who were too young to participate. Hugo B. Margáin, Ambassador to the United States and Secretary of the Treasury in the early 1970s, recalls that the campaign "was very important to me and others of my generation. My friends had participated in his movement, but I was too young. He was a romantic figure." Personal interview, Washington, D.C., March 14, 1977.

78. Personal interview, Praxedis Balboa Gojón, Mexico City, October 29, 1976. Hugo Margáin added that Cárdenas's expulsion of Calles from Mexico enhanced his reputation among many members of Margáin's generation. Personal interview, 1977.

79. For a personal view of the impact of the 1938 expropriation on an important public figure, see the account by the late Ambassador Vicente Sánchez Gavito, a graduate of the early thirties, in "La expropriación, úna crónica personal," *Excélsior*, May 18, 1976, p. 6.

Chapter 4

1. Dean Jaros, *Socialization to Politics* (New York: Praeger, 1973), p. 100.

2. "Political Socialization in Universities," in Seymour Martin Lipset and Aldo Solari, eds. *Elites in Latin America* (New York: Oxford University Press, 1967), p. 428. Another study of Latin American socialization experiences suggested that the "principal factors in political socialization of the middle classes are the schools, the nature of the economy, and the political system itself." See Arthur L. Stinchcombe, "Political Socialization in the South American Middle Class," *Harvard Educational Review*, Vol. 38 (1968), p. 527. Since most political leaders in Mexico and Latin America are from the middle class, it would not be unfair to apply his conclusions to political leaders in general.

3. Rafael Segovia, *La politización del niño mexicano* (Mexico: El Colegio de México, 1975), p. 15. However, in a study of English schoolchildren attending the traditional "public schools," McQuail and his colleagues found that children did not ask teachers for advice on voting, although teachers were consulted for advice on careers. Although his question does not get directly at the presence of political topics at the school, it tends to imply that English children do not discuss political topics with teachers. See D. McQuail, L. O'Sullivan, and W. G. Quine, "Elite Education and Political Values," *Political Studies*, Vol. 16 (1968), p. 261.

4. Heinz Eulau, "Recollections," in John C. Wahlke et al., *The Legislative System* (New York: John Wiley and Sons, 1962), p. 85. Kenneth Prewitt also found that among council members in the United States who claimed to have been politically socialized as pre-adults, 31 percent attributed their political activism solely to their school experience. Next in importance was the political family at 14 percent. "The school's impact on who joins the politically active stratum is not just as a complementary agency supporting dispositions already learned in the family. Clearly, the school has an independent relationship to leadership selection processes." *The Recruitment of Political Leaders: A Study of Citizen-Politicians* (Indianapolis: Bobbs-Merrill Co., 1970), pp. 65, 70.

5. For example, see Jerome Davis's figures, which show that of the outstanding Soviet revolutionary leaders, at least 60 percent had some university work, a remarkable figure given the difficult access to higher education among the masses in Russia during this period. "A Study of One Hundred and Sixty-three Outstanding Communist Leaders," in Glenn Paige, ed., *Political Leadership* (New York: Free Press, 1972), pp. 267–268. For equally striking figures among Chinese party leaders, see Robert C. North, "Kuomintang and Chinese Communist Elites," in Harold D. Lasswell and Daniel Lerner, eds., *World Revolutionary Elites* (Cambridge: MIT, 1966), p. 376ff.

6. A study of boarding schools in Tanzania suggested that the insulation of students from competing agencies of socialization was an important factor in deter-

mining the variety of civic attitudes among students from various schools. See Kenneth Prewitt, George Vonder Muhll, and David Court, "School Experiences and Political Socialization," in Jack Dennis and Kent Jennings, eds., *Comparative Political Socialization* (Beverly Hills: Sage, 1970), p. 93.

7. *World Revolutionary Elites*, p. 13.

8. Social background does play an important part in participation. David Ziblatt found that students whose fathers had never gone beyond the eighth grade were three times as likely as students with college-educated fathers to be inactive in high-school groups. "High School Extracurricular Activities and Political Socialization," *The Annals of the American Academy of Political and Social Science*, Vol. 361 (September, 1965), p. 27.

9. Antonio Delhumeau, "Elites culturales y educación de masas en México," *Revista Mexicana de Ciencias Políticas*, Vol. XIX (No. 73, 1973), p. 23. An extreme example of the political nature of professional education at the National University has been suggested by Jesús Silva Herzog, a public man and professor emeritus of the National School of Economics. While serving on the nominating board for a new dean of the National School of Economics, he led the effort to prevent one candidate from becoming dean. In retaliation, the candidate, a professor at the school, purposely failed one of Silva Herzog's sons who was studying in his field. (See his autobiographical *Mis ultimas andanzas, 1947–1972* (Mexico: Siglo XXI, 1973), pp. 107–8. For a similar example from the University of Nuevo León, see the realistic novel by Josefina Niggli, *Step Down, Elder Brother* (New York: Rinehart and Co., 1947), p. 63.

10. For the political recruitment implications of such an experience, see my "Education and Political Recruitment in Mexico: The Alemán Generation," *Journal of Inter-American Studies and World Affairs* (August, 1976), pp. 295–321.

11. See his "The Problem of Generations," in his *Essays on the Sociology of Knowledge* (London: Routledge and Kegan, 1952), p. 291.

12. Personal interview with a former cabinet secretary, Mexico City, October 29, 1976.

13. In his study of Algerian revolutionaries, William Quandt found that both education and the school itself were instrumental in transforming vague, family-based sentiments into political beliefs. *Revolution and Political Leadership: Algeria, 1954–1968* (Cambridge: MIT Press, 1969), p. 28.

14. *La politización*, p. 79. In his study of British schoolchildren, however, McQuail found in comparing students from grammar school and public schools that there was a general lack of interest in political affairs, and that there was no special difference between the two groups in their interest or their sense of duty to participate in politics (p. 265).

15. Arthur Liebman, Kenneth Walker, and Myron Glazer, *Latin American University Students: A Six Nation Study* (Cambridge: Harvard University Press, 1972), p. 161.

16. "The Guatemalan National Congress: An Elite Analysis," in Weston H. Agor, ed., *Latin American Legislatures: Their Role and Influence* (New York: Praeger, 1971), pp. 318–320.

17. Kenneth Prewitt, Heinz Eulau, and Betty H. Zisk, "Political Socialization and Political Roles," *Public Opinion Quarterly*, Vol. 30 (Winter, 1966–67), p. 574.

18. See J. E. Goldthorpe, *An African Elite: Makerere College Students, 1922–1960* (Nairobi: Oxford University Press, 1965), p. 79.

19. Kent M. Jennings and Richard G. Niemi, *The Political Character of Adoles-*

cence, The Influence of Families and Schools (Princeton: Princeton University Press, 1974), p. 40.

20. Kenneth Prewitt et al., "Political Socialization," p. 575.

21. See the author's *Mexico's Leaders: Their Education and Recruitment* (Tucson: University of Arizona Press, 1980). For evidence that this practice extends into the nineteenth century, see the following letter from Gabino Barreda, the founder of the National Preparatory School in the nineteenth century, to Mariano Riva, governor of the state of Mexico: "And I must also add that nothing is more convenient for the students, particularly from the standpoint of their individual careers. Because the innumerable relationships that they establish with their contemporaries will continue as they enter public and professional lives, providing an added factor that will resound to their collective benefit. Concomitantly, the public men who must utilize every intellectual resource in the service of the nation will find an inexhaustible supply among the companions of their school years." See Alonso Portuondo, "The Universidad Nacional Autónomo de México in the Post-Independence Period: A Political and Structural Review," (master's thesis, University of Miami, Coral Gables, Florida, 1972), p. 27, citing Gabino Barreda, *Estudios* (Mexico: UNAM, 1941), p. 66.

22. "A Theory of Political Ambition: Career Choices and the Role of Structure Incentive," *American Political Science Review*, Vol. 66 (March, 1972), p. 158.

23. "Sponsored and Contest Mobility and the School System," *American Sociological Review*, Vol. 25 (December, 1960), p. 860.

24. This is not to suggest that the preparatory schools and the universities can easily dominate the socialization process of most youngsters. Even the most isolated institution has limitations. In an analysis of the military training program, the authors concluded that "the military does not work with empty slates when it receives its young recruits. They come in with sets of pre-existing attitudes, albeit for many of them these attitudes are labile. . . . These pre-existing states of mind constrain the potential impact which even a 'total' institution such as the military might have." "The Effect of Military Service on Political Attitudes: A Panel Study," Paper presented to the Annual Meeting of the American Political Science Association, Chicago, August 29–September 2, 1974, p. 26.

25. For evidence of this variety, see Jorge Siegrist Clamont, *En Defensa de la autonomia universitaria; trayectoría histórico-jurídico de la universidad mexicana* (Mexico: Universidad Nacional, 1955), p. 189.

26. Personal interview, Mexico City, July 29, 1974.

27. Personal interview with Enrique Beltrán, Mexico City, August 13, 1974.

28. Personal interview with Adolfo Zamora, Mexico City, July 24, 1974.

29. For more information on this subject, see Alonso Portuondo, pp. 86–87; Josefina Vázquez de Knauth, *Nacionalismo y educación en Mexico* (Mexico: El Colegio de Mexico, 1970), and Clark C. Gill, "The Role of the Federal Government in Public Education in Mexico," unpublished Ph.D. dissertation, University of Minnesota, 1948.

30. Personal interview, Mexico City, July 25, 1974.

31. For various examples from the 1920s and 1930s, see Jorge Vallejo y Arizmendi, *Testimonio 1930–34* (Mexico: Editorial Stylo, 1947), and Ciriaco Pacheco Calvo, *La organización estudiantil en México* (Mexico: Confederación Nacional de Estudiantes, 1934).

32. Personal interviews with Julio Faesler and Jesús Puente Leyva, Mexico City, July 2, 1975, and June 17, 1975.

33. See Jorge Prieto Laurens, *Cincuenta años de política mexicana, memorias políticas* (Mexico, 1968), pp. 14, 18. For an excellent survey of the growing antipositivist movement in Mexico, and the implications of that movement, see William D. Raat, "The Antipositivist Movement in Prerevolutionary Mexico, 1892–1911," *Journal of Inter-American Studies*, Vol. 19 (February, 1977), especially pp. 95–96.

34. Personal interview, Mexico City, July 24, 1974.

35. See an autobiographical account of his childhood, entitled *Niño, Child of the Mexican Revolution* (New York: Praeger, 1971), pp. 133, 143.

36. Personal letter from Arturo Gómez Arias, Mexico City, September 27, 1973.

37. For comments on Turkey, see Byron G. Massialas, *Education and the Political System* (Reading: Addison-Wesley, 1969), p. 96.

38. See his insightful book, *Gentlemanly Power: British Leadership and the Public School Tradition* (New York: Oxford University Press, 1964), p. 341.

39. *The Comparative Study of Political Elites* (Englewood Cliffs: Prentice-Hall, 1976), p. 96. Personal interview, Mexico City, June 26, 1975. Mexico's recent political

40. Personal interview, Mexico City, June 26, 1975. Mexico's recent political leadership has also been criticized for its lack of imagination and flexibility by several insiders, most notably Manuel Moreno Sánchez, leader of the Senate under President Adolfo López Mateos and author of *Mexico: 1968–72* (Austin: Institute of Latin American Studies, 1973).

41. *Education and the Political System*, p. 87.

42. Personal interview, Mexico City, June 24, 1975.

43. Personal interview with Alfonso Pulido Islas, Mexico City, August 12, 1974.

44. Personal interview, Mexico City, June 20, 1976.

45. Personal interviews with Manuel Hinojosa Ortiz and Manuel González Ramírez, Mexico City, June 19, 1975, and August 15, 1974, respectively. For an earlier example, see Manuel Guevara Oropesa, "El estudiante," in *Doctor Salvador Zubirán, 50 años de vida profesional* (Mexico: Asociación de Médicos del Instituto Nacional de la Nutrición, 1973), p. 17.

46. Personal letter from Mario Colín Sánchez, Mexico City, May 3, 1974. For another account of the impact of the National Preparatory School on a variety of student generations, see Octavio González Cárdenas' *Los cien años de la Escuela Nacional Preparatoria* (Mexico: Editorial Porrúa, 1972).

47. For example, Raúl Rángel Frias, who later became Governor of Nuevo León, studied at the Colegio Civil of Monterrey. He was influenced by that experience because of the opportunity he had to argue with philosophy professors who were defenders of positivism. Personal interview, Monterrey, July 18, 1974.

48. *Comparative Study of Political Elites*, p. 96.

49. For relevant comments on the British public schools in this regard, see Robert Putnam, *Comparative Study of Political Elites*, p. 96, and Rupert Wilkinson, *Gentlemanly Power*, pp. 337–338.

50. Allan Kornberg and Norman Thomas, "The Political Socialization of National Legislative Elites in the United States and Canada," *Journal of Politics*, Vol. 27 (November, 1965), p. 770.

51. See Carlos Vejar Lacave and Amparo Espinosa de Serrano, eds., *El pensamiento contemporáneo en México* (Mexico: Editorial Porrúa, 1974), p. 177.

52. See the author's *Mexico's Leaders: Their Education and Recruitment* (Tucson: University of Arizona Press, 1980).

53. See the author's "La campaña presidencial de 1929 y el liderazgo en México," *Historia Mexicana*, (Vol. 27, No. 2, 1977). For a vivid description of the intellectual and social environmet of the National Law School during the 1920s and 1930s, see the following accounts: Gilberto F. Aguilar, *El barrio estudiantil de México* (Mexico: Editorial Latina, 1951); Antonio Armendáriz, *Semblanzas* (Mexico, 1968); Juan Bustillo Oro, *Vientos de los veintes* (Mexico: SepSetentas, 1973); Baltasar Dromundo, *Mi calle de San Ildefonso* (Mexico: Editorial Guarania, 1956) and *Los oradores del 29* (Mexico: ARS, 1949); Lucio Mendieta y Núñez, *Historia de la Facultad de Derecho* (Mexico: UNAM, 1956); Ciriaco Pacheco Calvo, *La organización estudiantil en México* (Mexico: Confederación Nacional de Estudiantes, 1934); and Manuel Ramírez Vázquez, *En torno de una generación: glosa de 1929* (Mexico: Ediciones "Una Generación," 1949).

54. Personal interview, Raúl Cardiel Reyes, October 22, 1976.

55. Personal interview with José Castro Estrada, Mexico City, August 4, 1974.

56. Personal interview with Alfonso Pulido Islas, former Dean of the National School of Economics, Mexico City, August 12, 1974.

57. For supporting evidence, see the author's "The National School of Economics and Public Life in Mexico," *Latin American Research Review*, Vol. 10 (Fall, 1975), pp. 137–151.

58. Ruben Vargas Austin, "The Development of Economic Policy in Mexico With Special Reference to Economic Doctrines," (Ph.D. dissertation, Iowa State University, 1958), p. 74.

59. See the comments by Charles N. Myers, *Education and National Development in Mexico* (Princeton: Princeton University Press, 1965), p. 105. Another school which falls into such a specialized category is the Autonomous University of Guadalajara, an institution often mentioned in United States newspaper articles because of the number of North Americans in its medical school. This school is not to be confused with the public University of Guadalajara, located in the same city.

60. Personal interview with Eduardo Bustamante, Mexico City, October 28, 1976, who attended the School in the 1910s.

61. See Agustín Arriaga Rivera, "El movimiento juvenil," in *Mexico, Cincuenta años de revolución*, Vol. II (Mexico: Fondo de Cultura Económica, 1963), p. 359.

62. Letter from Alfonso Pulido Islas, Mexico City, March 21, 1974, who attended preparatory school at the University. Also see David C. Bailey, *Viva Cristo Rey!* (Austin: University of Texas, 1974), p. 33, and Jean A. Meyer, *The Cristero Rebellion: The Mexican People Between Church and State* (Cambridge: Cambridge University Press, 1976), for evidence of the influence of the Catholic Youth Movement in the University of Guadalajara and in the leadership of the Cristero movement. In later years, the University of Guadalajara continued to contribute to opposition political leadership in the form of the National Action Party, a party which originally drew heavily from Catholic Youth groups for its membership. See Donald J. Mabry, *Mexico's Acción Nacional: A Catholic Alternative to Revolution* (Syracuse: Syracuse University Press, 1973), and Franz A. von Sauer, *The Alienated "Loyal" Opposition, Mexico's Partido Acción Nacional* (Albuquerque: University of New Mexico Press, 1974).

63. See Lázaro Cárdenas, *Obras, Apuntes 1913–1940*, Vol. I (Mexico: UNAM, 1972), p. 184; and Sebastian Mayo, *La educación socialista en México: el asalto a la Universidad Nacional* (Rosario, Argentina: Editorial Bear, 1964), p. 190.

64. Personal interview with Ernesto Enríquez, Mexico City, October 26, 1976; personal letter from Gilberto Loyo, Mexico City, September 14, 1972; and from Miguel Bustamante, Mexico City, March 13, 1975.

65. Mexico City, June 17, 1975.

66. Reo M. Christenson and Patrick J. Capretta, "The Impact of College on Political Attitudes, A Research Note," *Social Science Quarterly*, Vol. 49 (1968), p. 320.

67. Kenneth N. Walker, "Political Socialization in Universities," p. 420.

68. C. G. McClintock and Henry A. Turner, "The Impact of College upon Political Knowledge, Participation, and Values," *Human Relations*, Vol. 15 (1962), p. 173.

69. Prewitt et al., "Political Socialization and Political Roles," p. 574.

70. Personal interview with Agustín Salvat, Mexico City, October 20, 1976.

71. Manuel Hinojosa Ortiz, later SubSecretary of Forest Resources in the Secretariat of Agriculture, believed his educational experience was decisive in determining his attitude toward the role of government in economic development. Personal interview, Mexico City, June 19, 1975.

72. Willis D. Hawley, "The Implicit Civics Curriculum: Teacher Behavior and Political Learning," (paper prepared for delivery at the 1976 Annual Meeting of the American Political Science Association, Chicago, Illinois, September, 1976), p. 15.

73. See Gabriel Almond and Sidney Verba's discussion of Mexicans in *The Civic Culture* (Princeton: Princeton University Press, 1963).

74. *Gentlemanly Power: British Leadership and the Public School Tradition*, p. 36.

75. Carlos G. Vélez, "An Evening in Ciudad Reyes: A Processual Approach to Mexican Politics," *The New Scholar*, Vol. 5 (No. 1, 1975), p. 14.

76. *Mexico's Leaders: Their Education and Recruitment*.

77. See, for example, Allen H. Barton, "Determinants of Leadership Attitudes in a Socialist Society," in Allen H. Barton, Bogdan Denitch, and Charles Kadushin, eds., *Opinion-Making Elites in Yugoslavia* (New York: Praeger, 1973), p. 259.

78. Daniel Cosío Villegas, *El sistema político mexicano* (Mexico: Joaquín Mortiz, 1972), p. 105ff.

Chapter 5

1. Jerome Davis, "A Study of One Hundred and Sixty-three Outstanding Communist Leaders," in Glenn Paige, ed., *Political Leadership* (New York: Free Press, 1972), p. 271.

2. Richard Dawson and Kenneth Prewitt, *Political Socialization* (Boston: Little-Brown, 1969), p. 147, citing C. Arnold Anderson and Suellen Fisher, "The Curriculum as an Instrument for Inculcating Attitudes and Values," Comparative Education Center, University of Chicago, unpublished manuscript, 1967.

3. Charles Garrison, "Political Involvement and Political Science: A Note on the Basic Course as an Agent of Political Socialization," *Social Science Quarterly*, Vol. 49 (September, 1968), p. 313.

4. See Edgar Litt, "Civic Education, Community Norms, and Political Indoctrination," *American Sociological Review*, Vol. XXVIII (1963), pp. 69–75.

5. Alex S. Edelstein, "Since Bennington: Evidence of Change in Student Political Behavior," in Roberta S. Sigel, ed., *Learning About Politics* (New York: Random House, 1970), p. 396.

6. See Universidad Nacional, *Plan de estudios de la Escuela Nacional Preparatoria* (Mexico: Universidad Nacional, 1924), p. 4. For various examples of the curriculum of the National Preparatory School during these years, see the documents in Uni-

versidad Nacional, *Plan de estudios de la Escuela Nacional Preparatoria* (Mexico: Universidad Nacional, 1920); Universidad Nacional, *Catalogo de la Universidad Nacional de México, 1926–27* (Mexico: Talleres Gráficos de la Nación, 1926), pp. 157ff.; and Universidad Nacional Autónomo de México, *Anuario 1931–32* (Mexico: Universidad Nacional Autónomode México, 1931), pp. 191–192.

7. Esther L. Brown, *Lawyers, Law Schools and the Public Service* (New York: Russell Sage Foundation, 1948), p. 114. See Harold D. Lasswell and M. S. McDougal, "Legal Education and Public Policy," in Harold D. Lasswell, ed., *The Analysis of Political Behavior* (London: Routledge, Kegan Paul, Ltd., 1948), p. 22, for their statement that "any relation between the factual problems that incidentally creep into particular fields or courses, in a curriculum so 'organized,' and the important problems of contemporary society is purely coincidental; and all attempts to relate such fields or courses to each other are frustrated by lack of clear social goals. . . ."

8. For evidence of these requirements, see Mexico City, Universidad Nacional Autónomo de México, *Anuario de la Escuela Nacional de Jurisprudencia,* p. 58ff.

9. For evidence of their use, see Chico Goerne's course syllabus in Universidad Nacional Autónomo de México, Facultad de Derecho y Ciencias Sociales, *Plan de estudios, programas y reglamentos de reconocimientos* (Mexico: Talleres Gráficos de la Nación, 1929), pp. 36–37.

10. Personal interview with Eduardo Bustamante, Mexico City, October 28, 1976. Some of the South American writers who might have been discussed during these years included, among others, José Ingenieros (Argentina), Alcides Arguedas (Bolivia), José Carlos Mariátegui (Peru), and Euclydes da Cunha (Brazil). Since Mexican political leaders have not indicated any substantial influence from South American writers in this field, their works will not be discussed. For a detailed analysis of such works, see William Rex Crawford, *A Century of Latin American Thought* (New York: Praeger, 1966); Leopoldo Zea, *The Latin American Mind* (Norman: University of Oklahoma Press, 1963); Harold E. Davis, *Latin American Social Thought* (Washington, D.C.: The University Press of Washington, D.C., 1963); and Miguel Jorrín and John D. Martz, eds., *Latin American Political Thought and Ideology* (Chapel Hill: University of North Carolina Press, 1970).

11. Leopoldo Solis, "Mexican Economic Policy in the Post-War Period: The Views of Mexican Economists," *The American Economic Review,* Vol. 61, supplement (June, 1971), p. 60.

12. In fact, as late as 1933 there was an almost total lack of economic studies in Mexico. Eduardo Villaseñor, "XX aniversario de *El Trimestre Económico*," *El Trimestre Económico,* Vol. XX (October–December, 1953), p. 549.

13. See Ruben Vargas Austin, p. 224.

14. Personal interview with Sealtiel Alatriste, Mexico City, July 23, 1974.

15. For evidence of this issue and the use of Mexican sources, see Mexico City, Universidad Nacional Autónomo de México, Facultad de Derecho y Ciencias Sociales, *Plan de estudios,* p. 31, and Jorge Vallejo y Arizmendi, *Testimonio 1930–34,* p. 19, who says that students taking the political economy course were required to learn the prologue to the 1915 law.

16. Jesús Silva Herzog, *El pensamiento económico, social y político de México, 1810–1964* (Mexico: Instituto Mexicano de Investigaciones Económics, 1967), p. 334. Sobral's text was also used by other professors to prepare their classes. For example, see Jesús Silva Herzog, *Una vida en la vida de México* (Mexico: Siglo XXI, 1972), p. 79. Silva Herzog also used the classic work by Andrés Molina Enríquez, *The Fundamental*

National Problems (1909), which has been mentioned several times as a book read outside of class by Mexican politicians. It is considered by many scholars to be one of the books most influential to Mexican revolutionaries.

17. Arthur W. Kornhauser, "Changes in the Information and Attitudes of Students in an Economic Class," *Journal of Educational Research*, Vol. 22 (June–December, 1930), pp. 294, 296.

18. Personal interviews with José Ricardo Zevada, Mexico City, June 27, 1975, and Manuel Hinojosa Ortiz, Mexico City, August 15, 1974.

19. Personal interview, Mexico City, June 26, 1975.

20. Jorge Vallejo y Arizmendi, pp. 11–13.

21. For example, Hugo B. Margáin told the author that "I read Marx, Engels, and Lenin, but they did not convince me. We had our own revolution and Constitution to serve as a basis for our development. When I grew up I was influenced by the idea that we had to achieve the most prominent articles of the 1917 Constitution. . . ." Personal interview, Washington, D.C., March 14, 1977.

22. This statement is based on an analysis of law theses from this period maintained by the Hispanic Law Division of the Library of Congress. For some reason, the Hispanic Law Division has a much more complete collection of these during these years than does the National University.

23. Personal interview, Mexico City, October 27, 1976. Other prominent political leaders from this period who wrote on agrarian and labor matters include Ángel Carvajal, Secretary of Government, 1952–58; Carlos Zapata Vela, Federal Deputy 1940–43, 1961–64; Fausto Acosta Romo, Assistant Attorney General of Mexico, 1964–67; and José de Jesús Castorena, Governor of Guanajuato, 1947–48. For a description of student intellectual life by a prominent Mexican intellectual who wrote his thesis in 1925 on an agrarian topic, see Manuel Maples Arce, *Soberana Juventud* (Madrid: Editorial Plenitud, 1967), p. 183.

24. Examples include works by Miguel Lanz Duret and Eduardo Pallares, and Bernardino de Sahagún's *General History of the Things of New Spain*, a classic colonial work. But even such a standard text as Duret's *Derecho Constitucional Mexicano, y consideraciones sobre la realidad política de nuestro régimen* argues for the supremacy of law and the right of a people to revolt when law disappears. Furthermore, Duret integrated examples from the Soviet Union and Europe in his text. See the 1933 edition, p. 6.

25. Personal interview with Daniel Pedro Martínez, Mexico City, June 20, 1975.

26. Justo Sierra, *The Political Evolution of the Mexican People* (Austin: University of Texas Press, 1969), p. 367.

27. For an analysis of James's concept, see Andrew J. Reck, *Introduction to William James* (Bloomington: Indiana University Press, 1967), p. 84ff.

28. Karl Britton, *John Stuart Mill, Life and Philosophy* (New York: Dover Books, 1969), p. 92.

29. Personal interview with the late Martin Luis Guzmán, October 21, 1976, Mexico City.

30. Jorge Vallejo y Arizmendi, *Testimonio 1930–34*, p. 18.

31. Mexico City, Universidad Nacional Autónomo de México, Facultad de Derecho . . . , *Plan de Estudios*, pp. 33–46.

32. Gabriel de Tarde, in his *La Logique Sociale* (Paris; F. Alcan, 1895), whose

work was discussed in both sociology classes, is considered the founder of the social behaviorism movement in sociology. As such, however his contributions were not ideological. See Donald Martindale, *The Nature and Types of Sociological Theory* (Cambridge: Riverside Press, 1960), pp. 305–309.

33. John Herman Randall, *The Making of the Modern Mind* (Cambridge: Riverside Press, 1954), pp. 399–400. Furthermore, Patrick Romanell, the most prominent student of Mexican twentieth-century philosophers, concludes that Bergson was the most influential source of the anti-positivist movement in Mexico. He considers both Antonio Caso and José Vasconcelos to be disciples of Bergson. See his "Bergson in Mexico: A Tribute to José Vasconcelos," *Philosophy and Phenomenological Research*, XXI (June, 1961), pp. 502.

34. See John Haddox's discussion of a group of Mexican intellectuals, including Antonio Caso, whose goals included the destruction of Porfirism, the removal of foreign economic controls in Mexico, the lessening of the influences of positivism on the cultural life and educational system, the discovery of the authentic reality of Mexico, and the formulation of ideals that could be used to improve this reality. *Vasconcelos of Mexico* (Austin: University of Texas, 1967), pp. 4, 17.

35. Dominick La Capra, *Emile Durkheim, Sociologist and Philosopher* (Ithaca: Cornell University Press, 1972), p. 18, which contains an excellent analysis of his political philosophy.

36. Ibid., p. 20.

37. See Frank Brandenburg, *The Making of Modern Mexico* (Englewood Cliffs: Prentice-Hall, 1964), p. 83ff., and José Luis Reyna, "Redefining the Established Authoritarian Regime: Perspectives of the Mexican Policy," draft of an unpublished paper prepared for the Center for Inter-American Relations, New York, February, 1975.

38. For a view of the ideological boundaries of the Institutional Revolutionary Party (PRI), see Lorenzo Meyer's statement that, "Only the most extreme right or left are excluded and not necessarily by the party but by themselves. The PRI has room for Marxists (as long as they are not members of the PC) as well as for classical liberals who believe that a strict observance of the doctrines of Adam Smith or Milton Friedman are the only way out of underdevelopment." "The Origins of Mexico's Authoritarian State, Political Control in the Old and New Regimes," unpublished paper presented at the Center for Inter-American Relations, New York, June 6–7, 1975, p. 21.

39. The North American theorist James Mark Baldwin was largely responsible for the idea of studying the social person, and, like de Tarde, did not contribute to ideological viewpoints in his sociological writings.

40. Henry Steele Commager, *Lester Ward and the Welfare State* (Indianapolis: Bobbs-Merrill Co., 1967), p. xviii.

41. Ibid.

42. Ibid., p. xxxiv; for a discussion of his views on the superiority of government over private administration of public concerns see his *Dynamic Sociology*, Vol. II (New York: Appleton, 1883, 1887), p. 578ff. Also see Samuel Chugerman, *Lester F. Ward, The American Aristotle* (Durham: Duke University Press, 1939).

43. J. D. Y. Peel, *Herbert Spencer the Evolution of a Sociologist* (New York: Basic Books, 1971), p. 213ff.

44. A contemporary example of the diversity of such views might be represented by the two men who directed the treasury ministry for President Echeverría from 1970 to 1975, Hugo B. Margáin and José López Portillo, both graduates of the

School of Law, in 1937 and 1947, respectively. It has been suggested that Margáin resigned from the ministry in May of 1973 because his more fiscally conservative views collided too strongly with those of the President. *Excélsior*, June 4, 1973, p. 7.

45. H. Stuart Hughes, *Oswald Spengler, A Critical Estimate* (New York: Charles Scribner's Sons, 1952), p. 102.

46. Ibid., p. 103.

47. Donald Martindale, *The Nature and Types*, p. 184.

48. Other important economic writers who were mentioned less often included Henry George, Harold Laski, and Charles Gide. See Ruben Vargas Austin, "The Development of Economic Policy in Mexico," p. 211, for comments about Henry George. Daniel Cosío Villegas and Jesús Silva Herzog, both of whom taught during these years, were also influenced by these writers. Charles Gide's book was used as a text for the political economy course at the Law School prior to 1930, and his ideas were examined in Chico Goerne's sociology class in 1929. After 1930, Lucio Mendieta y Núñez describes this course as an examination of Marxism. Personal interview with Daniel Cosío Villegas, Mexico City, June 30, 1975; Lucio Mendieta y Núñez, *Historia de la Facultad de Derecho* (Mexico: UNAM, 1956), pp. 320–321.

49. Robert L. Heilbroner, *The Worldly Philosophers* (New York: Time Inc., 1962), p. 64.

50. Roberto Robles Martínez, an economics graduate of the National Polytechnical Institute, mentions being strongly influenced by David Ricardo. Personal interview, Mexico City, October 29, 1976.

51. Clark Kerr, *Marshall, Marx and Modern Times* (Cambridge: Cambridge University Press, 1969), p. 70.

52. There is some dispute as to when Marx first was available to Mexican readers. The late Vicente Lombardo Toledano told James Wilkie and Edna Mouzón de Wilkie in an interview that in the late 1920s it was impossible to find the works of Marx in Mexico and that he himself first read them in New York in English translation. See their *México Visto en el siglo xx* (Mexico: Instituto Mexicano de Investigaciones Económics, 1969). However, Vicente Lombardo Toledano did not become an avowed Marxist until 1931, and he may have rationalized this situation as an explanation for his not becoming a Marxist until such a late date. It is quite definite, however, that the students graduating in the mid 1920s were being exposed to Marx's ideas in *Das Kapital* and *The Critique of Economic Policy*, and, that by 1929, Marx was discussed in all three sociology classes and thoroughly examined in the political economy class.

53. Seymour E. Harris, ed., *The New Economics, Keynes' Influence and Public Policy* (London: Dennis Dobson Ltd., 1960), p. 14. The works of Beatrice and Sidney Webb were also quite important to the Mexicans. Writing at the turn of the century, they were careful critics of the abuses of industrial capitalism. See, for example, their *Problems of Modern Industry* (London: Longmans, Green, 1906).

54. Keynes, pp. 155–56, 235.

55. For numerous examples of problems and policies, see Roger D. Hansen, *The Politics of Mexican Development* (Baltimore: John Hopkins University Press, 1971).

56. Jorge Vallejo y Arizmendi, *Testimonio 1930–34*, pp. 13–14.

57. Mendieta y Núñez, *Historia de la Facultad de Derecho*, pp. 318–319; interview with José Ricardo Zevada, Mexico City, June 27, 1975. A similar situation could be found in the Free Law School, the major private competitor of the National Law School in Mexico City. Ernesto Enríquez, who graduated from that institution in

1924, remembers that "all of the texts at this time were in French. I always have had difficulties with languages, but I had to learn French because my professional training was in this language." Personal interview, Mexico City, October 26, 1976.

58. Interview with Antonio Martínez Báez, 1925 Law Class, Mexico City, June 27, 1975.

59. Interview with Antonio Carrillo Flores.

60. Julius Stone, *Social Dimensions of Law and Justice* (Stanford: University Press, 1966), p. 105.

61. Gustav Radbruch, *Introducción a la ciencia del derecho* (Madrid: Revista de derecho privado, 1930), p. 22.

62. Javier Malagón, "Four Centuries of the Faculty of Law in Mexico," *Hispanic American Historical Review* (August, 1952), p. 448. Some of the works which replaced French texts and reference books included books by Radbruch, Kelsen, Del Vecchio, Jellinek, Spann, Recasens Siches, Alcala-Zamora, Jímenez de Asua, Kisch, Goldschmidt, Chiovenda, Carnelutti, Calamandrey, Sohn, and Laski. I have chosen not to discuss Spanish authors because their influence came during the last half of the 1930s, and because such works are more closely related to the Mexican legal tradition. See Mendieta y Núñez, *Historia de la Facultad de Derecho*, pp. 336–337, for a more detailed list of these works.

63. Jorge Vallejo y Arizmendi, *Testimonio 1930–34*, pp. 37–38. In footnote 19, p. 37, Vallejo provides a concrete example of the change of tendencies in Mexico from 1930 to 1935 by looking at the thesis of and a book published in those years by Eduardo García Máynez.

64. See, for example, Hans Kelsen, *Pure Theory of Law* (Berkeley: University of California Press, 1967).

65. Mexico City, Universidad Nacional Autónomo de México, Escuela Nacional Preparatoria, *Plan de estudios*, 1940, p. 123ff.

66. Jorge Vallejo y Arizmendi, *Testimonio 1930–34*, p. 31. As one professor noted, the majority of books purchased for the Law Library were from Europe. Virgilio Domínguez, "La enseñanza del derecho y la Biblioteca Antonio Caso," *Revista de la Escuela Nacional de Jurisprudencia*, Vol. 37 (enero–marzo, 1948), p. 12.

67. Stone, p. 126. John Austin, who presented the philosophy of positive law in his *Lectures on Jurisprudence*, also was discussed in several courses.

68. Mexico City, August 12, 1974. For a similar statement see Valentín Campa, *Mi Testimonio* (Mexico: Ediciones de Cultura Popular, 1978), p. 14.

69. Frederic C. Turner, *The Dynamic of Mexican Nationalism* (Chapel Hill: University of North Carolina Press, 1968).

70. Jesús Silva Herzog, *El Pensamiento*, p. 387.

71. *La constitución y la dictadura, estudio sobre la organización política en México* (Mexico: Revistas de Revistas, 1912), p. 330.

72. See Moises González Navarro, *Vallarta y su ambiente político jurídico* (Mexico: UNAM, 1949), p. 151.

73. E. V. Niemeyer, Jr., *Revolution at Querétaro* (Austin: University of Texas Press, 1974), pp. 233–234.

74. Personal interview, Mexico City, October 25, 1976.

75. Both Miguel Alemán and Praxedis Balboa Gojón, from different social circumstances and parts of Mexico, echoed Armendáriz's sentiments concerning the influence of these two brothers. Flores Magón's works influenced the earlier revolution-

ary generation, too, and such leaders as General Alvaro Obregón have identified this influence. See Narciso Bassols Batalla, *Obregón* (Mexico: Editorial Nuestro Tiempo, 1967), p. 13.

76. See Charles Cumberland's *Mexican Revolution, Genesis under Madero* (Austin: University of Texas, 1952), Chapter III, "The Book and the Parties," p. 55ff, for comments on the importance of Madero's work.

77. For examples of theses, see Jorge Vallejo y Arizmendi, *Testimonio 1930–34*, pp. 40–41.

78. Personal interviews with Miguel Alemán, Mexico City, October 27, 1976; Manuel R. Palacios, Mexico City, July 1, 1975; Agustín Salvat, Mexico City, June 23, 1975.

79. Personal interview, Mexico City, October 25, 1976.

80. Personal letter, Mexico City, March 21, 1974.

81. See Pedro Henríquez Ureña's comments on the intellectual currents of his generation in *Universidad y educación* (Mexico: UNAM, 1969), p. 1965.

82. Gordon Brotherson, ed., *José Enrique Rodó, Ariel* (Cambridge: Cambridge University Press, 1967), p. 14.

83. Irving Howe, "Dostoevsky: The Politics of Salvation," in Rene Wellek, ed., *Dostoevsky* (New York: Prentice-Hall, 1962), pp. 55–56.

84. Janko Lavrin, *Tolstoy, An Approach* (New York: Macmillan, 1946), p. 145.

85. Personal interviews with Manuel González Ramírez, Mexico City, October 23, 1976; Raúl Cardiel Reyes, Mexico City, October 22, 1976; Agustín Salvat, Mexico City, October 20, 1976; Víctor Manuel Villaseñor, Mexico City, June 26, 1975; and Miguel Alemán, Mexico City, October 27, 1976.

86. For example, see *Revista Centro*, official paper of the Student Association of San Luis Potosí, January, 1936, pp. 39–40, for reviews of such works. In the April edition of that student newspaper, for the same year, one of the respondents, Raúl Cardiel Reyes, wrote an article on the "Marxist Theory of Value," pp. 152–157.

87. *The Making of the Modern Mind* (Cambridge: Riverside Press, 1954), p. 608.

88. See Karl Jaspers, *Nietzsche, An Introduction to the Understanding of His Philosophical Activity* (Tucson: University of Arizona Press, 1965), p. 273.

89. Harold C. Raley, *José Ortega y Gasset: Philosopher of European Unity* (University: University of Alabama Press, 1971), pp. 146–47, 206, has an excellent analysis of his works.

90. See Francisco J. Gaxiola, *Memorias* (Mexico: Editorial Porrúa, 1975), p. 69, for a comment on the influence of this magazine.

Chapter 6

1. See my *Mexico's Leaders: Their Education and Recruitment* (Tucson: University of Arizona Press, 1980), chapters 4–5.

2. David C. Schwartz, "Toward a Theory of Political Recruitment," *Western Political Quarterly*, Vol. 22 (September, 1969), p. 553.

3. For evidence of this role, see Donald Mabry, *Mexico's Acción Nacional: A Catholic Alternative to Revolution* (Syracuse: Syracuse University Press, 1973), pp. 34, 51, 72. It is surmised that professors are equally important throughout Latin America, even in regimes dominated by military officers. See, for example, the importance of military academies as a locus for recruitment in Argentina in José Luis de Imaz, *Those Who Rule* (Albany: State University of New York Press, 1970), pp. 24–25.

4. Kenneth Prewitt, *The Recruitment of Political Leaders: A Study of Citizen-Politicians* (Indianapolis: Bobbs-Merrill Co., 1970), p. 120.

5. Dean Jaros, *Socialization to Politics* (New York: Praeger, 1973), p. 110.

6. See, for example, my "Education and Political Recruitment in Mexico: The Alemán Generation," *Journal of Inter-American Studies and World Affairs*, Vol. 18 (August, 1976), pp. 295–321, and "The National School of Economics and Public Life in Mexico," *Latin American Research Review*, Vol. 10 (Fall, 1975), pp. 137–151.

7. Rafael Segovia, *La politización del niño mexicano* (Mexico: El Colegio de México, 1975), p. 13. Richard Dawson and Kenneth Prewitt reported that primary and secondary students in Kenya, Tanzania, and Uganda overwhelmingly chose their teachers as having taught them most about being a good citizen. See their *Political Socialization* (Boston: Little, Brown, 1969), p. 161.

8. For further discussion on the relation between parental occupation and the influence of teachers, see Rafael Segovia, *La politización del niño*, p. 16.

9. Personal interview, Mexico City, October 25, 1976.

10. *Mis ultimas andanzas, 1947–1972* (Mexico: Siglo XXI, 1973), p. 99.

11. Dean Jaros and R. Darcy, "The Elusive Impact of Political Science: More Negative Findings," *Experimental Study of Politics*, Vol. 2, No. 1 (1973), pp. 19–23.

12. "The Implicit Civics Curriculum: Teacher Behavior and Political Learning," paper prepared for delivery at the 1976 Annual Meeting of the American Political Science Association, Chicago, Illinois, September, 1976, pp. 14–17.

13. "Since Bennington: Evidence of Change in Student Political Behavior," in Roberta Sigel, ed., *Learning About Politics* (New York: Random House, 1970), p. 397.

14. Personal letter from Carlos Novoa, Mexico City, January 13, 1975.

15. Personal interview, Mexico City, October 21, 1976.

16. Personal interview with Manuel González Ramírez, Mexico City, October 23, 1976.

17. M. Kent Jennings and Richard G. Niemi, *The Political Character of Adolescence, The Influence of Families and Schools* (Princeton: University Press, 1974), p. 211.

18. Willis D. Hawley, "The Implicit Civics Curriculum," p. 11.

19. For evidence of this finding, even among the general contemporary student population, see Arthur B. Liebman, Kenneth Walker, and Myron Glazer, *Latin American University Students: A Six Nation Study* (Cambridge: Harvard University Press, 1972), pp. 80–83.

20. For a more positive view of provincial professors, see Richard G. King, *The Provincial Universities of Mexico: An Analysis of Growth and Development* (New York: Praeger, 1971), p. 83.

21. Dean Jaros, *Socialization*, p. 102.

22. Personal letter, Mexico City, July 10, 1974.

23. The only study which attempts to deal with variations in teaching style, but without examining the effectiveness of the individual teacher, is that by Albert Somit, Joseph Tannenhaus, Walter Wilke, and Rita Couley, "The Effect of the Introductory Political Science Course on Student Attitudes Toward Personal Participation," in Roberta Sigel, ed., *Learning About Politics* (New York: Random House, 1970), p. 407.

24. "The Implicit Civics Curriculum," p. 9.

25. Dean Jaros, *Socialization*, p. 106.

26. Personal letter from Manuel Ulloa Ortiz, Mexico City, 1974.

27. Manuel Maples Arce, *Soberana juventud* (Madrid: Editorial Plenitud, 1967), p. 27.

28. Personal interview with Alfonso Pulido Islas, Mexico City, October 28, 1976. Miguel Alemán, although strongly influenced by his father, also came under the influence of two professors who were revolutionaries. See George S. Wise, *El Mexico de Alemán* (Mexico: Editorial Atlante, 1952), pp. 57–58, and personal interview, Mexico City, October 2, 1976.

29. Myron Glazer, "Chile," in Donald K. Emmerson, ed., *Students and Politics in Developing Nations* (New York: Praeger, 1968), p. 311.

30. Personal interview, Mexico City, July 24, 1974.

31. For an example, see Luis Garrido, *El Tiempo de mi vida, memorias* (Mexico: Porrúa, 1974), p. 205.

32. Personal letter, Alfonso Pulido Islas, Mexico City, August 12, 1974.

33. For a description of this change, see Jorge Vallejo y Arizmendi, *Testimonio 1930–34* (Mexico: Editorial Stylo, 1947), p. 13.

34. Personal letter, Mexico City, January 17, 1974.

35. Personal letter from Antonio Armendáriz, Mexico City, April 10, 1972.

36. Myron Glazer, "Chile," p. 311. The lack of discussion of controversial or political questions appears to be fairly common. Byron Messialas found that only about half of the American teachers examined in his study spent more than 10 percent of their time on controversial subjects. *Education and the Political System* (Reading: Addison-Wesley, 1969), p. 170.

37. Byron G. Massialas, *Education and the Political System*, pp. 180–181.

38. Personal interview with Sealtiel Alatriste, Mexico City, June 24, 1975.

39. Personal interview with Daniel Pedro Martínez, Mexico City, June 20, 1975; also a letter to the author from Miguel Bustamante, Mexico City, March 13, 1975, who indicated that some of his professors at the medical school had a negative effect on him.

40. Personal letter from Manuel Hinojosa Ortiz, Mexico City, April 16, 1974.

41. For these findings, see Dean Jaros, p. 119, and Jaros and Darcy, pp. 46–47.

42. Liebman et al. found that the older the student, the greater the decline in leftist orientations. This finding can be explained by the pragmatic nature of the student as he nears graduation, and the need to have his views fit within the broad framework of the PRI-dominated political system if he wants to enter a public career (p. 110). William Tuohy and Barry Ames also reached similar conclusions in their "Mexican University Students in Politics: Rebels Without Allies?" (Denver: Monograph Series in World Affairs, University of Colorado, 1970).

43. Personal interview with Ricardo Rivera Pérez, Mexico City, June 19, 1975.

44. Personal interview with Antonio Armendáriz, Mexico City, June 24, 1975.

45. Personal letter from Víctor Manuel Correa Racho, Mexico City, April 6, 1975.

46. Personal letter from Sealtiel Alatriste, Mexico City, January 17, 1974. Even before the 1920s, in prominent intellectual circles, Enrique Krauze describes the "Generation of 1915" as receiving a legacy of action, movement, and political culture in place of a doctrine, and that was to protect, improve, and increase the public educational institutions founded by the previous generations. *Caudillos culturales en la revolución mexicana* (Mexico: Siglo XXI, 1976).

47. Personal interview with Ángel Carvajal, Mexico City, October 25, 1976; and with Mario Colín Sánchez, Mexico City, July 28, 1974. In one study of schoolchildren cited by Dean Jaros as indicative of the importance of the conventional values of teachers, he noted that, as youngsters proceed through their years of schooling, their values come increasingly to approximate those of their teachers. He suggests the

possibility of a causal link. And, since many of the professors are themselves public men, such conventional values would be even more significant. *Socialization*, p. 105.

48. For some comment on this understanding in the 1930s, see Carlos Fuentes, *Tiempo mexicano* (Mexico: Joaquín Mortiz, 1972), p. 80.

49. Sebastian Mayo, *La educación socialista en México: el asalto a la universidad nacional* (Rosario: Editorial Bear, 1964), p. 78.

50. See my *Mexico's Leaders: Their Education and Recruitment*, chapter 6.

51. Each professor considered in this group was named by three or more respondents as having been influential in this regard. Several individuals were named by more than twenty respondents.

52. It is interesting to note that an excellent study of the North American academic system found that at least 8 percent of the social science professors surveyed were the sons and daughters of teachers, and nearly half came from other professional or managerial backgrounds, while somewhat less than one-third were the children of farmers or manual workers. See Paul F. Lazarsfeld and Wagner Thielens, Jr., *The Academic Mind* (Glencoe: Free Press, 1958), pp. 6–7.

53. Jorge Prieto Laurens, *Cincuenta años de política mexicana, memorias políticas* (Mexico, 1968), pp. 17, 54.

54. Personal interview, Mexico City, October 27, 1976.

55. Antonio Carrillo Flores, "Mi Colaboración a *Pensamiento de Mexico*," in Carlos Véjar Lacave and Amparo Espinosa de Serrano, eds., *El pensamiento contemporáneo en México* (Mexico: Editorial Porrúa, 1974), pp. 177–78, has a vivid description of a confrontation over this issue.

56. Personal interview with Manuel Hinojosa Ortiz, Mexico City, June 19, 1975.

57. *Diccionario Porrúa* (Mexico: Porrúa, 1970), p. 948.

58. See Leticia Chávez, *Recordando a mi padre* (Mexico: Asociación Civil E. A. Chávez, 1967), Vol. V.

59. Leticia Chávez presents considerable evidence that he was not a "true believer" of positivism and makes claims for his constant Christianity. The religious overtone of some of her memoirs begs for some caution. See *Recordando a mi padre*, Vol. I, p. 8ff.

60. See his *Los últimos sesenta años de la historia de México y sus enseñanzas relativos a México, Francia y el mundo latino* (Paris: Lahure, 1926), pp. 10–11.

61. Personal letter from Emilio Portes Gil, Mexico City, October 20, 1972.

62. Andres Iduarte, *Niño, Child of the Mexican Revolution* (New York: Praeger, 1971), p. 133.

63. Personal letter from Roberto Arias y Soria, Pachuca, Hidalgo, August 16, 1974.

64. *Excélsior*, October 10, 1975, 2B.

65. Alonso Portuondo, "The Universidad Nacional Autónomo de México in the Post-Independence Period: A Political and Structural Review," master's thesis, University of Miami, Coral Gables, Florida, 1972, p. 60.

66. *El pensamiento económico, social y político de México, 1810–1964* (Mexico: Instituto Mexicano de Investigaciones Económicas, 1967), p. 624.

67. Alfonso Reyes, *Mexico in a Nutshell* (Berkeley: University of California Press, 1964), p. 12.

68. Personal letter from Daniel Cosío Villegas, Mexico City, April 18, 1973; Jaime Torres Bodet, *Obras Escogidas* (Mexico: Fondo de Cultura Económica, 1961), p. 239ff.

69. José Vasconcelos, *A Mexican Ulysses* (Bloomington: Indiana University Press, 1963), p. 56.

70. María Rosa Uría-Santos, "El Ateneo de la Juventud: su influencia en la vida intellectual de México," Ph.D. dissertation, University of Florida, Gainesville, 1965, p. 78.

71. Alonso Portuondo, "The Universidad Nacional Autónomo de Mexico," pp. 60, 66.

72. Leopoldo Zea, *Latin America and the World* (Norman: University of Oklahoma Press, 1969), p. viii.

73. From a description by Concha Alvarez, in Enrique Krauze, *Caudillos culturales*, p. 69. See Luis Garrido, *Antonio Caso: una vida profunda* (Mexico: UNAM, 1961), p. 24, for an equally vivid description. As Eduardo Villaseñor has noted, Caso taught night classes at the graduate school, allowing many students who might otherwise have missed him to take his courses. *Memorias-Testimonio* (Mexico: Fondo de Cultura Económica, 1974), p. 35.

74. Edith Flower, "The Mexican Revolt Against Positivism," *Journal of the History of Ideas*, Vol. X (January, 1949), p. 115.

75. Personal interview with Raúl Rangel Frias, Monterrey, July 18, 1974.

76. Personal interview, Mexico City, June 26, 1975.

77. Ignacio Chávez, "Discurso pronunciado en la ceremonia conmemorativa del xxv aniversario de la fundación de El Colegio Nacional," *Memoria de El Colegio Nacional*, Vol. VI, No. 2–3 (1967–68), p. 253; John Haddox, *Antonio Caso, Philosopher of Mexico* (Austin: University of Texas Press, 1971), p. 8.

78. María Rosa Uría-Santos, "El Ateneo de la Juventud," p. 73.

79. John Haddox, *Antonio Caso*, pp. 6, 17.

80. Personal interview with Manuel González Ramírez, Mexico City, August 15, 1974.

81. Enrique Krauze, *Caudillos Culturales*, p. 70.

82. "Democracía como método y fin," in *La persona humana y el estado totalitario* (Mexico: UNAM, 1941), pp. 191–192. He also expressed these views in the text he used in his sociology classes. See his *Sociología* (Mexico: Porrúa, 1945), p. 355. In the 1930s, however, he did become a leading spokesman against President Cárdenas's attempt to introduce socialism into the National University. When he was removed for opposing this policy, there was such an outcry from his former students in government and in intellectual circles that he was quickly reinstated, an accomplishment which attests to his great influence and popularity. His stand against socialism can be seen in two lights. The standard reason is that he was attempting to protect academic freedom. However, another interpretation sees Caso as a humanist, conservative, who by keeping the University independent was promoting the continuation of a conservative professorship and student body critical of the social measures introduced by the Cárdenas regime. For comments on this view see John Haddox, *Antonio Caso*, p. 8, and Alonso Portuondo, "The Universidad Nacional Autónomo de Mexico," p. 60.

83. *Sociología*, p. 356–357.

84. John Haddox, *Antonio Caso*, p. 38.

85. *La persona*, p. 129; John Haddox, *Antonio Caso*, pp. 38–39.

86. Personal letter from Manuel R. Palacios, Mexico City, February 1, 1973.

87. María Rosa Uría-Santos, "El Ateneo de la Juventud," p. 74.

88. Delia L. M. Sutton, *Antonio Caso y su impacto cultural en el intelecto mexicano* (Mexico: SHCP, 1971), p. 76.

89. Henry C. Schmidt, "Antecedents to Samuel Ramos, Mexicanist Thought in the 1920s," *Journal of Inter-American Studies and World Affairs*, Vol. 18 (May, 1976), p. 187.

90. Personal letter from Ricardo J. Zevada, Mexico City, May 4, 1973; and personal interview, Mexico City, June 27, 1975.

91. See his *Teoría general de las obligaciones* (Mexico: Porrúa, 1959), 2 vols.

92. Enrique Krauze, *Caudillos culturales*, p. 279.

93. Personal interview with Sealtiel Alatriste, Mexico City, June 24, 1975.

94. Like Palacios, Martínez Sobral was considered an outstanding member of his generation in Guatemala, many other members of which became prominent in public life. He received a law degree in Guatemala, another in international law in Chile, a third in Mexico, as well as an LL.D. and a Ph.D. in economics in Mexico. He returned to Guatemala only once, from 1924 to 1927, when he served as a technical advisor on that country's monetary reform law.

95. Amilcar Echeverría, *Enrique Martínez Sobral* (Guatemala, 1964), pp. 67–69.

96. See his *Principios de economía, con especial referencia a las condiciones mexicanas* (Mexico: Libería Franco-Americano, 1926), pp. 30–64.

97. Jesús Silva Herzog, *El pensamiento economico*, p. 338.

98. Amilcar Echeverría, *Enrique Martínez Sobral*, p. 88.

99. Personal letter from Manuel Ulloa Ortiz.

100. Roberto A. Esteva Ruiz, *Los títulos de crédito en el derecho mexicano* (Mexico: Editorial Cultura, 1938), p. 376.

101. Jesús Silva Herzog, *Pensamiento económico*, pp. 537, 540.

102. Albert Michaels, "Mexican Politics and Nationalism from Calles to Cárdenas," Ph.D. dissertation, University of Pennsylvania, 1966, p. 296.

103. For an excellent analysis of his growing conservatism, and then a brief revival at the end of his life, see Vol. 1 of Víctor Manuel Villaseñor, *Memorias de un hombre de izquierda* (Mexico: Editorial Grijalbo, 1976).

104. For some background on the political involvement of his family, see Alan M. Kirshner, "Tomas Garrido Canabal and the Mexican Red Shirt Movement," Ph.D. dissertation, New York University, 1970; and the memoirs of Andrés Iduarte, who was Brito Foucher's cousin and contemporary.

105. Praxedis Balboa, *Apuntes de mi vida* (Mexico, 1975).

106. Jorge Vallejo, *Testimonios, 1930–34* (Mexico: Editorial Stylo, 1947), p. 31.

107. He was, however, an active supporter of the 1929 Autonomy Movement within the National University, a campaign which took on national political overtones and was widely supported by student activists.

108. Trinidad García Aguirre, *Introducción al estudio del derecho* (Mexico: M. de J. Nucamendi, 1935), p. 37.

109. Personal letter from César Sepulveda, Mexico City, 1974.

110. María del Carmen Millán, "Introduction," in Leopoldo Zea, *Latin America and the World* (Norman: University of Oklahoma Press, 1969), p. ix. Zea, who is a disciple of Ramos, has continued this same tradition by proposing a philosophy of Mexicanism.

111. These themes are best expressed in his *Profile of Man and Culture in Mexico* (Austin: University of Texas Press, 1962).

112. For the latter, see my *Mexico's Leaders*, chapter 4.

113. Personal interview with Mario de la Cueva, Mexico City, August 9, 1978.

114. Luis Calderón Vega, *Los 7 sabios de México* (Mexico, 1961), p. 30.

115. Personal interview with Ernesto Enríquez Coyro, Mexico City, June 18, 1975.

116. Enrique Krauze, *Caudillos culturales*, p. 97.

117. Ricardo J. Zevada, "Su Trayectoría," in Narciso Bassols, *Obras* (Mexico: Fondo de Cultura Económica, 1964), p. 13. Daniel Cosío Villegas also pointed out to the author that Bassols had never studied outside of Mexico. Personal interview, Mexico City, June 30, 1975.

118. Enrique Krauze, *Caudillos culturales*, pp. 64–65.

119. Personal letter from Manuel R. Palacios, Mexico City, February 1, 1973.

120. Personal interview with Antonio Carrillo Flores, Mexico City, June 26, 1975.

121. Narciso Bassols, *Obras*, p. 15.

122. Bassols's talents continued to be appreciated, and Manuel Avila Camacho first offered him the post of Secretary of Industry and Commerce, and, when he refused, an appointment to the Supreme Court. Bassols refused this offer too. Víctor Manuel Villaseñor, *Memorias*, Vol. I, pp. 461, 468–70.

123. Antonio Carrillo Flores, "La herencia," in Narciso Bassols, *Obras*, p. 95; and Jesús Silva Herzog, *Pensamiento económico*, p. 564.

124. Jesús Silva Herzog, *Pensamiento económico*, p. 568; Narciso Bassols, *Obras*, especially on the New Agrarian Law.

125. Ricardo J. Zevada, *Calles el presidente* (Mexico: Editorial Nuestro Tiempo, 1971), pp. 111–112.

126. Enrique Krauze, *Caudillos culturales*, pp. 193–194.

127. Based on an interview he gave to *El Universal* in 1929, Narciso Bassols, *Obras*, p. 47, in which he also criticized capitalism.

128. Jesús Silva Herzog, *Pensamiento económico*, p. 573.

129. Alonso Aguilar, "Bassols y los problemas económicas nacionales," in Narciso Bassols, *Obras*, p. 11.

130. Enrique Krauze, *Caudillos culturales*, p. 194.

131. Unlike most of the younger professors, Beteta became directly involved in revolutionary history when he accompanied his brother on Carranza's flight from Mexico City in 1920 (see his description of this experience in *Camino a Tlaxcalantongo* (Mexico: Fondo de Cultura Económica, 1961).

132. Ramón Beteta, "Some Economic Aspects of Mexico's Six-Year Plan," in Hubert C. Herring and Herbert Weinstock, eds., *Renascent Mexico* (New York: Covici-Friede, 1935), p. 102.

133. *The Mexican Revolution: A Defense* (Mexico: DAPP, 1937), p. 58.

134. Personal interview with Antonio Carrillo Flores.

135. "Social Forces in Mexican Life," in Hubert C. Herring and Katharine Terrill, eds., *The Genius of Mexico* (New York: Committee on Cultural Relations with Latin America, 1931), pp. 34–35.

136. *The Mexican Revolution*, pp. 55–56.

137. Beteta's personal sensitivity to persons and events is strongly reflected in the entertaining memoirs of his youth, entitled *Járano* (Austin: University of Texas Press, 1970).

138. *The New York Times*, July 28, 1957, p. 2.

139. Antonio Carrillo Flores, "La Constitución y la acción económica del estado," *Investigación Económica*, No. 3 (1941), p. 296.

140. *La responsabilidad de la iniciativa privada en la industrialización de México* (Mexico: Editorial Cultura, 1950).

141. "La civilización industrial norteamericana: reflexiones de un mexicano," *El Trimestre Económico*, Vol. 18, No. 3 (July–September, 1951), p. 407.

142. Personal letter from Hugo B. Margáin.

143. Jorge Prieto Laurens, *Cincuenta años de política mexicana*, p. 34.

144. Personal letter from Manuel Ulloa Ortiz.

145. Narciso Bassols, *Obras*, viii.

146. Ricardo Zevada, *Calles*, p. 108.

147. *Derecho Administrativo* (Mexico: Porrúa, 1934).

148. Personal interview with Antonio Taracena.

149. Personal interview with Guillermo Ibarra, Manuel Hinojosa Ortiz, and Carlos Román Celis, Mexico City, August 6, 1974. After his retirement, students visited him daily at his home to use his library. (Personal interview with Andrés Serra Rojas, Mexico City, June 8, 1978).

150. See John Womack, Jr., *Zapata and the Mexican Revolution* (New York: Alfred A. Knopf, 1969), for comments on Díaz Soto y Gama's role in this movement.

151. Personal letter from Amando Beltrán, Mexico City, August 24, 1974.

152. "The Agrarian Movement in Mexico," in Hubert Herring and Katharine Terrill, eds., *The Genius of Mexico* (New York: Committee on Cultural Cooperation with Latin America, 1931), pp. 178–180.

153. Personal interview.

154. *Excélsior*, September 20, 1976, p. 3B.

155. Ricardo J. Zevada, *Calles*, p. 93.

156. Ibid., p. 116.

157. Gómez Morín was also thought to be one of the secret logistical supporters of the de la Huerta rebellion. But because of his expertise and ability, Secretary of the Treasury Alberto Pani insisted to Obregón and Calles that Gómez Morín be asked to help the government. Enrique Krauze, *Caudillos culturales*, p.221.

158. Personal letter from Manuel R. Palacios, February 1, 1973; personal interview with Eduardo Bustamante, Mexico City, July 24, 1974; with Antonio Armendáriz, June 24, 1975. As Krauze suggests, by 1920 Gómez Morín was aware of the possibility of a new social organization growing out of the Russian experience. "No other member of his generation showed equal awareness of the importance which the Russian Revolution had as a comparative model for the Mexican revolution." *Caudillos culturales*, p. 86. During the year 1928 he served as a lawyer for the Soviet commercial delegation in Mexico City. Jesús Silva Herzog, *Una vida*, p. 90; personal interview with Antonio Armendáriz, June 24, 1975; Luis Calderón Vega, *Los 7 sabios*, p. 65.

159. Donald Mabry, *Mexico's Acción Nacional: A Catholic Alternative to Revolution*, p. 23.

160. *Memorias*, p. 100; personal interview, 1975.

161. Eduardo Villaseñor, p. 123; personal interview with Eduardo Bustamante, Mexico City, October 28, 1976.

162. Enrique Krauze, *Caudillos culturales* p. 216.

163. Ibid., p. 205.

164. Ibid., p. 206ff.

165. Ibid., p. 217.

166. Ibid., p. 199.

167. See my "La campaña presidencial de 1929 y el liderazgo político en México," *Historia Mexicana*, Vol. 27 (No. 2, 1977), pp. 231–259, for further details of the impact of the Vasconcelos campaign.

168. Personal interview with Mariano Azuela, who worked in Gómez Morín's law office from 1930 to 1935, Mexico City, October 24, 1976.

169. Enrique Krauze, *Caudillos culturales*, p. 117.

170. Personal interview with Mariano Azuela.

171. For a description of how this change occurred, see Gómez Morín's own analysis in *Excélsior*, July 16, 1973, p. 4A.

172. Enrique Krauze, *Caudillos culturales*, p. 309.

173. José Vallejo y Arizmendi, *Testimonio 1930–34*, p. 33.

174. Vicente Lombardo Toledano, "The Labor Movement," *Annals of the American Academy of Political and Social Science* (March, 1940), p. 50; Enrique Krauze, *Caudillos culturales*, p. 302.

175. Lombardo Toledano did not, however, always remain true to his political principles. He was a pragmatic politician, and his behavior followed the dictates of the moment. For evidence, see Víctor Manuel Villaseñor, *Memorias*, Vol. I, especially the sections for 1934 to 1940.

176. Lucio Mendieta y Núñez, *Historia de la Facultad de Derecho* (Mexico: UNAM, 1956), p. 247.

177. Víctor Alba, *Las ideas sociales contemporáneas en México* (Mexico: Fondo de Cultura Económica, 1960), pp. 229–230.

178. Gabriella de Beer claims that it was Vasconcelos who was responsible for the Madero campaign slogan "Effective Suffrage and No Reelection." *José Vasconcelos and his World* (New York: Las Americas Publishing Co., 1966), p. 100.

179. "Antecedents to Samuel Ramos," p. 185.

180. "The Universidad Nacional Autónomo de México," p. 60.

181. Daniel Cosío Villegas, *Memorias*, p. 109.

182. Salvador Azuela, "El Valor Cívico de las luchas de 1929," in *En torno de una generación* (Mexico: Ediciones "Una Generación," 1949), p. 41.

183. Henry Schmidt, "Antecedents to Samuel Ramos," p. 182ff.

184. De Beer, *José Vasconcelos*, p. 97.

185. Albert Michaels, "Mexican Politics and Nationalism," p. 302.

186. John Haddox, *Vasconcelos of Mexico*, pp. 7–8.

187. See Hugo Pineda, *José Vasconcelos, político mexicano, 1928–29* (Mexico: Edutex, 1975); and Mauricio Magdaleno, *Las palabras perdidas* (Mexico: Fondo de Cultura Económica), p. 9.

188. Alfonso Portuondo, "The Universidad Nacional Autónomo de Mexico," pp. 78, 67.

189. Personal interview with Antonio Armendáriz, 1975.

190. Personal interview with Emilio Portes Gil, Mexico City, August 1, 1974.

191. Jesús Silva Herzog, *El pensamiento económico*, pp. 485–486.

192. Fernando González Roa, *Las questiones fundamentales de actualidad en México* (Mexico: Secretaria de Relaciones Exteriores, 1927), p. 243.

193. See González Roa's *Chapters on the Agrarian Question in Mexico* (New York: State Department of Social Welfare, 1927), p. 96.

194. Jesús Silva Herzog, *Pensamiento económico*, p. 483.

195. Jesús Silva Herzog, *El pensamiento económico en México* (Mexico: Fondo de Cultura Económica, 1947), pp. 159–160.

196. Jesús Silva Herzog, *Pensamiento económico*, p. 480.

197. Ibid., p. 484.

198. Fedro Guillén, *Jesús Silva Herzog* (Mexico: Empresas Editoriales, 1969), p. 22.

199. James Wilkie and Edna Monzón de Wilkie, p. 706.

200. Fedro Guillén, *Jesús Silva Herzog*, p. 39; Victor Alba, *Las ideas sociales*, p. 232.

201. Jesús Silva Herzog, *Petroleo Mexicano, historia de un problema* (Mexico: Fondo de Cultura Económica, 1941), p. 305.

202. Personal letter from Alfonso Pulido Islas, March 21, 1974.

203. *Nuestro petroleo* (Mexico: Editorial Masas, 1938), p. 15.

204. Albert Michaels, "Mexican Politics and Nationalism," pp. 95, 218.

205. Personal interview with Víctor Manuel Villaseñor, June 26, 1975.

206. Mexico City, Universidad Nacional, Escuela Nacional de Económica, *2 conferencias sobre el problema petroleo* (Mexico: Imprenta Universitaria, 1938), p. 10.

Chapter 7

1. M. Brewster Smith, "Personal Values as Determinants of a Political Attitude," *The Journal of Psychology*, Vol. 28 (1949), p. 477.

2. Ibid., p. 481.

3. Robert E. Scott, "Mexico: The Established Revolution," in Lucian Pye and Sidney Verba, eds., *Political Culture and Political Development* (Princeton: Princeton University Press, 1965), p. 331.

4. See Robert D. Putnam, *The Comparative Study of Political Elites* (Englewood Cliffs: Prentice-Hall, 1976), p. 80, for comments on this point.

5. Richard Fagen and William Tuohy, *Politics and Privilege in a Mexican City* (Stanford: Stanford University Press, 1972), p. 26, explains this characteristic in some ꞉tail.

6. Julio Labastida Martín del Campo, "El régimen de Echeverría: perspectivas de cambio en la estrategía de desarrollo y en la estructura de poder," *Revista Mexicana de Sociología*, Vol. 34 (July–December, 1972), p. 881; also see Juan Felipe Leal, "The Mexican State: 1915–1973, A Historical Interpretation," *Latin American Perspectives*, Vol. 2, No. 2 (Summer, 1975), pp. 48–63, for en elucidation of how this centralization of power occurred.

7. "Measuring Politicians' Values: Administration and Assessment of a Ranking Technique in the British House of Commons," Paper presented to the American Political Science Association Annual Meeting, Chicago, 1976.

8. Robert Putnam, *Comparative Study*, p. 88.

9. Daniel Cosío Villegas, *Memorias* (Mexico: Joaquín Mortiz, 1976), p. 9.

10. Profile of Man and Culture in Mexico (Mexico: University of Texas Press, 1962), p. 146.

11. Daniel Cosío Villegas, *Ensayos y notas*, Vol. 1 (Mexico: Editorial Hermes, 1966), p. 15.

12. Personal interview with Martín Luis Guzmán, Mexico City, October 21, 1976; and with Javier Gaxiola, Mexico City, October 22, 1976.

13. Susan K. Purcell, *The Mexican Profit-Sharing Decision, Politics in an Authoritarian Regime* (Berkeley: University of California Press, 1975), p. 16.

14. Samuel Barnes demonstrates the impact of the political environment on elites in Italy, where those socialized during the 1920s and who received a higher education and were most exposed to Fascism were those who most strongly identified with the right. See his "The Legacy of Fascism: Generational Differences in Italian Political Attitudes and Behavior," *Comparative Political Studies*, Vol. 5 (April, 1972), p. 55.

15. Personal interview with Antonio Taracena, Mexico City, October 20, 1976, and with Praxedis Balboa Gojón, October 29, 1976.

16. Personal interview with Daniel Pedro Martínez, Mexico City, October 20, 1976.

17. Personal interview, Mexico City, October 28, 1976.

18. For a detailed description of this group and the positions its members held, see my "Education and Political Recruitment in Mexico: The Alemán Generation," *Journal of Inter-American Studies and World Affairs*, Vol. 18 (August, 1976), pp. 295–321.

19. Personal interview with Sealtiel Alatriste, Mexico City, June 24, 1975.

20. Manuel R. Palacios, Mexico City, October 22, 1976.

21. Personal interview, Mexico City, October 27, 1976.

22. *The Failure of Elites* (Cambridge: MIT Press, 1970), p. 280.

23. Personal interview with Manuel Hinojosa Ortiz, Mexico City, October 28, 1976; Luis de la Peña, October 27, 1976; César Sepulveda, October 26, 1976; and Agustín Salvat, October 20, 1976.

24. "M. Kent Jenning and Richard G. Niemi, "Continuity and Change in Political Orientations: A Longitudinal Study of Two Generations," *American Political Science Review* (December, 1975), p. 1335.

25. International Studies of Values in Politics, *Values and the Active Community* (New York: Free Press, 1971), p. 69.

26. Personal interview with Raúl Rángel Frias, Monterrey, July 18, 1974.

27. For evidence, see Robert Scott's statement that authoritarian values are deeply embedded in the culture, and Rafael Segovia's more recent conclusion that authoritarian attitudes dominate among Mexican children. "Mexico," p. 358; *La politización del niño mexicano* (Mexico: El Colegio de México, 1975), p. 124.

28. Personal interview with Salvador Aceves Parra, Mexico City, July 22, 1974.

29. Personal interview with Agustín Salvat, Mexico City, June 23, 1975.

30. Personal interview with Julián Garza Tijerina, Mexico City, July 28, 1974.

31. Personal interview, Mexico City, July 28, 1974.

32. Personal interview with Sealtiel Alatriste, Mexico City, July 23, 1974.

33. Personal interview, Mexico City, July 29, 1974.

34. Personal interview, Mexico City, October 25, 1976.

35. Personal interview with Salvador Azuela, Mexico City, June 26, 1975; and with Sealtiel Alatriste, June 24, 1975.

36. Personal interview with Adolfo Zamora, Mexico City, July 24, 1974.

37. I did not use a predetermined list from which the respondents could choose, nor did I ask that their choices be ranked in order of priority. It was believed these methods would be restrictive and encourage the omission of possibly significant beliefs, such as anti-militarism, from the more traditional choices of politicians in other cultures. Donald Searing ran into this problem in his interviews with British MP's. See "Measuring Politicians' Values," p. 7.

38. "The Development of Economic Policy in Mexico With Special Reference to Economic Doctrines," Ph.D. dissertation, Iowa State University, 1958, p. 115.

39. Personal interview, Mexico City, October 28, 1976.

40. Personal interview with Antonio Carrillo Flores, Mexico City, June 26, 1975.

41. Pan American Union, *Constitution of the United Mexican States 1917* (Washington, D.C.: OAS, 1964); for an enlightened comparison of the original 1917 Constitution (without amendments) with the 1857 document, see H. N. Branch, "The Mexican Constitution of 1917 Compared with the Constitution of 1857," *The Annals of the American Academy of Political and Social Science* (supplement), May, 1917.

42. Personal interview, Washington, D.C., March 14, 1977.

43. *El movimiento estudiantil y los problemas nacionales* (Mexico: Editorial Nuestro Tiempo, 1971), p. 127.

44. Personal interview with Ezequiel Burguete, Mexico City, June 19, 1975.

45. Personal interview with Roberto Robles Martínez, Mexico City, October 2, 1976.

46. Personal interview with Manuel Hinojosa Ortiz, Mexico City, October 28, 1976.

47. "Political Socialization in Universities," in Seymour Martin Lipset and Aldo Solari, eds., *Elites in Latin America* (New York: Oxford University Press, 1967), p. 423.

48. Personal interview, Mexico City, June 26, 1975.

49. See Daniel Cosío Villegas's description attesting to this career with his comment to Miguel Alemán that Carrillo Flores will probably die in public office. Miguel Alemán, *Miguel Alemán Contesta* (Austin: Institute of Latin American Studies, 1975), p. 26.

50. Personal interview with Víctor Manuel Villaseñor, Mexico City, October 27, 1976. Alemán himself did not actively participate in the Vasconcelos campaign, but he was a prominent student campaigner in the 1927 opposition ranks, and his father, General Alemán, was killed opposing the reelection of Obregón in 1929. Many of his collaborators were Vasconcelistas. See the author's "La campaña presidencial de 1929 y el liderazgo político en México," *Historia Mexicana* Vol. 27, No. 2 (1977), pp. 231–59, for details about the participants and their political careers.

51. Personal interview with Angel Carvajal, October 25, 1976.

52. Personal interview with former cabinet secretary, 1976.

53. Personal interview with Daniel Pedro Martínez, 1976.

54. Personal interview with Antonio Armendáriz, Mexico City, October 25, 1976.

55. For evidence of this theme, see Justo Sierra, *The Political Evolution of the Mexican People* (Austin: University of Texas Press, 1969).

56. Personal interview with Sealtiel Alatriste, 1975.

57. Personal interview with Antonio Taracena, 1975.

58. Personal interview with Antonio Armendáriz, 1975.

59. Personal interview with Raúl Cardiel Reyes, Mexico City, October 22, 1976.

60. M. Kent Jennings and Richard Niemi, citing David Easton and Jack Dennis, *Children in the Political System* (New York: McGraw Hill, 1969), chapter 2.

61. *El movimiento estudiantil*, p. 126.

62. *Sons of the Establishment: Elite Youth in Panama and Costa Rica* (Chicago: Rand-McNally, 1966), p. 113.

63. Personal interview, 1975.

64. Personal interview with Raúl Cardiel Reyes, 1974.

65. *Revolution and Political Leadership: Algeria, 1954–1968* (Cambridge: MIT Press, 1969), p. 267.

66. Personal interview with Salvador Azuela, Mexico City, June 26, 1975.

67. Miguel Alemán suggested that social peace was the object of his generation, and that he believed they had succeeded in accomplishing that goal. See his *Miguel Alemán Contesta*, p. 18.

68. For an excellent analysis of the source and importance of democratic principles and individual liberty among political leaders in the National Action Party, see Franz A. Von Sauer, *The Alienated "Loyal" Opposition, Mexico's Partido Acción Nacional* (Albuquerque: University of New Mexico Press, 1974).

69. Jaime Torres Bodet, *Discursos, 1941–64* (Porrúa, 1965), p. 845.

70. For this precursor era, see Charles C. Cumberland, *Mexican Revolution, Genesis Under Madero* (Austin: University of Texas Press, 1974); Jesús Silva Herzog, *Breve historia de la revolución mexicana, los antecedentes y la etapa maderista*, Vol. I (Mexico: Fondo de Cultura Económica, 1960), and James D. Cockcroft, *Intellectual Precursors of the Mexican Revolution, 1900–1913* (Austin: University of Texas Press, 1968).

71. Personal interview, 1976; for a similar view see Baltasar Dromundo, "El ideal común. Respuestas a la época," in *En torno de una generación* (Mexico: Ediciones "Una Generación," 1949), p. 30. Some political leaders praised certain individuals for their willingness to abandon political power once their terms had ended.

72. Personal interview with Efraín Brito Rosado, Mexico City, August 11, 1974.

73. Personal interview with Raúl Cardiel Reyes, 1976.

74. Personal interview with Agustín Salvat, 1976.

75. *The Making of Modern Mexico* (Englewood Cliffs: Prentice-Hall, 1964), pp. 10–11.

76. Personal interview, 1977.

77. Personal interview, 1975.

78. Personal interview with Antonio Taracena, Mexico City, June 21, 1975.

79. Measured in terms of high-level office holders, Alemán more than halved the percentage of this group compared to the previous regime. See the author's *Mexico's Leaders: Their Education and Recruitment* (Tucson: University of Arizona Press, 1980), chapter 2. This happened at all political levels: in the cabinet, excluding defense and navy (traditionally held by career officers in Mexico), he had no officers, one of two presidents to do so from 1935 to 1976; among governors, he reduced the percentage from 40 to 13, a figure lower than the following two administrations; and among senators, only 5 percent were officers, again the lowest figure for all administrations from 1935 to 1976. See Table 3704 in the author's "Mexican Military Leadership in Statistical Perspective Since the 1930s," in James W. Wilkie and Peter Reich, eds., *Statistical Abstract of Latin America Supplement Series*, Vol. 20 (Los Angeles: UCLA Latin America Center, 1980), pp. 595–606.

80. Personal interview, Mariano Azuela, 1976.

81. The administration had little choice concerning the interim replacement, since, according to the Oaxacan constitution, that individual must be one of the two senators. In 1976 the official party decided to further coopt the Popular Socialist Party by selecting one of its leaders as one of the two senatorial candidates. When the resignation of the governor became imminent, it was apparent that the official party had only one choice, the remaining senator; otherwise the first opposition party leader

since 1929 would have become a governor in Mexico. For more information, see *Excélsior*, March 4, 1977; and *Hispano Americano*, March 14, 1977, p. 20.

82. For a summary and analysis of these many issues see Howard F. Cline, *The United States and Mexico* (New York: Atheneum, 1963), and Karl M. Schmitt, *Mexico and the United States, 1821–1973* (New York: John Wiley, 1974).

83. Leopoldo Zea, *Latin America and the World* (Norman: University of Oklahoma Press, 1969), p. 28.

84. See, for example, Frederick Turner's statement that "the capture and subsequent occupation of Veracruz between April and November, 1914, generated deeper xenophobia in Mexico than any other single occurrence during the Revolution." *The Dynamic of Mexican Nationalism* (Chapel Hill: University of North Carolina, 1968), p. 223. For more details about the occupation, see Robert E. Quirk's excellent *An Affair of Honor: Woodrow Wilson and the Occupation of Veracruz* (Lexington: University of Kentucky Press, 1962). For the effect of the Pershing expedition, see Turner, p. 228ff, and Frank Tompkins, *Chasing Villa* (Harrisburg: Military Service Publishing Co., 1934).

85. Personal interview, Manuel González Ramírez, 1976.

86. Personal interview with Luis de la Peña Porth, Mexico City, October 27, 1976.

87. Personal interview, 1976.

88. Interviews with Agustín Salvat and Alfonso Pulido Islas, 1976.

89. International Studies of Values in Politics, *Values and the Active Community*, p. 71.

90. Personal interview, 1976.

91. Personal interview, Agustín Salvat, 1976.

92. For an interesting selection of published views on this issue, including those of prominent intellectuals and public leaders, see Stanley R. Ross, ed., *Is the Mexican Revolution Dead?* (New York: Knopf, 1967), and the second edition published in 1971.

93. Beteta was mentioned as an important influence on the ideas of almost all of the respondents who studied economics.

94. *The Mexican Revolution, A Defense* (Mexico: DAPP, 1937), pp. 18–19.

95. Personal interview, Luis de la Peña Porth, 1976.

96. Personal interview, Manuel Hinojosa Ortiz, 1976.

97. Personal interview, Alfonso Pulido Islas, 1976.

98. Personal interview, Manuel R. Palacios, 1976.

99. Personal interview, Daniel Pedro Martínez, 1976.

100. Personal interview, Antonio Taracena, 1976.

101. Personal interview, Javier Gaxiola, 1976.

102. Personal interview, Agustín Salvat, 1976.

103. Personal interview, César Sepulveda, 1976.

104. Rosalio Wences Reza, *El movimiento estudiantil*, p. 119; for evidence of support among less educated migrants in Mexico City, see Wayne Cornelius, *Politics and the Migrant Poor in Mexico City* (Stanford: Stanford University Press, 1975).

105. Antonio Taracena, "Mexico: sus problemas," unpublished paper, 1976, p. 7.

106. Many of the respondents, interviewed in the fall of 1976, may have been inclined to view this problem as important because of the serious confrontations then taking place between peasants and landowners in northern Mexico. These situations had and will continue to have serious political repercussions.

107. Personal interview, 1976.

108. Personal interview, 1976.

109. For an excellent, up-to-date account of government activity in this policy area, see Marvin Alisky, "Mexico's Population Pressures," *Current History* (March, 1977), pp. 106–110, 131.

110. Personal interview, 1976. Guzmán himself, as the owner of *Tiempo*, began to advertise "responsible paternity" in 1968, long before the government took public action. Eduardo Villaseñor, another respondent, also helped organize a private foundation which produced several important studies of this problem in the early 1970s.

111. Personal interview, Manuel R. Palacios, 1976.

112. Personal interview, Raúl Cardiel Reyes, 1976.

113. Personal interview, Antonio Martínez Baez, 1976.

114. Personal interview, Eduardo Bustamante, 1976.

115. Donald D. Searing, "Measuring," p. 20.

116. For some background on the public-private sector conflict, see John Womack, "The Spoils of the Mexican Revolution," *Foreign Affairs*, Vol. 48 (July, 1970), pp. 680–681; "Mexico: The Old Guard," *Latin American Political Report*, Vol. 11, February 11, 1977, pp. 42–44; Susan and John Purcell, "Mexican Business and Public Policy," in James Malloy, ed., *Authoritarianism and Corporatism in Latin America* (Pittsburgh, Pittsburgh University Press, 1977); and their "The State and Economic Enterprise in Mexico: The Limits of Reform," in *Nueva Política*, Vol. I, No. 2 (abril–junio, 1976), pp. 229–250. For some of the political problems and the transfer of power in 1976, see Salvatore Bizzarro, "Mexico's Government in Crisis," *Current History* (March, 1977), pp. 102–105, 130.

117. Personal interview, 1976.

118. Personal interview, Manuel Hinojosa Ortiz, 1976.

119. Personal interview, Praxedis Balboa Gojón, 1976.

120. Personal interview, Agustín Salvat, 1976.

121. Personal interview, Raúl Cardiel Reyes, 1976.

122. William B. Quandt, *Revolution and Political Leadership*, p. 273.

123. Personal interview, Manuel Hinojosa Ortiz, 1976.

124. Personal interview, Miguel Alemán, 1976.

125. Personal interview, Antonio Armendáriz, 1976.

126. Personal interview, Daniel Pedro Martínez, 1976.

127. Personal interview, 1976.

Chapter 8

1. Richard Sennett and Jonathan Cobb, *The Hidden Injuries of Class* (New York: Knopf, 1972), p. 24.

2. *The Recruitment of Political Leaders: A Study of Citizen-Politicians* (Indianapolis: Bobbs-Merrill Co., 1970), p. 10.

3. Robert D. Putnam, *The Beliefs of Politicians: Ideology, Conflict, and Democracy in Britain and Italy* (New Haven: Yale University Press, 1973), p. 148.

4. See Peter H. Smith, "La movilidad política en el México contemporáneo," *Foro Internacional*, Vol. 15 (No. 3, 1975), pp. 379–413.

5. Carlos G. Vélez, "An Evening in Ciudad Reyes: A Processual Approach to Mexican Politics," *The New Scholar*, Vol. 5 (No. 1, 1975), p. 14.

6. "Persistence and Regression of Changed Attitudes: Long-Range Studies," in Jack Dennis, ed., *Socialization to Politics* (New York: Wiley, 1973), pp. 416, 422.

7. One study of the socialization of elites in Yugoslavia claimed that values did not come from parents, early experiences, or even adult readings, but that they occurred in the individual's working environment. In reaching that conclusion, the author stated that, in general, *"the influence of previous work in a sector is to socialize people to support the attitude now current in that sector, even when they move into other fields."* This finding again suggests the importance of supportive behavior. Allen H. Barton, "Determinants of Leadership Attitudes in a Socialist Society," in Allen H. Barton, Bogdan Denitch, and Charles Kadusin, eds., *Opinion-Making Elites in Yugoslavia* (New York: Praeger, 1973), p. 259. Several other studies have commented on the influence of the structure and culture of the political system and its relationship to belief patterns of elites and decision-making. See Erwin C. Hargrove, "Values and Change: A Comparison of Young Elites in England and America," *Political Studies,* Vol. 17 (September, 1969), p. 343; and Jeffrey Hart, "Geopolitics and Dependency: Cognitive Maps of Latin American Foreign Policy Elites," paper presented at the 1976 Annual Meeting of the American Political Science Association, Chicago, Illinois, September 25, 1976, p. 26.

8. A classic example of this relationship is Gustavo Díaz Ordaz, president of Mexico from 1964–70, whose grandfather, General José María Díaz Ordaz, was a direct descendant of two Spanish conquistadores and one of Benito Juárez's important collaborators. The president of Mexico from 1976 to 1982, José López Portillo, also had a grandfather prominent in nineteenth-century politics; he was a federal deputy, senator, and governor, and also served in the cabinet as Secretary of Public Education and of Foreign Relations.

9. Personal interview with Fernando Zertuche Muñoz, Mexico City, July 26, 1978; with José Juan de Olloqui, Mexico City, July 12, 1978; with Julio Faesler, Mexico City, July 2, 1975; with Pedro Ramírez Vázquez, Mexico City, July 19, 1978; with Jesús Reyes Heroles, Mexico City, July 18, 1978; with María Emilia Téllez, Mexico City, July 28, 1974; and with Rosa Luz Alegría, Mexico City, August 7, 1978.

10. For example, see José Vasconcelos's memoirs, *Ulises Criollo* (Mexico: Editorial Jus, 1978).

11. See also Roderic A. Camp, *Mexico's Leaders, Their Education and Recruitment* (Tucson: University of Arizona Press, 1980), p. 197.

12. For changes among Mexican political leaders, see Peter H. Smith, *Labyrinths of Power: Political Recruitment in Twentieth-Century Mexico* (Princeton: Princeton University Press, 1979) and my article, "Quines alcanzan la cumbre: la elite política mexicana," *Foro Internacional,* Vol. 18 (July–September, 1978), pp. 24–61.

Bibliography

Agor, Weston H. *Latin American Legislatures: Their Role and Influence.* New York: Praeger, 1971.

Alatriste de la Fuente, Miguel. *Un liberal de la reforma, ensayo biográfico del General Miguel C. de Alatriste.* Mexico: Secretaría del Patrimonio Nacional, 1962.

Alba, Víctor. *Las ideas sociales contemporáneas en México.* Mexico: Fondo de Cultura Económica, 1960.

Alemán, Miguel. *Miguel Alemán Contesta.* Austin: Institute of Latin American Studies, University of Texas, 1975.

———. *Program of Government.* San Antonio, 1946.

Alisky, Marvin. "Mexico's Population Pressures." *Current History* (March, 1977), pp. 106–110, 131.

———. "U.S.-Mexican Governments in Transition." *Latin American Digest,* Vol. 11, No. 1 (Fall, 1976), pp. 1–4.

Almond, Gabriel A., and Sidney Verba. *The Civic Culture: Political Attitudes and Democracy in Five Nations.* Princeton: Princeton University Press, 1963.

Álvarez, Concha. *Asi paso mi vida.* Mexico: Porrúa, 1962.

Ames, Barry. "Bases of Support for Mexico's Dominant Party." *American Political Science Review,* Vol. 64 (March, 1970), pp. 153–167.

Anderson, Charles W. "Bankers as Revolutionaries." In William P. Glade, Jr., and Charles W. Anderson, eds., *The Political Economy of Mexico.* Madison: University of Wisconsin, 1963.

Anderson, Rodney D. *Outcasts in Their Own Land: Mexican Industrial Workers, 1906–1911.* DeKalb: Northern Illinois University Press, 1976.

Anderson, Roger C. "The Functional Role of the Governors and Their States in the Political Development of Mexico, 1940–64." Ph.D. dissertation, University of Wisconsin, 1971.

La Antorcha, Vol. 1–4 (1931).

Aponte, Barbara B. *Alfonso Reyes and Spain.* Austin: University of Texas, 1972.

Armendáriz, Antonio. *El método de la doctrina del estado.* Mexico, 1930.

———. "Evocación al Maestro Caso." *Universidad de México,* Vol. 3 (May, 1949), p. 9.

———. *Semblanzas.* Mexico, 1968.

Aronson, Sidney H. *Status and Kinship in the Higher Civil Service.* Cambridge: Harvard University Press, 1964.

Arriola, Carlos. "El Partido Acción Nacional (orígen y circunstancia)." *Foro Internacional,* Vol. 16 (October–December, 1975), pp. 233–251.

Asociación Civil "Ezequiel A. Chávez." *Breves notas acerca de la vida de E. A. Chávez, 1868–1946.* Mexico: Asociación Civil Ezequiel A. Chávez, 1968.

Austin, Ruben Vargas. "The Development of Economic Policy in Mexico With Special Reference to Economic Doctrines." Ph.D. dissertation, Iowa State University, 1958.

Bailey, David C. *Viva Cristo Rey!* Austin: University of Texas Press, 1974.

Balán, Jorge, Harley Browning, and Elizabeth Jelin. *Men in a Developing Society: Geographic and Social Mobility in Monterrey, Mexico.* Austin: University of Texas Press, 1973.

Balboa, Praxedis. *Apuntes de Mi Vida.* Mexico, 1975.

Baldwin, James Mark. *Social and Ethical Interpretations in Mental Development.* New York: Macmillan Company, 1897.

Barnes, Samuel H. "The Legacy of Fascism: Generational Differences in Italian Political Attitudes and Behavior." *Comparative Political Studies,* Vol. 5 (April, 1972), pp. 41–57.

Barocio, Alberto. *México y la cultura.* Mexico: SEP, 1946.

Barton, Allen H. "Determinants of Leadership Attitudes in a Socialist Society." In Allen H. Barton et al., eds., *Opinion-Making Elites in Yugoslavia.* New York: Praeger, 1973, pp. 220–262.

Barton, Allen H., Bogdan Denitch, and Charles Kadushin, eds. *Opinion-Making Elites in Yugoslavia.* New York: Praeger, 1973.

Bassols, Narciso. *La nueva ley agraria, antecedentes.* Mexico: Editorial Cultura, 1927.

———. *Obras.* Mexico: Fondo de Cultura Económica, 1964.

———. "Qué son, por fin, las juntas de conciliación y arbitraje?" *Revista General de Derecho y Jurisprudencia* (1930), pp. 185–211.

Bassols Batalla, Narciso. *Obregón.* Mexico: Editorial Nuestro Tiempo, 1967.

Beck, Carl. "Leadership Attributes in Eastern Europe: The Effects of Country and Time." In Carl Beck et al., *Comparative Political Leadership*. New York: David McKay, 1973, pp. 86–153.

Beck, Paul A., and M. Kent Jennings. "Parents as 'Middlepersons' in Political Socialization." *Journal of Politics*, Vol. 37 (February, 1975), pp. 83–107.

Benveniste, Guy. *Bureaucracy and National Planning, A Sociological Case Study in Mexico*. New York: Praeger, 1970.

Bermúdez, Antonio J., and Octavio Véjar Vázquez. *No dejes crecer la hierba*. Mexico: Costa Amic, 1969.

Bernal Sahagun, Víctor M. *Anatomía de la publicidad en México*. Mexico: Editorial Nuestro Tiempo, 1974.

Beteta, Ramón. *Jarano*. Austin: University of Texas Press, 1970.

————. *The Mexican Revolution: A Defense*. Mexico: DAPP, 1937.

————. "Social Forces in Mexican Life." In H. C. Herring and Katharine Terrill, eds., *The Genius of Mexico*. New York: Committee on Cultural Relations with Latin America, 1931, pp. 33–45.

————. "Some Economic Aspects of Mexico's Six-Year Plan." In Hubert C. Herring and Herbert Weinstock, eds., *Renascent Mexico*. New York: Covici-Friede, 1935, pp. 88–109.

Bezdek, Robert R. "Electoral Oppositions in Mexico: Emergence, Suppression, and Impact on Political Processes." Ph.D. dissertation, Ohio State University, 1973.

Bibliografía Historia Mexicana. Mexico: Colegio de México, 1967–76.

Bizzarro, Salvatore. "Mexico's Government in Crisis." *Current History* (March, 1977), pp. 102–105, 130.

Black, Gordon S. "A Theory of Political Ambition: Career Choices and the Role of Structure Incentive." *American Political Science Review*, Vol. 66 (March, 1972), pp. 144–159.

Bonilla, Frank. *The Failure of Elites*. Cambridge: MIT Press, 1970.

Borja Soriano, Manuel. *Teoría general de las obligaciones*. 2 Vols. Mexico: Porrúa, 1939.

Brandenburg, Frank. *Making of Modern Mexico*. Englewood Cliffs: Prentice-Hall, 1964.

————. "Mexico, An Experiment in One-Party Democracy." Ph.D. dissertation, University of Pennsylvania, 1956.

Bravo Ugarte, José. *Historia sucinta de Michoacán*. Mexico, Editorial Jus, 1964.

Bremauntz, Alberto. *Setenta años de mi vida*. Mexico: Ediciones Jurídico Sociales, 1968.

Britton, Karl. *John Stuart Mill, Life and Philosophy*. New York: Dover Books, 1969.

Brotherston, Gordon, ed. *José Enrique Rodó, Ariel*. Cambridge: Cambridge University Press, 1967.

Brown, Ester L. *Lawyers, Law Schools and the Public Service*. New York: Russell Sage Foundation, 1948.

Brown, Lyle C. "General Lázaro Cárdenas and Mexican Presidential Politics, 1933–40." Ph.D. dissertation, University of Texas, 1964.

Brush, David Allen. "The De la Huerta Rebellion in Mexico, 1923–24." Ph.D. dissertation, Syracuse University, 1975.

Bustillo Oro, Juan. *Vientos de los Veintes*. Mexico: SepSetentas, 1973.

Cadena Z., Daniel. *El candidato presidencial, 1976*. Mexico, 1975.

Calderón Vega, Luis. *Los 7 sabios de Mexico*. Mexico, 1961.

Camacho, Manuel. "El poder: estado o 'feudos' políticos." *Foro International,* Vol 14, 1974, pp. 331–351.

Camp, Roderic A. "Autobiography and Decision-Making in Mexico: A Review Essay." *Journal of Inter-American Studies and World Affairs,* Vol. 19 (May, 1977), pp. 275–283.

———. "La Campaña presidencial de 1929 y el liderazgo político en México." *Historia Mexicana,* Vol. 27 (No. 2, 1977), pp. 231–259.

———. "Education and Political Recruitment in Mexico: the Alemán Generation." *Journal of Inter-American Studies and World Affairs,* Vol. 18 (August, 1976), pp. 295–321.

———. "Mexican Governors Since Cárdenas: Education and Career Contacts." Journal of Inter-American Studies and World Affairs, Vol. 16 (November, 1974), pp. 454–481.

———. *Mexican Political Biographies, 1935–1975*. Tucson: University of Arizona Press, 1976.

———. *Mexico's Leaders, Their Education and Recruitment*. Tucson: University of Arizona Press, 1980.

———. "The National School of Economics and Public Life in Mexico." *Latin American Research Review,* Vol. 10 (Fall, 1975), pp. 137–151.

———. "A Reexamination of the Political Leadership and Allocation of Federal Revenues in Mexico, 1934–1973." *Journal of Developing Areas,* Vol. 10 (January, 1976), pp. 193–213.

———. *The Role of Economists in Policy-making: A Comparative Case Study of Mexico and the United States*. Tucson: University of Arizona Press, 1977.

———. "El sistema mexicano y las decisiones sobre el personal político." *Foro Internacional,* Vol. 17 (July–September, 1976), pp. 51–82.

Campa, Valentin. *Mi testimonio*. Mexico: Ediciones de Cultura Popular, 1978.

Cárdenas, Lázaro. *Obras-Apuntes 1913/1940*. Mexico: UNAM, 1972.

Carrasco Puente, Rafael. *La Caricatura en México*. Mexico: Imprenta Universitaria, 1953.

Carrillo Flores, Antonio. "La civilización industrial norteamericana: reflexiones de un mexicano." *El Trimestre Económico,* Vol. 38 (July–September, 1951), pp. 403–414.

———. "La Constitución y la acción económica del estado." *Investigación Económica,* No. 3 (1941), pp. 277–296.

———. *La defensa de los derechos del hombre en la coyuntura del México de hoy.* Mexico, 1971.

———. *La defensa jurídica de los particulares frente a la administración en México*. Mexico: Porrúa, 1939.

———. *La responsabilidad de la iniciativa privada en la industrialización de México*. Mexico: Editorial Cultura, 1960.

Caso, Antonio. *El concepto de la historia universal y la filosofía de los valores.* Mexico: Ediciones Bota, 1933.

––––––. "Democracía como método y fin." In *La persona humana y el estado totalitario.* Mexico: UNAM, 1941, pp. 27–31.

––––––. *Sociología.* Mexico: Porrúa, 1946.

––––––. *Sociología genética y sistemática.* Talleres Gráficos de la Nación, Mexico, 1927.

Castro, Eusebio. *Centenario de la Escuela Nacional Preparatoria.* Mexico: 1968.

Ceballos, Miguel Angel. *La Escuela Nacional Preparatoria.* Mexico: Imprenta Mundial, 1933.

Ceceña, José Luis. *México en la orbita imperial.* Mexico: Ediciones "El Caballito," 1975.

Centers, Richard. "Children of the New Deal: Social Stratification and Adolescent Attitudes." In R. Bendix and S. M. Lipset, eds., *Class, Status and Power.* New York: Free Press, 1953, pp. 359–370.

Centro de Estudios Internacionales. *La vida política en México (1970–1973).* Mexico: El Colegio de México, 1974.

Chaffee, Wilber A., Jr. "Entrepreneurs and Economic Behavior: A New Aproach to the Study of Latin American Politics." *Latin American Research Review,* Vol. 11, No. 3 (1976), pp. 55–68.

Chávez, Ezequiel A. *Relexionado para que la vida suba de nivel.* Mexico: Asociación Civil "Ezequiel A. Chávez," 1968.

––––––. *Los últimos sesenta años de la historia de México y sus enseñanzas relativas a México, Francia y el Mundo Latino.* Paris: Lahure, 1926.

Chávez, Ignacio. "Discurso pronunciado en la ceremonia conmemorativa del xxv aniversario de la fundación de El Colegio Nacional." *Memoria de El Colegio Nacional,* Vol. 6, Nos. 2–3 (1967–68), pp. 249–56.

Chávez, Leticia. *Recordando a mi padre.* 10 vols. Mexico: Asociación Civil E. A. Chávez, 1967.

Christenson, Reo M., and Patrick J. Capretta. "The Impact of College on Political Attitudes, A Research Note." *Social Science Quarterly,* Vol. 49 (1968), pp. 315–320.

Clark, Mary J. "A Biography of Miguel Alemán, President of Mexico." Master's thesis, Texas College of Arts and Industries, 1951.

Clarke, James W. "Family Structure and Political Socialization Among Urban Black Children." *American Journal of Political Science,* Vol. 17 (May, 1973), pp. 302–315.

Cline, Howard F. *Mexico: Revolution to Evolution: 1940–1960.* New York: Oxford University Press, 1963.

Clubok, Alfred B., Norman M. Wilensky, and Forrest J. Berghorn. "Family Relationships, Congressional Recruitment, and Political Modernization." *Journal of Politics,* Vol. 31 (November, 1969), pp. 1035–1062.

Coatsworth, John H. "Los orígenes del autoritarismo moderno en México." *Foro Internacional,* Vol. 16 (October–December, 1975), pp. 205–232.

Cockcroft, J. D. "Coercion and Ideology in Mexican Politics." In John D. Cockcroft et al., eds., *Dependence and Underdevelopment: Latin Amer-*

ica's Political Economy. Garden City: Doubleday, 1972, pp. 245–268.
Cohen, Marshall, ed. The Philosophy of John Stuart Mill. New York: The Modern Library, 1961.
Coleman, Kenneth M. "Diffuse Support in Mexico: The Potential for Crisis." Sage Professional Papers in Comparative Politics. Vol. 5. Beverly Hills: Sage Publications, 1976.
Connell, R. W. "Political Socialization and the American Family: The Evidence Re-examined." Public Opinion Quarterly, Vol. 36 (Fall, 1972), pp. 323–333.
Corbett, John G. "The Context of Politics in a Mexican Community: A Study in Constraints on System Capacity." Ph.D. dissertation, Stanford University, 1974.
Cornelius, Wayne A., Jr. "Contemporary Mexico: A Structural Analysis of Urban Caciquismo." In Robert Kern, ed., The Caciques. Albuquerque: University of New Mexico Press, 1973, pp. 135–150.
———. "Nation-building, Participation and Distribution: The Politics of Social Reform Under Lázaro Cárdenas." In G. Almond et al., eds., Crisis, Choice and Change: Historical Studies of Political Development. Boston: Little, Brown, 1973, pp. 392–498.
———. Politics of the Migrant Poor in Mexico City. Stanford: Stanford University Press, 1975.
Cosío Villegas, Daniel. Ensayos y notas. Vol. 1. Mexico: Editorial Hermes, 1966.
———. El estilo personal de gobernar. Mexico: Joaquín Mortiz, 1974.
———. Memorias. Mexico: Joaquín Mortiz, 1976.
———. El sistema político mexicano. Mexico: Joaquín Mortiz, 1973.
———. La sucesión: desenlace y perspectivas. Mexico: Joaquín Mortiz, 1976.
———. La sucesión presidencial. Mexico: Joaquín Mortiz, 1975.
Crosby, Charles. "The Mexican Political Cartoon From 1867 to 1920: A Reflection of Unrest and Revolt." Ph.D. dissertation, New York University, 1976.
Cumberland, Charles C. Mexican Revolution, Genesis under Madero. Austin: University of Texas, 1952.
D'Antonio, William V., and William H. Form. Influentials in Two Border Cities: A Study in Community Decision-making. Notre Dame: University of Notre Dame Press, 1965.
Davis, Charles L. "The Mobilization of Public Support for an Authoritarian Regime: The Case of the Lower Class in Mexico City." American Journal of Political Science, Vol. 20, No. 4 (November, 1976), pp. 653–670.
———. "The Regime Legitimating Function of External Political Efficacy in an Authoritarian Regime: The Case of Mexico." Paper delivered at the Annual Meeting of the American Political Science Association, New Orleans, 1974.
———. "Social Mistrust as a Determinant of Political Cynicism in a Transitional Society: An Empirical Examination." Journal of Developing Areas, Vol. 11 (October, 1976), pp. 91–102.

————. "Toward an Explanation of Mass Support for Authoritarian Regimes: A Case Study of Political Attitudes in Mexico City." Ph.D. dissertation, University of Kentucky, 1974.

Davis, Jerome. "A Study of One Hundred and Sixty-three Outstanding Communist Leaders." In Glenn Paige, ed., *Political Leadership*. New York: Free Press, 1972, pp. 262–272.

Dawson, Richard, and Kenneth Prewitt. *Political Socialization*. Boston: Little, Brown, 1969.

Dawson, Richard, Kenneth Prewitt, and Karen Dawson. *Political Socialization*. Boston: Little, Brown, 1977.

De Beer, Gabriella. *José Vasconcelos and His World*. New York: Las Américas Publishing Company, 1966.

De Flores, Louis J. "The Evolution of the Role of Government in the Economic Development of Mexico." Ph.D. dissertation, University of Southern California, 1968.

De la Garza, Rudolph O. "La función reclutadora de la cámara de diputados." *Revista Mexicana de Ciencias Políticas*, Vol. 11 (April–June, 1975), pp. 65–74.

————. "The Mexican Chamber of Deputies and the Mexican Political System." Ph.D. dissertation, University of Arizona, 1972.

Delhumeau, Antonio. "Elites culturales y educación de masas en México." *Revista Mexicana de Ciencias Políticas*, Vol. 19, No. 73 (1973), pp. 21–26.

Dennis, Jack. "Major Problems of Political Socialization Research." In Jack Dennis, ed., *Socialization to Politics*. New York: Wiley, 1973.

Dennis, Jack, ed. *Socialization to Politics*. New York: Wiley, 1973.

Dennis, Jack, and Kent Jennings, eds. *Comparative Political Socialization*. Beverly Hills: Sage, 1970.

Díaz Guerrero, Rogelio. *Psychology of the Mexican*. Austin: University of Texas Press, 1975.

Díaz Soto y Gama, Antonio. "The Agrarian Movement in Mexico." In H. C. Herring and Katharine Terrill, eds., *The Genius of Mexico*. New York: Committee on Cultural Cooperation with Latin America, 1931, pp. 177–84.

Domínguez, Virgilio. "La enseñanza del derecho y la Biblioteca Antonio Caso." *Revista de la Escuela Nacional de Jurisprudencia*, Vol. 37 (enero–marzo, 1948).

Dromundo, Baltasar. *La Escuela Nacional Preparatoria Nocturna y José María de los Reyes*. Mexico: Porrúa, 1973.

————. *Los oradores del 29*. Mexico: Ediciones "Una Generación," ARS, 1949.

————. *Mi barrio de San Miguel*. Mexico: Antigua Librería Robredo, 1951.

————. *Mi calle de San Ildefonso*. Mexico, Editorial Guaranía, 1956.

Dulles, John W. F. *Yesterday in Mexico*. Austin: University of Texas Press, 1961.

Echeverría, Amilcar. *Enrique Martínez Sobral*. Guatemala, 1964.

Edelstein, Alex S. "Since Bennington: Evidence of Change in Student Political Behavior." In Roberta S. Sigel, ed., *Learning About Politics*. New York: Random House, 1970.

Edinger, Lewis J., and Donald D. Searing. "Social Background in Elite Analysis: A Methodological Inquiry." *American Political Science Review*, Vol. 61 (June, 1967), pp. 428–445.

Escarcega, Alfonso. *Gómez Morín (Anecdotario Chihuahuense)*. Mexico: Editorial Jus, 1973.

Esteva Ruiz, Roberto A. *Los títulos de crédito en el Derecho Mexicano*. Mexico: Editorial Cultura, 1938.

Eulau, Heinz. "Recollections." In John C. Wahlke, Heinz Eulau, William Buchanan, and LeRoy Ferguson, *The Legislative System*. New York: Wiley, 1962, pp. 77–95.

Eulau, Heinz, William Buchanan, Leroy Ferguson, and John C. Wahlke. "The Political Socialization of American State Legislators." *Midwest Journal of Political Science*, Vol. 3 (1959), pp. 188–206.

Everett, Michael D. "The Role of the Mexican Trade Unions, 1950–1963." Ph.D. dissertation, Washington University, Missouri, 1967.

Fagen, Richard, and William Tuohy. *Politics and Privilege in a Mexican City*. Stanford: Stanford University Press, 1972.

Falkwowski, Daniel C. "Nacional Financiera, S. A., de México: A Study of a Development Bank." Ph.D. dissertation, New York University, 1972.

Felix, David. "Income Inequality in Mexico." *Current History* (March, 1977), pp. 111–114.

Fennelly, John F. *Twilight of the Evening Lands*. New York: Brookdale Press, 1972.

Fernández del Castillo, Antonio. "Palabras del Señor Lic. Antonio Fernández del Castillo." Mexico: Academia Nacional de Historia y Geografía, 1968.

Flores Zavala, Ernesto. *El estudiante inquieto*. Mexico, 1972.

Flower, Edith. "The Mexican Revolt Against Positivism." *Journal of the History of Ideas*, Vol. 10 (January, 1949), pp. 115–129.

Forster, Merlin H. "The 'Contemporáneos,' 1915–1932: A Study in Twentieth-Century Mexican Letters." Ph.D. dissertation, University of Illinois, 1960.

Fraga, Gabino. *Derecho administrativo*. Mexico: Porrúa, 1934.

Fuentes, Carlos. *The Death of Artemio Cruz*. New York: Noonday Press, 1964.

———. *The Good Conscience*. New York: Noonday Press, 1970.

———. *Tiempo mexicano*. Mexico: Joaquín Mortiz, 1972.

Fuentes Díaz, Vicente. *Los partidos políticos en México*. Mexico: Editorial Altiplano, 1969.

Gabbert, Jack Benton. "The Evolution of the Mexican Presidency." Ph.D. dissertation, University of Texas, 1963.

García Aguirre, Trinidad. *Introdución al estudio del derecho*. Mexico: M. de J. Nucamendi, 1935.

García Cantú, Gastón. *Política mexicana*. Mexico: UNAM, 1974.

Garrido Díaz, Luis. *Antonio Caso: una vida profunda*. Mexico: UNAM, 1961.

————. *El tiempo de mi vida: memorias*. Mexico: Porrúa, 1974.

Garrison, Charles. "Political Involvement and Political Science: A Note on the Basic Course as an Agent of Political Socialization." *Social Science Quarterly*, Vol. 49 (September, 1968), pp. 305–14.

Gaxiola, Francisco Javier. *Memorias*. Mexico: Editorial Porrúa, 1975.

Glade, William P., Jr. "The Role of Government Enterprise in the Economic Development of Underdeveloped Regions: Mexico, A Case Study." Ph.D. dissertation, University of Texas, 1955.

Glade, William P., Jr., and Charles W. Anderson. *The Political Economy of Mexico*. Madison: University of Wisconsin, 1963.

Glade, William P., Jr., and Stanley R. Ross, eds. *Críticas constructivas del sistema político mexicano*. Austin: Institute of Latin American Studies, 1973.

Glass, Elliot S. "Mexico in the Works of Emilio Rabasa." Ph.D. dissertation, Columbia University, 1972.

Goldrich, Daniel. *Sons of the Establishment: Elite Youth in Panama and Costa Rica*. Chicago: Rand-McNally, 1966.

Goldthorpe, J. E. *An African Elite: Makerere College Students, 1922–1960*. Nairobi: Oxford University Press, 1965.

Gómez Morín, Manuel. *El credito agrícola en México*. Madrid: Espasa Calpe, 1928.

————. *1915 y otros ensayos*. Mexico: Editorial Jus, 1973.

González, Luis. *San José de Gracia, Mexican Village in Transition*. Austin: University of Texas Press, 1975.

González Aparicio, Enrique. *Nuestro petroleo*. Mexico: Editorial Masas, 1938.

González Cárdenas, Octavio. *Los cien años de la Escuela Nacional Preparatoria*. Mexico: Editorial Porrúa, 1972.

González Casanova, Pablo. *La democracia en México*. Mexico: ERA, 1965.

González de la Vega, Francisco. "El Aula 'Manuel Borja Soriano.'" In *La Universidad*. Vol. 3, No. 33, September, 1949, p. 5.

González Graf, Jaime. *La perspectiva política en México*. Mexico: Instituto Mexicano de Estudios Políticos, 1974.

González Llaca, Edmundo. "El presidencialismo o la personalización del poder." *Revista Mexicana de Ciencias Políticas*, Vol. 21 (April–June, 1975), pp. 35–42.

González Navarro, Moises. *Vallarata y su ambiente político jurídico*. Thesis, University of Mexico, 1949.

González Ramírez, Manuel. *Mexico, litografía de la ciudad que se fue*. Mexico, 1962.

González Roa, Fernando. *Chapters on the Agrarian Question in Mexico*. New York: State Department of Social Welfare, 1927.

————. *La cuestiones fundamentales de actualidad en México*. Mexico: Secretaría de Relaciones Exteriores, 1927.

Graham, Lawrence S. *Mexican State Government: A Prefectural System in Action*. Austin: Bureau of Government Research, LBJ School of Public Affairs, 1971.

——. *Politics in a Mexican Community*. Gainesville: University of Florida Press, 1968.

Graham, Richard, and Peter H. Smith. *New Approaches to Latin American History*. Austin: University of Texas Press, 1974.

Grayson, George W. "The Making of a Mexican President, 1976." *Current History*, Vol. 70 (February, 1976), pp. 49–52, 83–84.

Greenberg, Martin H. *Bureaucracy and Development: A Mexican Case Study*. Lexington: D. C. Heath, 1970.

Greene, Graham. *The Lawless Roads*. London: William Heinemann, 1955.

——. *The Power and the Glory*. New York: Time Incorporated, 1962.

Greenleaf, Richard E., and Michael C. Meyer. *Research in Mexican History*. Lincoln: University of Nebraska Press, 1973.

Grindle, Merilee S. *Bureacrats, Politicians, and Peasants in Mexico: A Case Study in Public Policy*. Berkeley: University of California Press, 1977.

——. "Patrons and Clients in the Bureaucracy: Career Networks in Mexico." *Latin American Research Review*, Vol. 12 (No. 1, 1977), pp. 37–66.

Gruber, Wilfried. "Career Patterns of Mexico's Political Elite." *Western Political Quarterly*, Vol. 24 (September, 1971), pp. 467–482.

Guerrero, Julio. *La génesis del crimen en México*. Paris: C. Bouret, 1901.

Guillén, Fedro. *Jesús Silva Herzog*. Mexico: Empresas Editoriales, 1969.

Guzmán, Martín Luis. *Apunte sobre una personalidad*. Mexico, 1955.

Haddox, John H. *Antonio Caso, Philosopher of Mexico*. Austin: University of Texas Press, 1971.

——. *Vasconcelos of Mexico*. Austin: University of Texas, 1967.

Halsey, A. H., and Martin Trow. *The British Academics*. Cambridge: Harvard University Press, 1971.

Hansen, Roger D. *The Politics of Mexican Development*. Baltimore: John Hopkins University Press, 1971.

——. "PRI Politics in the 1970's: Crisis or Continuity?" In James W. Wilkie, Michael C. Meyer, and Edna Monzón de Wilkie et al., eds., *Contemporary Mexico*. Los Angeles: University of California at Los Angeles Latin American Center, 1976, pp. 389–402.

Hargrove, Erwin C. "Values and Change: A Comparison of Young *Elites* in England and America." *Political Studies*, Vol. 17 (September, 1969), pp. 339–344.

Harris, Seymour E., ed. *The New Economics: Keynes' Influence on Theory and Public Policy*. London: Dennis Dobson Ltd., 1960.

Hart, Jeffrey. "Geopolitics and Dependency: Cognitive Maps of Latin American Foreign Policy Elites." Paper prepared for delivery at the 1976 Annual Meeting of the American Political Science Association, Chicago, Illinois, September 25, 1976.

Hawley, Willis D. "The Implicit Civics Curriculum: Teacher Behavior and Political Learning." Paper prepared for delivery at the 1976 Annual Meeting of the American Political Science Association, Chicago, Illinois, September, 1976.

Heggan, Jon Parker. "Political Socialization in a Discontinuous Setting: The Experience of Three Colombian Secondary Schools." In Byron Massialas, ed., *Political Youth, Traditional Schools*. Englewood Cliffs: Prentice-Hall, 1972.

Henríquez Ureña, Pedro. "The Revolution in Intellectual Life." *Survey Grafic* (May, 1924), pp. 165–166.

————. *Universidad y educación*. Mexico: UNAM, 1969.

Hernández Luna, Juan. *Conferencias del Ateneo de la Juventud por Antonio Caso et al.* Mexico: UNAM, 1962.

Holtzman, Wayne H., Rogelio Díaz-Guerrero, and Jon D. Swartz. *Personality Development in Two Cultures*. Austin: University of Texas Press, 1975.

Howe, Irving. "Dostoevsky: The Politics of Salvation." In Rene Wellek, ed., *Dostoevsky*. New York: Prentice-Hall, 1962, pp. 53–70.

Iduarte, Andrés, *Niño, Child of the Mexican Revolution*. New York: Praeger, 1971.

Innes, John S. "The Universidad Popular Mexicana." *The Americas*, Vol. 30 (July, 1973), pp. 110–122.

International Studies of Values in Politics. *Values and the Active Community*. New York: Free Press, 1971.

Investigaciones contemporáneos sobre historia de México. Memorias de la tercera reunión de historiadores mexicanos y norteamericanos. Mexico: UNAM; Austin: University of Texas Press, 1971.

Jacobson, Peter. "Opposition and Political Reform in Mexico: An Assessment of the Partido Acción Nacional and the 'Apertura Democrática.'" *The New Scholar*, Vol. 5 (No. 1, 1975), pp. 19–30.

Jaros, Dean. *Socialization to Politics*. New York: Praeger, 1973.

————. "Transmitting the Civic Culture: The Teacher and Political Socialization." *Social Science Quarterly*, Vol. 49 (1968), pp. 284–295.

Jaros, Dean, and R. Darcy. "The Elusive Impact of Political Science: More Negative Findings." *Experimental Study of Politics*, Vol. 2 (No. 1, 1973), pp. 14–52.

Jaspers, Karl. *Nietzsche, An Introduction to the Understanding of His Philosophical Activity*. Tucson: University of Arizona Press, 1965.

Jennings, M. Kent, and Gregory B. Markus. "The Effect of Military Service on Political Attitudes: A Panel Study." Paper prepared for delivery at the 1974 Annual Meeting of the American Political Science Association, Chicago, Illinois, August 29–September 2, 1974.

Jennings, M. Kent, and Richard G. Niemi. "Continuity and Change in Political Orientations: A Longitudinal Study of Two Generations." *American Political Science Review* (December, 1975), pp. 1316–1335.

Jennings and Niemi (*continued*)
———. *The Political Character of Adolescence: The Influence of Families and Schools.* Princeton: Princeton University Press, 1974.

Johnson, John J. *Political Change in Latin America.* Stanford: Stanford University Press, 1958.

Johnson, Kenneth F. "Ideological Correlates of Right-Wing Political Alienation in Mexico." *American Political Science Review*, Vol. 59 (September, 1965), pp. 656–664.

———. *Mexican Democracy: A Critical View.* Boston: Allyn and Bacon, 1971.

Kahl, Joseph A. *The Measurement of Modernism.* Austin: University of Texas Press, 1974.

Karsen, Sonja. *Jaime Torres Bodet.* New York: Twayne Publishers, 1971.

Kautsky, John H. *Patterns of Modernizing Revolutions: Mexico and the Soviet Union.* Sage Professional Papers in Comparative Politics, Vol. 5. Beverly Hills: Sage Publications, 1975.

Kerr, Clark. *Marshall, Marx and Modern Times.* Cambridge: Cambridge University Press, 1969.

Kesselman, Mark. "Recruitment of Rival Party Activists in France: Party Cleavages and Cultural Differentiation." *Journal of Politics*, Vol. 35 (February, 1973), pp. 2–44.

Kirk, Betty. *Covering the Mexican Front.* Norman: Univ. of Okla. Press, 1942.

Kirshner, Alan M. "Tomás Garrido Canabal and the Mexican Red Shirt Movement." Ph.D. dissertation, New York University, 1970.

Kornberg, Allan, Joel Smith, and David Bromley. "Some Differences in the Political Socialization Patterns of Canadian and American Party Officials." In Jack Dennis, ed., *Socialization to Politics.* New York: Wiley, 1973, pp. 426–461.

Kornberg, Allan, and Norman Thomas. "The Political Socialization of National Legislative Elites in the United States and Canada." *Journal of Politics*, Vol. 27 (November, 1965), pp. 761–775.

Kornhauser, Arthur W. "Changes in the Information and Attitudes of Students in an Economics Class." *Journal of Educational Research*, Vol. 22 (June–December, 1930), pp. 288–308.

Krauze, Enrique. *Caudillos culturales en la revolución mexicana.* Mexico: Siglo XXI, 1976.

Kubota, Akira, and Robert E. Ward. "Family Influence and Political Socialization in Japan." In Jack Dennis and Kent Jennings, eds., *Comparative Political Socialization.* Beverly Hills: Sage, 1970, pp. 11–46.

Labastida Martín del Campo, Julio. "Algunas hipótesises sobre el modelo político mexicano y sus perspectivas." *Revista Mexicana de Sociología*, Vol. 36 (July–September, 1974), pp. 629–642.

———. "El régimen de Echeverría." *Revista Mexicana de Sociología*, Vol. 34 (July–December, 1972), pp. 881–907.

La Capra, Dominick. *Emile Durkheim, Sociologist and Philosopher.* Ithaca: Cornell University Press, 1972.

Ladd, Everett C., and Seymour M. Lipset. *The Divided Academy: Professors and Politics.* New York: W. W. Norton, 1976.

Lamare, James W. "Using Political Science Courses to Inculcate Political Orientations: A Historical Assessment." *Teaching Political Science*, Vol. 2 (July, 1975), pp. 409–432.

Langton, Kenneth P. "Peer Group and School and the Political Socialization Process." *American Political Science Review*, Vol. 61 (September, 1967), pp. 751–58.

Lanz Duret, Miguel. *Derecho constitucional mexicano, y consideraciones sobre la realidad política de nuestro régimen.* Mexico, 1933.

Lasswell, Harold D., and Daniel Lerner. *World Revolutionary Elites: Studies in Coercive Ideological Movements.* Cambridge: MIT Press, 1966.

Lasswell, Harold D., and M. S. McDougal. "Legal Education and Public Policy." In H. Lasswell, ed., *The Analysis of Political Behavior.* London: Routledge, Kegan Paul, Ltd., 1948.

Lavrin, Janko. *Tolstoy, An Approach.* New York: Macmillan, 1946.

Lazarsfeld, Paul F., and Wagner Thielens, Jr. *The Academic Mind.* Glencoe: Free Press, 1958.

Leal, Juan Felipe. "The Mexican State, 1915–1973: A Historical Interpretation." *Latin American Perspectives*, Vol. 2 (Summer, 1975), pp. 48–63.

Lewis, George K. "An Analysis of the Institutional Status and Role of the Petroleum Industry in Mexico's Evolving System of Political Economy." Ph.D. dissertation, University of Texas, 1959.

Liebman, Arthur, Kenneth Walker, and Myron Glazer. *Latin American University Students: A Six Nation Study.* Cambridge: Harvard University Press, 1972.

Lieuwen, Edwin. *Mexican Militarism.* Albuquerque: University of New Mexico Press, 1968.

Litt, Edgar. "Civic Education, Community Norms, and Political Indoctrination." *American Sociological Review*, Vol. 28 (1963), pp. 69–75.

Loaeza, Soledad. "El partido Acción Nacional." *Foro Internacional*, Vol. 14 (No. 3, 1974), pp. 351–373.

Lombardo Toledano, Vicente. *En torno al problema agraria.* Mexico: CNC, 1974.

———. "The Labor Movement." *Annals* (March, 1940), pp. 48–54.

Lomeli Garduño, Antonio. *Anecdotario Político Mexicano.* Mexico: Costa-Amic, 1974.

López Gallo, Manuel. *Economía y política en la historia de México.* Mexico: Ediciones Solidaridad, 1965.

López Reyes, Amalia, and Guadalupe Pérez San Vicente. *Joaquín Ramírez Cabañas, el maestro y su obra.* Mexico: 1948.

Loyo Brambila, Aurora, and Ricardo Pozas Horcasitas. "Notes on the Mechanisms of Control Exercised by the Mexican State Over the Organized Sector of the Working Class, A Case Study: The Political Crisis of

1958." Paper presented to the Center for Inter-American Relations, April, 1975.

Lozoya, Jorge Alberto. *El ejercito mexicano (1911–1963)*. Mexico: El Colegio de México, 1970.

Mabry, Donald J. "Changing Models of Mexican Politics, A Review Essay." *The New Scholar*, Vol. 5 (No. 1, 1975), pp. 31–37.

———. *Mexico's Acción Nacional: A Catholic Alternative to Revolution*. Syracuse: Syracuse University Press, 1973.

Mabry, Donald, and Roderic A. Camp. "Mexican Political Elites, 1935–1973: A Comparative Study." *The Americas: A Quarterly Journal of Inter-American Cultural History*, Vol 31 (April, 1975), pp. 452–469.

Machado, Mario B. "Political Socialization in Authoritarian Systems: The Case of Brazil." Ph.D. dissertation, University of Chicago, 1975.

McClintock, C. G., and Henry A. Turner. "The Impact of College Upon Political Knowlege, Participation and Values." *Human Relations*, Vol. 15 (1962), pp. 163–176.

McFarland, Floyd Brant. "An Analysis of Relationships between Foreign Economic Policy and Economic Development in Mexico." Ph.D. dissertation, University of Texas, 1964.

McQuail, D., L. O'Sullivan, and W. G. Quine. "Elite Education and Political Values." *Political Studies*, Vol. 16 (1968), pp. 257–266.

Magdaleno, Mauricio, *Las palabras perdidas*. Mexico: Fondo de Cultura Económica, 1956.

Malagón Barcelo, Javier. "Breve Reseña Histórica de la Escuela Nacional de Jurisprudencia." *Revista de la Facultad de Derecho de México*, Vol. 1, Nos. 1–2 (January–June, 1951), pp. 163–188.

———. "Four Centuries of the Faculty of Law in Mexico." *Hispanic American Historical Review*, Vol. 32 (August, 1952), pp 442–51.

Maldonado, Braulio. *Baja California: comentarios políticos*. Mexico: Costa Amic, 1960.

Mannheim, Karl. "The Problem of Generations." In Karl Mannheim, ed., *Essays on the Sociology of Knowledge*. London: Routledge and Kegan, 1952, pp. 276–322.

Maples Arce, Manuel. *Soberana juventud*. Madrid: Editorial Plenitud, 1967.

Margiotta, Franklin D. "Changing Patterns of Political Influence: The Mexican Military and Politics." Paper prepared for delivery at the Annual Meeting of the American Political Science Association, New Orleans, 1973.

———. "The Mexican Military: A Case Study in Non-intervention." Master's thesis, Georgetown University, 1968.

Martindale, Donald. *The Nature and Types of Sociological Theory*. Cambridge: Riverside Press, 1960.

Martínez Sobral, Enrique. *Compendio de económica*. 7th edition. Mexico: Ediciones Botas, 1949.

———. *Elementos de hacienda pública*. Mexico: Editorial Botas, 1939.

————. *Principios de económica, con especial referencia a las condiciones mejicanas*. Mexico: Lib. Franco-Americano, 1926.

Marvick, Dwaine. "Political Recruitment and Careers." *International Encyclopedia of the Social Sciences*. Vol. 12. New York: Crowell, Collier and Macmillan, 1968, pp. 273–282.

Marvick, Dwaine, ed. *Political Decision-Makers*. New York: Free Press, 1961.

Massialas, Byron G. *Education and the Political System*. Reading: Addison-Wesley, 1969.

Massialas, Byron G., ed. *Political Youth, Traditional Schools*. Englewood Cliffs: Prentice-Hall, 1972.

Matthews, Donald F. *The Social Background of Political Decision-Makers*. New York: Garden City, 1954.

Mayo, Sebastian. *La educación socialista en México: el asalto a la Universidad Nacional*. Rosario, Argentina: Editorial Bear, 1964.

Medin, Tzvi. *Ideología y praxis política de Lázaro Cárdenas*. Mexico: Siglo XXI, 1975.

Medina, Luis. "Origen y circunstancia de la idea de unidad nacional." In Centro de Estudios Internacionales, *La vida política en México (1970–1973)*. Mexico: El Colegio de México, 1974.

Mendieta y Núñez, Lucio. "Apuntes para la historia de derecho de la Facultad de Derecho." *Revista de la Escuela Nacional de Jurisprudencia*, Vol. 1 (September–December, 1939), pp. 385–419.

————. "Un Balance Objectivo de la Revolución Mexicana." In Lucio Mendieta y Núñez, ed., *Tres ensayos de sociología política nacional*. Mexico: UNAM, 1961, pp. 129–166.

————. *Historia de la Facultad de Derecho*. Mexico: UNAM, 1956.

Mendoza, Vicente T. *El corrido mexicano*. Mexico: Fondo de Cultura Económica, 1976.

México, cincuenta años de revolución. 4 vols. Mexico: Fondo de Cultura Económica, 1960.

Mexico, realización y esperanza. Mexico: Editorial Superación, 1952.

Mexico. Secretaría de Educación Pública. *México y la cultura*. Mexico, 1961.

Mexico City. Escuela Nacional Preparatoria. *Memoria del primer congreso de escuela preparatorias de la República*. Mexico City: Editorial Cultura, 1922.

Mexico City. Universidad Nacional. *Catalogo de la Universidad de México, 1926–27*. Mexico: Talleres Gráfico de la Nación, 1926.

————. *Plan de estudios, 1924*. Mexico: UNAM, 1924.

Mexico City. Universidad Nacional. Escuela Nacional Preparatoria. *Plan de Estudios de la ENP*. Mexico: Universidad Nacional, 1920.

————. *Plan de Estudios de la ENP*. Mexico: Universidad Nacional, 1924.

Mexico City. Universidad Nacional Autónomo de México. *Anuario de la Escuela Nacional de Jurisprudencia, 1940*. Mexico, 1940.

————. *Anuario de la Escuela Nacional Preparatoria, 1940*. Mexico, 1940.

————. *Anuario General (1931–54)*. Mexico: UNAM, 1931–54.

Mexico City. Universidad Nacional Autónomo de México (continued)
———. Anuario 1931–1932. Mexico: UNAM, 1931.
Mexico City. Universidad Nacional Autónomo de México. Escuela Nacional de Economía. Anuario, 1959. Mexico: UNAM, 1959.
———. 2 conferencias sobre el problema petroleo. Mexico City: Imprenta Universitaria, 1938.
Mexico City. Universidad Autónomo de México. Facultad de derecho y ciencias sociales. Plan de estudios, programas y reglamentos de reconocimientos. Mexico: Talleres Gráficos de la Nación, 1929.
Meyer, Jean A. The Cristero Rebellion: The Mexican People Between Church and State (1926–1929). Cambridge: Cambridge University Press, 1976.
Meyer, Lorenzo. "Continuidades e innovaciones en la vida política mexicana del siglo xx, el antiguo y el nuevo régimen." Foro Internacional, Vol. 16 (julio–septiembre, 1975), pp. 37–63.
———. "The Origins of Mexico's Authoritarian State, Political Control in the Old and New Regimes." Paper presented at the Center for Inter-American Relations, New York, June 6–7, 1975.
Michaels, Albert L. "The Mexican Election of 1940." Special Studies No. 5, Council on International Studies, Buffalo: State University of New York, 1971.
———. "Mexican Politics and Nationalism from Calles to Cárdenas." Ph.D. dissertation, University of Pennsylvania, 1966.
Miller, Richard Ulric. "The Role of Labor Organizations in a Developing Country: The Case of Mexico." Ph.D. dissertation, Cornell University, 1964.
Millon, Robert P. Mexican Marxist—Vicente Lombardo Toledano. Chapel Hill: University of North Carolina Press, 1966.
Miranda, José P. Marx en México. Mexico: Siglo XXI, 1972.
Monson, Robert. "Political Stability in Mexico: The Changing Role of Traditional Rightists." Journal of Politics, Vol. 35 (August, 1973), pp. 594–614.
Moreno Sánchez, Manuel. Crisis política de México. Mexico: Editorial Extemporáneos, 1970.
———. Mexico: 1968–72. Austin: Institute of Latin American Studies, 1973.
Morton, Ward. Woman Suffrage in Mexico. Gainesville: University of Florida Press, 1962.
Moskos, Charles C., Jr., and Wendell Bell. "Attitudes Toward Democracy Among Leaders in Four Emerging Nations." British Journal of Sociology, Vol. 15 (1964), pp. 317–337.
Myers, Charles N. Education and National Development in Mexico. Princeton: Princeton University Press, 1965.
Narciso Bassols en memoria. Mexico, 1960.
Needleman, Carolyn, and Martin Needleman. "Who Rules Mexico? A Critique of Some Current Views on the Mexican Political Process." Journal of Politics, Vol. 31 (November, 1969), pp. 1011–1034.

Needler, Martin C. "A Critical Time for Mexico." *Current History* (February, 1972), pp. 81–85.

―――. "Daniel Cosío Villegas and the Interpretation of Mexico's Political System." *Journal of Inter-American Studies*, Vol. 18 (April, 1976), pp. 245–252.

―――. *Politics and Society in Mexico*. Albuquerque: University of New Mexico Press, 1971.

―――. "Problems in the Evaluation of the Mexican Political System." In James W. Wilkie et al., eds., *Contemporary Mexico*. Los Angeles: UCLA Latin American Center, 1976, pp. 339–347.

Newcomb, Theodore. "Persistence and Regression of Changed Attitudes: Long-Range Studies." In Jack Dennis, ed., *Socialization to Politics*. New York: Wiley, 1973, pp. 413–426.

Niemeyer, E. V., Jr. *Revolution at Querétaro*. Austin: University of Texas Press, 1974.

Niggli, Josephine. *Step Down, Elder Brother*. New York: Rinehart, 1947.

Ortega Molina, Gregorio. *El sindicalismo contemporáneo en México*. Mexico: Fondo de Cultura Económica, 1975.

Ortiz Rubio, Pascual. *Memorias, 1895–1928*. Mexico: Editorial Periodística y Impresora de México, 1963.

Pacheco Calvo, Ciriaco. *La organización estudiantil en México*. Mexico: Confederación Nacional de Estudiantes, 1934.

Padgett, Leon. *The Mexican Political System*, 2d edition. Boston: Houghton Mifflin Company, 1976.

Pallares Ramírez, Manuel. *La Escuela Nacional de Economía, esbozo histórico 1929–1952*. Mexico, 1952.

Parsons, R. Wayne, and Allen H. Barton. "Social Background and Policy Attitudes of American Leaders." Paper presented at the Seventieth Annual Meeting of the American Political Science Association, Chicago, September, 1974.

Paz, Octavio. "Mexico: Freedom as Fiction." *Atlas World Press Review*, October, 1976, p. 44.

―――. *The Other Mexico: Critique of the Pyramid*. New York: Grove Press, 1972.

Pazos, Felipe. "Veinte años de pensamiento económico en la América Latina." *El Trimestre Económico*, Vol. 20 (October–December, 1953), pp. 552–570.

Peel, J. D. Y. *Herbert Spencer: The Evolution of a Sociologist*. New York: Basic Books, 1971.

Pineda, Hugo. "José Vasconcelos Político Mexicano." Ph.D. dissertation, The George Washington University, 1971.

―――. *José Vasconcelos, Político Mexicano, 1928–1929*. Mexico: Edutex, 1975.

Pineda, Salvador, et al. *Problemas universitarios y agonía de la ENP*. Mexico: Stylo, 1950.

Porras y López, Armando. *Luis Cabrera, revolucionario e intelectual.* Mexico: Biblioteca Mexicana, 1968.

Portes Gil, Emilio. *Quince años de política mexicana.* Mexico City: Ediciones Botas, 1954.

————. *Raigambre de la revolución en Tamaulipas, autobiografía en acción.* Mexico, 1972.

Portuondo, Alonso. "The Universidad Nacional Autónomo de México in the Post-Independence Period: A Political and Structural Review." Master's thesis, University of Miami, Coral Gables, Florida, 1972.

Prewitt, Kenneth. "Political Socialization and Leadership Selection." *The Annals of the American Academy of Political and Social Science,* Vol. 361 (September, 1965), pp. 96–111.

————. *The Recruitment of Political Leaders: A Study of Citizen-Politicians.* Indianapolis: Bobbs-Merrill, 1970.

Prewitt, Kenneth, and Heinz Eulau. "Social Bias in Leadership Selection, Political Recruitment, and Electoral Context." *Journal of Politics,* Vol. 33 (May, 1971), pp. 293–315.

Prewitt, Kenneth, Heinz Eulau, and Betty H. Zisk. "Political Socialization and Political Roles." *Public Opinion Quarterly,* Vol. 30 (Winter, 1966–67), pp. 569–582.

Prewitt, Kenneth, and Joseph Okello-Oculi. "Political Socialization and Political Education in the New Nations." In Roberta S. Sigel, ed., *Learning About Politics: A Reader in Political Socialization.* New York: Random House, 1970, pp. 607–621.

Prewitt, Kenneth, George Vonder Muhll, and David Court. "School Experiences and Political Socialization." In Jack Dennis and Kent Jennings, eds., *Comparative Political Socialization.* Beverly Hills: Sage, 1970, pp. 75–97.

Prieto Laurens, Jorge. *Cincuenta años de política mexicana: memorias políticas.* Mexico, 1968.

Purcell, John F., and Susan Purcell. "Mexican Business and Public Policy." In James Malloy, ed., *Authoritarianism and Corporatism in Latin America.* Pittsburgh: University of Pittsburgh Press, 1977.

————. "The State and Economic Enterprise in Mexico: The Limits of Reform." *Nueva Política,* Vol. I (abril–junio, 1976), pp. 229–250.

Purcell, Susan K. "The Future of the Mexican Political System." In José Luis Reyna and Richard S. Weinert, eds., *Authoritarianism in Mexico.* New York: ISHI Press, 1977, pp. 173–191.

————. *The Mexican Profit-Sharing Decision: Politics in an Authoritarian Regime.* Berkeley: University of California Press, 1975.

Putnam, Robert D. *The Beliefs of Politicians: Ideology, Conflict, and Democracy in Britain and Italy.* New Haven: Yale University Press, 1973.

————. *The Comparative Study of Political Elites.* New Jersey: Englewood Cliffs: Prentice-Hall, 1976.

Quandt, William B. "The Comparative Study of Political Elites." *Comparative Politics Series,* Vol. 1. Beverly Hills: Sage, 1970.

————. *Revolution and Political Leadership: Algeria, 1954–1968.* Cambridge: MIT Press, 1969.

Quirk, Robert E. *An Affair of Honor: Woodrow Wilson and the Occupation of Veracruz.* New York: Norton, 1967.

Rabasa, Emilio. *La Constitución y la dictadura: estudio sobre la organización política de México.* Mexico: Revistas de Revistas, 1912.

Radbruch, Gustav. *Introducción a la ciencia del derecho.* Madrid: Revista de derecho privado, 1930.

Raley, Harold C. *José Ortega y Gasset: Philosopher of European Unity.* University: University of Alabama Press, 1971.

Ramírez Vázquez, Manuel. *En torno de una generación; glosa de 1929.* Mexico: Ediciones "Una Generación." 1949.

Ramos, Samuel. *Profile of Man and Culture in Mexico.* Mexico: University of Texas Press, 1962.

————. *Veinte años de educación en Mexico.* Mexico, 1941.

Randall, John Herman. *The Making of the Modern Mind.* Cambridge: Riverside Press, 1954.

Raat, William Dirk. "The Antipositivist Movement in Prerevolutionary Mexico, 1892–1911." *Journal of Inter-American Studies and World Affairs,* Vol. 19 (February, 1977), pp. 83–98.

Reading, Reid. "Political Socialization in Colombia and the United States: An Exploratory Study." *Midwest Journal of Political Science,* Vol. 12 (1968), pp. 352–381.

Recaséns Siches, Luis, et al. *Latin-American Legal Philosophy.* Cambridge: Harvard University Press, 1948.

Reck, Andrew J. *Introduction to William James.* Bloomington: Indiana University Press, 1967.

Requeña, José Luis. "Recuerdos de la Escuela Nacional de Jurisprudencia." *Revista de la Escuela Nacional de Jurisprudencia,* Vol. 4 (March–May, 1939), pp. 127–134.

Reyes, Alfonso. *Mexico in a Nutshell.* Berkeley: University of California Press, 1964.

————. "Pasado inmediato." *Obras Completas,* Vol. 12. Mexico, 1941, pp. 182–216.

Reyna, José Luis. "Redefining the Established Authoritarian Regime: Perspectives of the Mexican Polity." Paper prepared for the Center for Inter-American Relations. New York, February, 1975.

Reynolds, Clark W. *The Mexican Economy: Twentieth Century Structure and Growth.* New Haven: Yale University Press, 1970.

Richmond, Patricia M. "Mexico: A Case Study of One-Party Politics." Ph.D. dissertation, University of California, Berkeley, 1965.

Rivera Silva, Manuel. *Perspectivas de una vida, biografía de una generación.* Mexico: Porrúa, 1974.

Rodríguez, Valdemar. "National University of Mexico: Rebirth and Role of the Universitarios, 1910–1957." Ph.D. dissertation, University of Texas, 1958.

Romanell, Patrick. "Bergson in Mexico: A Tribute to José Vasconcelos." *Philosophy and Phenomenological Research*, Vol. 21 (June, 1961), pp. 501–513.

————. *Making of the Mexican Mind.* Notre Dame: University of Notre Dame Press, 1967.

Ronfeldt, David. *Atencingo: The Politics of Agrarian Struggle in a Mexican Ejido.* Stanford, Stanford University Press, 1973.

————. *The Mexican Army and Political Order Since 1940.* Santa Monica: Rand, 1973.

Rose, Richard. "The Political Ideas of English Party Activsts." *American Political Science Review*, Vol. 56 (June, 1962), pp. 360–371.

Sanders, Thomas G. *Mexico in the '70's.* Hanover: American Universities Field Staff, 1976.

Schers, David. "The Popular Sector of the Mexican *PRI.*" Ph.D. dissertation, University of New Mexico, August, 1972.

Schlesinger, Joseph A. *Ambition and Politics: Political Careers in the United States.* Chicago: Rand McNally, 1966.

————. "Lawyers and American Politics: A Clarified View." *The Midwest Journal of Political Science*, Vol. 1 (May, 1957), pp. 26–39.

Schmidt, Henry C. "Antecedents to Samuel Ramos: Mexicanist Thought in the 1920's." *Journal of Inter-American Studies and World Affairs* (May, 1976), pp. 179–202.

Schmitt, Karl M. "Congressional Campaigning in Mexico: A View From the Provinces." *Journal of Inter-American Studies*, Vol. 11 (January, 1969), pp. 93–110.

Schopenhauer, Arthur. *On the Basis of Morality.* Indianapolis: Bobbs-Merrill, 1965.

Schwartz, David C. "Toward a Theory of Political Recruitment." *Western Political Quarterly*, Vol. 22 (September, 1969), pp. 552–571.

Scott, Robert E. *Mexican Government in Transition.* 2nd edition. Urbana: University of Illinois Press, 1964.

————. "Mexico." In G. Almond, ed., *Comparative Politics Today.* Boston: Little, Brown, 1974, pp. 366–403.

————. "Mexico: The Established Revolution." In Lucian Pye and Sidney Verba, eds., *Political Culture and Political Development.* Princeton: Princeton University Press, 1965, pp. 330–395.

Scott, Robert E., ed. *Latin American Modernization Problems.* Urbana: University of Illinois Press, 1973.

Searing, Donald D. "The Comparative Study of Elite Socialization." *Comparative Political Studies*, Vol. 1 (January, 1969), pp. 471–500.

————. "Measuring Politicians' Values: Administration and Assessment of a Ranking Technique in the British House of Commons." *American Political Science Review*, Vol. 72 (March, 1978), pp. 65–95.

————. "Models and Images of Man and Society in Leadership Theory." *Journal of Politics*, Vol. 31 (February, 1969), pp. 3–30.

Segovia, Rafael. *La politización del niño mexicano*. Mexico: El Colegio de Mexico, 1975.

————. "La reforma política: el ejecutivo federal, el PRI." *Foro Internacional*, Vol. 14 (No. 3, 1974), pp. 305–330.

————. "Las Tendencias Políticas en México de los Proximos Diez Años." Paper presented at the American University, School of International Service, March 18, 1976.

Sennett, Richard, and Jonathan Cobb. *The Hidden Injuries of Class*. New York: Knopf, 1972.

Shafer, Robert J. *Mexican Business Organizations*. Syracuse: Syracuse University Press, 1973.

Siegrist Clamont, Jorge. *En defensa de la autonomía universitaria; trayectoria historico-jurídica de la universidad mexicana*. 2 vols. Mexico: Universidad Nacional, 1955.

Sierra, Justo. *The Political Evolution of the Mexican People*. Austin: University of Texas Press, 1969.

Sigel, Roberta S., ed. *Learning About Politics*. New York: Random House, 1970.

Silva Herzog, Jesús. "El desarrollo de la enseñanza de las ciencias económicas en México, 1929–1953." *El Trimestre Económico*, Vol. 21 (January–March, 1954), pp. 1–5.

————. *Una historia de la Universidad de México y sus problemas*. Mexico: Siglo XXI, 1974.

————. *Mis últimas andanzas, 1947–1972*. Mexico: Siglo XXI, 1973.

————. *El pensamiento económico en México*. Mexico: Fondo de Cultura Económica, 1947.

————. *El pensamiento económico, social y político de México, 1810–1964*. Mexico: Instituto Mexicano de Investigaciones Económicas, 1967.

————. *Petroleo mexicano, historia de un problema*. Mexico: Fondo de Cultura Económica, 1941.

————. *Una vida en la vida de México*. Mexico, Siglo XXI Editores, 1972.

Simmons, Merle E. *The Mexican Corrido as a Source for Interpretive Study of Modern Mexico, 1870–1950*. Bloomington: Indiana University Press, 1957.

Smith, Donald L. "Pre-PRI: The Mexican Government Party, 1929–46." Ph.D dissertation, Texas Christian University, 1974.

Smith, M. Brewster. "Personal Values as Determinants of a Political Attitude." *The Journal of Psychology*, Vol. 28 (1949), pp. 477–486.

Smith, Peter H. "Continuity and Turnover Within the Mexican Political Elite, 1900–1971." Paper presented at IV International Congress of Mexican Studies, Santa Monica, California, October 17–21, 1973.

————. *Labyrinths of Power: Political Recruitment in Twentieth-Century Mexico*. Princeton: Princeton University Press, 1979.

————. "Making it in Mexico: Aspects of Political Mobility Since 1946." Paper prepared for delivery at the Annual Meeting of the American

Political Science Association, August 28–September 2, 1974.

Smith, Peter H. "La movilidad política en el México contemporáneo." *Foro Internacional*, Vol. 15 (No. 3, 1975), pp. 379–413.

Solari, Aldo. "Secondary Education and the Development of Elites." In Seymour Martin Lipset and Aldo Solari, eds., *Elites in Latin America*. New York: Oxford University Press, 1967, pp. 457–483.

Solis, Leopoldo. "Mexican Economic Policy in the Post-War Period: The Views of Mexican Economists." *The American Economic Review*, Vol. 61 (June, 1971), pp. 1–67 supplement.

Somit, Albert, Joseph Tannenhaus, Walter Wilke, and Rita Couley. "The Effect of the Introductory Political Science Course on Student Attitudes Toward Personal Participation." In Roberta Sigel, ed., *Learning About Politics*. New York: Random House, 1970, pp. 404–410.

Stanislawski, Dan. *The Anatomy of Eleven Towns in Michoacán*. New York: Greenwood Press, 1969.

Stansfield, David E. "The Mexican Cabinet, An Indicator of Change." Unpublished paper, 1974.

Steele Commager, Henry. *Lester Ward and the Welfare State*. Indianapolis: Bobbs-Merrill, 1967.

Stevens, Evelyn P. "Information and Decision Making in Mexico." Ph.D. dissertation, University of California, Berkeley, 1968.

———. "Mexico's PRI: The Institutionalization of Corporatism." In James Malloy, ed., *Authoritarianism and Corporatism in Latin America*. Pittsburgh: University of Pittsburgh Press, 1977.

———. *Protest and Response in Mexico*. Cambridge: MIT Press, 1974.

Stinchcombe, Arthur L. "Political Socialization in the South American Middle Class." *Harvard Educational Review*, Vol. 38 (1968), pp. 506–527.

Stone, Julius. *Social Dimensions of Law and Justice*. Stanford: Stanford University Press, 1966.

Stuart Hughes, H. *Oswald Spengler: A Critical Estimate*. New York: Charles Scribner's Sons, 1952.

Sugges, Peter R., Jr. "Beliefs About the Multinational Enterprise: A Factor Analytic Study of British, Canadian, French, and Mexican Elites." Ph.D. dissertation, New York University, 1976.

Sutton, Delia L. M. *Antonio Caso y su impacto cultural en el intelecto mexicano*. Mexico: SHCP, 1971.

Tamayo, Jorge. *Breve reseña sobre la Escuela Nacional de Ingeniería*. Mexico: Universidad Nacional, 1958.

Tapper, Ted. *Political Education and Stability: Elite Responses to Political Conflict*. New York: John Wiley, 1976.

Taracena, Alfonso. *Cartas políticas de José Vasconcelos*. Mexico: Editorial Librera, 1959.

Taracena, Antonio. "Mexico—Sus Problemas." Unpublished paper, 1976.

Tedin, K. L. "The Influence of Parents on the Political Attitudes of Adolescents." *American Political Science Review*, Vol. 68 (December, 1974), pp. 1579–92.

Testimonio en la muerte de Manuel Gómez Morín. Mexico: Editorial Jus, 1973.

Tinker, Edward Laroque. *Corridos and Calaveras*. Austin: University of Texas Press, 1961.

Torres Bodet, Jaime. *Años contra el tiempo*. Mexico: Porrúa, 1969.

——. *Equinoccio*. Mexico: Porrúa, 1974.

——. "Tiempo de Arena." In *Obras Escogidas*. Mexico: Fondo de Cultura Económica, 1961, pp. 191–386.

——. *La tierra prometida*. Mexico: Porrúa, 1972.

Trevino, Jacinto B. *Memorias*. Mexico: Editorial Orión, 1961.

Tribukait, Albrecht. "El presidencialismo en México." *Revista Mexicana de Ciencia Política*, Vol. 18 (No. 70, 1972), pp. 39–60.

Tuohy, William S. "Centralism and Political Elite Behavior in Mexico." In Clarence E. Thurber and Lawrence S. Graham, eds., *Development Administration in Latin America*. Durham: Duke University Press, 1973, pp. 260–280.

——. "Psychology in Political Analysis: The Case of Mexico." *Western Political Quarterly*, Vol. 27 (June, 1974), pp. 289–307.

Tuohy, William, and Barry Ames. "Mexican University Students in Politics: Rebels Without Allies?" *Monograph Series in World Affairs*. Denver: University of Colorado, 1970.

Tuohy, William S., and David Ronfeldt. "Political Control and the Recruitment of Middle-Level Elites in Mexico: An Example from Agrarian Politics." *Western Political Quarterly*, Vol. 22 (June, 1969), pp. 365–374.

Turner, Frederick C. *The Dynamic of Mexican Nationalism*. Chapel Hill: University of North Carolina Press, 1968.

Turner, Ralph H. "Sponsored and Contest Mobility and the School System." *American Sociological Review*, Vol. 25 (December, 1960), pp. 855–867.

Ugalde, Antonio. "Contemporary Mexico: From Hacienda to PRI, Political Leadership in a Zapotec Village." In Robert Kern, ed., *The Caciques*. Albuquerque: University of New Mexico Press, 1973, pp. 119–134.

——. *Power and Conflict in a Mexican Community: A Study of Political Integration*. Albuquerque: University of New Mexico Press, 1970.

Universidad, Mensual de Cultura Popular. 1936–55.

Uría-Santos, María Rosa. "El Ateneo de la Juventud: Su influencia en la vida intelectual de México." Ph.D. dissertation, University of Florida, Gainesville, 1965.

Urióstegui Miranda, Píndaro. *Testimonios del proceso revolucionario de México*. Mexico: Argrin, 1970.

Valadés, José C. *El presidente de México en 1970*. Mexico: Editores Mexicanos Unidos, 1969.

Vallejo y Arizmendi, Jorge. *Testimonio 1930–34*. Mexico: Editorial Stylo, 1947.

Vargas Austin, Ruben. "The Development of Economic Policy in Mexico, with Special Reference to Economic Doctrines." Ph.D. dissertation, Iowa State University, 1958.

Vasconcelos, José. *En el ocaso de mi vida*. Mexico: Populibros la prensa, 1957.

———. *A Mexican Ulysses*. Translated by William Rex Crawford. Bloomington: Indiana University Press, 1963.

Vázquez de Knauth, Josefina. *Nacionalismo y educación en México*. Mexico: Colegio de México, 1970.

Vejar Lecave, Carlos, and Amparo Espinosa de Serrano. *El pensamiento contemporáneo en México*. Mexico: Porrúa, 1974.

Velasco, Gustavo R. *Al servicio de la Escuela Libre de Derecho*. Mexico: Editorial Humanidades, 1967.

Velez, Carlos G. "An Evening in Ciudad Reyes: A Processual Approach to Mexican Politics." *The New Scholar*, Vol. 5 (No. 1, 1975), pp. 5–18.

Verner, Joel G. "The Guatemalan National Congress: An Elite Analysis." In Weston H. Agor, ed., *Latin American Legislatures: Their Role and Influence*. New York: Praeger, 1971, pp. 293–324.

Vernon, Raymond. *The Dilemma of Mexico's Development*. Cambridge: Harvard University Press, 1963.

Villaseñor, Eduardo. *Memorias-Testimonio*. Mexico: Fondo de Cultura Económica, 1974.

———. "XX aniversario de El Trimestre Económico." *El Trimestre Económico*, Vol. 20 (October–December, 1953), pp. 547–551.

Villaseñor, Víctor Manuel. *Memorias de un hombre de izquierda*. 2 vols. Mexico: Editorial Grijalba, 1976.

Von Sauer, Franz A. *The Alienated "Loyal" Opposition: Mexico's Partido Acción Nacional*. Albuquerque: University of New Mexico Press, 1974.

Walker, Kenneth N. "Political Socialization in Universities." In Seymour Martin Lipset and Aldo Solari, eds., *Elites in Latin America*. New York: Oxford University Press, 1967, pp. 408–430.

Wallraff, Charles F. *Karl Jaspers: An Introduction to His Philosophy*. Princeton: Princeton University Press, 1970.

Wellhofer, E. Spencer. "Background Characteristics and Dissident Behavior: Tests with Argentine Party Elites." *Journal of Developing Areas*, Vol. 9 (January, 1975), pp. 237–252.

Welsh, William A. "Methodological Problems in the Study of Political Leadership in Latin America." *Latin American Research Review*, Vol. 5 (Fall, 1970), pp. 3–33.

———. "Toward Effective Typology Construction in the Study of Latin American Political Leadership." *Comparative Politics*, Vol. 3 (January, 1971), pp. 271–280.

Wences Reza, Rosalio. *El movimiento estudiantil y los problemas nacionales*. Mexico: Editorial Nuestro Tiempo, 1971.

Wilkie, James W. *Elitelore*. Los Angeles: UCLA Latin American Center, 1973.

————. *The Mexican Revolution: Federal Expenditure and Social Change Since 1910.* Berkeley: University of California Press, 1970, revised edition.

Wilkie, James W., Michael C. Meyer, and Edna Monzón de Wilkie, eds. *Contemporary Mexico.* Los Angeles: UCLA Latin American Center, 1976.

Wilkie, James, and Edna Monzón de Wilkie. *México visto en el siglo xx.* Mexico: Instituto Mexicano de Investigaciones Económicas, 1969.

Wilkinson, Rupert. *Gentlemanly Power: British Leadership and the Public School Tradition: A Comparative Study in the Making of Rulers.* New York: Oxford University Press, 1964.

————. "Political Leadership and the Late Victorian Public School." *British Journal of Sociology,* Vol. 13 (1962), pp. 320–330.

Williams, Edward J. "Mutation in the Mexican Revolution: Industrialism, Nationalism and Centralism." *Secolas Annals* (March, 1976), pp. 34–43.

Winter, David G., Stewart, Abigail J., and David C. McClelland. "Grading the Effects of a Liberal Arts Education." *Psychology Today* (September, 1978), pp. 69–70, 73–74.

Wise, George S. *El México de Alemán.* Mexico: Editorial Atlante, 1952.

Womack, John. "The Spoils of the Mexican Revolution." *Foreign Affairs,* Vol. 48 (July, 1970), pp. 677–687.

Zaragoza-Carbajal, Maximino. "Vicente Lombardo-Toledano: His Role in the Socio-Political Evolution of Mexico Since the 1920's." Ph.D. dissertation, St. Louis University, 1971.

Zea, Leopoldo. *Latin America and the World.* Norman: University of Oklahoma Press, 1969.

Ziblatt, David. "High School Extracurricular Activities and Political Socialization." *The Annals of the American Academy of Political and Social Science,* Vol. 361 (September, 1965), pp. 21–31.

Index

Age: importance of, in socialization, 50–51; when politicians leave parents, 29. *See also* Generations

Agrarian law, significance of, for law students, 14

Alatriste, Sealtiel: on preparatory school experiences, 54–55; on professors as models, 88

Alemán, Miguel: activity of, in student politics, 12; closeness of, to father, 31; father of, 167 n. 13; on his professors, 91; on importance of democracy, 137; on importance of the labor question, 69; reason of, for entering politics, 20; on unity of his generation, 127

Algerian leaders, views of, on unity, 136

Anglo-American influence: in law courses, 77; significance of, on politicians' views, 78; significance of, to teaching sociology, 72; why less important, 77–78

Anti-militarism: as expressed in office-holding trends, 198 n. 79; as value, 138–139

Apolitical professors, 97

Aragón, Octavio, importance of, as professor, 96

Armendáriz, Antonio: childhood interest of, in politics, 29; importance of indignation on career of, 168 n. 36; importance of mother of, 31; on National Preparatory School, 51; on peers, 37; on significance of Flores Magón brothers, 79; on why professors are important socializers, 84

Aronson, Sidney, study of North American politicians by, 170 n. 11

Article 27, importance of, in law courses, 68–69

Azuela, Mariano: importance of father of, 30; importance of professors of, 14

Azuela, Salvador, importance of Revolution to, 42

229